Sexuality and Socialism

Sexuality and Socialism

History, Politics, and Theory of LGBT Liberation

Sherry Wolf

HAYMARKET BOOKS
CHICAGO, ILLINOIS

Published in 2009 by Haymarket Books
P.O. Box 180165
Chicago, IL 60618
773-583-7884
www.haymarketbooks.org

ISBN 978-1931859-79-0

Cover design by Amy Balkin
Cover photograph of the 2006 Heritage of Pride Parade
in New York City © Bryan Smith.

This book has been published with the generous support
of the Wallace Global Fund.

Library of Congress Cataloging-in-Publication Data
is available.

Printed in Canada by union labor on recycled paper containing
100 percent post-consumer waste in accordance with the guidelines
of the Green Press Initiative, www.greenpressinitiative.org.

2 4 6 8 10 9 7 5 3 1

Contents

To Judy and Richard Wolf, my parents, who encouraged their tomboy daughter to play sports, think for herself, question authority (though perhaps not theirs), and believe that what we do can make a difference

Acknowledgments

From a distance, writing a book appears to be a pretty solitary affair, and in many ways it is. But my worldview and ideas about sexuality and socialism have been shaped by many political collaborators over the years. I have the great fortune of working alongside some excellent Marxist writers, thinkers, and activists who are among my dearest friends. First and foremost, I must thank Paul D'Amato, my editor, for his insights and questions that forced me to clarify concepts and refine some rough edges. I've no doubt that working with me is a trial, and whatever faults this book has are surely my own, though I'm certain some of its attributes are due to Paul's prodding editorial comments. In addition to Sharon Smith's writings and speeches on women and socialism, U.S. labor, and a jaw-dropping range of topics, conversations with Sharon helped form many of the ideas that wound up in this book. I must also thank Ahmed Shawki for asking me to write the book—and thinking that I could, despite the fact that I'd never written one before.

Regular discussions with Joel Geier, Elizabeth Schulte, Alan Maass, Lee Sustar, Marlene Martin, Bill Roberts, Shaun Harkin, Lance Selfa, and Eric Ruder forced me to think more sharply about the audience and goals for this work. I must also thank Jesse Sharkey, Jason Yanowitz, Annie Zirin, Julie Fain, Lauren Fleer, Keeanga-Yamahtta Taylor, and Susan Dwyer for mercifully saving me from having to endure my own cooking these last months; and also for pounding me with questions, arguments, rebuttals, and quizzical looks over many dinners. I'm not sure if they all realized they were helping me with the book as I ate their food and sipped wine, but those free-flowing discussions propelled me back into the library stacks more times than I care to admit. On a couple of chapters, I called upon the expertise of Dana Cloud, Aisha Karim, Matt Swagler, Phil Gasper, and David Whitehouse, all of whom made extremely useful comments. I also must acknowledge my new friends, *Inside Higher Ed*'s Scott McLemee and Ohio State's Christopher Phelps, for sending along helpful articles.

Thanks also to Barry Sheppard for introducing me to the folks at the Holt Labor Library in San Francisco. Dave Florey's sleuthing on my behalf in NYU's Tamiment archives was a great help as well. And Dave Zirin's advice to not think of it as writing a book, but just to work on seventy-two articles instead, was the kind of silly and spot-on help I needed from my pal the sportswriter for politicos who hate sports and athletes who hate politics.

Finally, I'd like to thank the folks at Haymarket Books, who accomplish extraordinary feats of publishing with a passion and persistence that live up to their mission of creating "books for changing the world": Julie Fain, Anthony Arnove, Sarah Macaraeg, Rachel Cohen, Joe Allen, Bill Roberts, and Dao Tran. It's an honor to be added to your list of authors.

Introduction

There is a contradiction that pervades the politics and culture of U.S. society regarding lesbian, gay, bisexual, and transgender (LGBT) people. On the one hand, top-rated TV shows and Academy Award–winning movies, such as *Will and Grace*, the *L Word*, and *Milk*, portray gays and lesbians in a favorable light. On the other, federal and most state legislation denies equal marriage, workplace, and civil rights protections for sexual minorities. Rates of violence against LGBT people remain alarmingly high, including incidents of murder.[1] Current opinion polls, however, show a marked increase in social acceptance of a wide range of sexual and gender-variant behaviors.[2] This contradiction is a product of both the emergence in modern capitalism of greater sexual freedom to form sexual identities outside the traditional family and capitalism's continued need to reinforce gender norms that bolster the "nuclear" family.

This work uses a Marxist worldview to examine this and other historical, political, and theoretical questions of sexual and gender oppression in order to frame an argument for how we can organize for LGBT liberation. Socialism's founders, Karl Marx and Frederick Engels, lived in the Victorian era, many decades before the notion of LGBT liberation took form. They (and other Marxists after them) did, however, provide the theoretical tools necessary to both analyze and wage a successful battle against this and other forms of oppression.

What was the gist of their argument? Homophobic, sexist, racist, nationalist, and other divisions in modern society reflect the interests of the dominant class in society. This class—the ruling class—constitutes a small minority of the population; it therefore must use the institutional and ideological tools at its disposal to divide the mass of the population against itself in order to prevent the majority from uniting and rising in unison to take back what is rightfully theirs. The former slave and Black abolitionist Frederick Douglass put it aptly when he said of the slaveholders' strategy against slaves and poor whites, "They divided both to conquer each."[3]

The ruling class depends, argued Marx, on promoting ideas that reinforce division and a sense of powerlessness among the exploited. "The ideas of the ruling class are in every epoch," Marx and Engels noted, "the ruling ideas, i.e., the class which is the ruling material force of society, is at the same time its ruling intellectual force."[4] This holds true also for ideas about social and legal "norms" of sexual behavior under capitalism. Ideological and legal repression and control of sexual behavior in the United States and other industrialized societies, therefore, grow from the needs of the class in power.

However, oppression is not merely ideological but also material. The oppression of immigrants, for example, allows capitalists to super-exploit cheap immigrant labor, which in turn allows them leverage to lower all workers' wages. As chapter 1 explains, the nuclear family provides an inexpensive way for the ruling class to foist the costs of reproduction, maintenance, and responsibility for disciplining the current and future generations of workers onto the class of the exploited. LGBT people are oppressed because their sexual and gender identities challenge the traditional family upon which capitalism continues to depend.

If we lived in a truly free society in which material and social constraints were removed, people would be neither oppressed nor even defined by their sexual or gender identities. Only then could we begin to see how a liberated human sexuality could evolve and express itself. But in a class society that requires certain behavioral norms to discipline its workforce and ideology to justify the nuclear family, reactionary sexual ideas—including gender norms—are means of stoking division and repressing society as a whole.

Although the dominant ideas are those of the ruling class and social control is concentrated in their institutions—the state, courts, police, etc.—the rest of us are not merely dupes and victims. From growing urbanization and immigration to global warfare, social forces set into motion from above have given rise to material and ideological means for people to drastically alter their intimate lives, as Chapters 2 and 3 explain. History shows that time and again, working-class people are capable of breaking out of the legal and social constraints imposed from above to challenge the status quo. While not the first incident of mass upheaval against sexual and gender norms, the Stonewall rebellion in New York City in 1969 marked a turning point for modern lesbians, gays, and bisexuals—and gave rise to the conditions for transgender people to assert their demands and launch their own organizations, as chapter 4 details.

The Stonewall Riots, occuring amid wider social explosions against the racial, imperial, and sexual order of U.S. society, gave expression to radical ideas of sexual liberation. Yet in the decades since there has been a narrowing of the debate and aims of the existing LGBT organizations that jettisoned all talk of liberation in favor of the aim of gradual civil rights reforms. LGBT civil rights were largely pursued within the confines of electoral politics, as chapter 5 examines. The minimalist demands of this era arose from political debates and organizations that viewed sexual freedom in terms of how individuals spoke, dressed, socialized, and consumed goods on the market, a positioning often referred to as lifestyle politics. These ideas reached their apex in the 1990s with the near-disappearance of class struggle in the United States and a steep decline of far left organizations to pose a collective alternative to the isolation and pessimism that characterized individual attempts to challenge LGBT oppression, discussed in chapter 6.

The dominance of biological determinist ideas to explain sexual and gender identities and behaviors in recent years is the topic of chapter 7. In it, I unpack some of the myths and mistaken assumptions using current scientific thinking to take on questions about whether people are "born gay," the rise of transgender identity, and the medical establishment's treatment of millions born with ambiguous genitalia, known as intersex people.

I feel as though I've experienced political whiplash in the final weeks of completing work on this book. From a seemingly apolitical and quiescent terrain a torrent of political organizing, protest, and healthy debate has arisen in and beyond LGBT circles in the United States. The background to it all is the worst economic collapse since the Great Depression of the

1930s and the election of the first African-American president in a nation built on Black slavery. A sense of hope and expectation mixes with deep fears about our economic, social, and environmental future.

When I first began to research and write this book, I was hopeful that scholars and activists alike would glean lessons to be debated and put to use in some future struggles. It appears the future is coming at us faster than I had ever anticipated. The electoral defeats of same-sex marriage in California, Florida, and Arizona in November 2008 now appear to be temporary setbacks that have stoked a genuine opposition that is more confrontational and less tepid than in recent years. The youth and spontaneity of the latest explosion of LGBT militancy in response to the defeat of same-sex marriage in California's Proposition 8 referendum are magnificent. The political outlook and social composition of this rising LGBT movement deserve comment as well. These young (and not so young) fighters are part of the growing army of café baristas with college degrees and itinerant low-wage workers that now populate every city and town of the United States. This newly forming movement is largely pro-labor, anticorporate, and explicitly welcoming non-LGBT folks into the struggle.

New movement activists, students, and socialists organized a gay marriage forum in Chicago on December 11, 2008, one day after the historic victory of the Republic Windows and Doors factory occupation in that city.[3] Fresh from winning nearly $2 million in severance and vacation pay for the multiracial group of nearly 250 factory workers, Raúl Flores addressed the crowd brilliantly, saying that our struggles are united and we must be too. "Our victory is yours," he said, "Now we must join with you in your battle for rights and return the solidarity you showed us."[6] Goodbye *Will and Grace*, hello Republic factory workers!

The day before, hundreds of gay protesters rallying for equal marriage rights as part of the national Day Without a Gay initiative linked their march with the Republic workers' protest outside Bank of America. Trade unionists, immigrant rights activists, and LGBT people rallied together in the most eloquent display of rainbow power Chicago has witnessed in decades. Orlando Sepulveda, a Chilean immigrant, described the day's action as "a school for struggle."[7] Even the name of the LGBT action expressed the cross-pollination of struggles— the historic mass immigrant workers' marches that hit the streets in 2006 were called A Day Without an Immigrant.

Gus Van Sant's award-winning biopic of the gay activist elected San Francisco supervisor in 1977, *Milk*, arrived in theaters in late November 2008, at a crucial teaching moment. The film alludes to a key aspect of the successful gay-labor struggles against Coors beer and the 1978 Briggs Initiative that would have banned gay and lesbian teachers and their allies from "advocating, soliciting, imposing, encouraging or promoting"[8] homosexuality in California's classrooms. By uniting with Teamsters in the Coors battle and forging lasting alliances with blue- and white-collar workers in the fight against the Briggs Initiative, Harvey Milk, along with tens of thousands of activists, advanced both the fight for gay civil rights and for labor unity.

The interaction between workplace organizing and the fight for LGBT rights has a long history. Harry Hay, the founder of the first U.S. gay organization, the Mattachine Society, got his start as a union organizer in the 1930s and 1940s in New York's Department Store Workers Union with the International Workers of the World (IWW).[9] Some of the research that historian

Allan Bérubé did on the Marine Cooks and Stewards Union (MCS) in the 1930s and 1940s shows how prior to the emergence of gay rights organizations in the United States, a largely gay and multiracial group of workers led by communists on passenger ships transformed a reactionary union into one that defended gay rights, challenged racism, and won material gains for all their workers until McCarthyite tactics tore the MCS apart in the 1950s.[10] The banner hanging in the hall of the twenty-thousand-strong, Black- and gay-led MCS union read: "Race-baiting, Red-baiting, and Queer-baiting Is Anti-Union."[11] Chapter 8 argues that class unity among LGBT and straight people is both possible and necessary in order to build a world in which we are all sexually liberated. The book concludes with an argument for sexual liberation for all.

A new movement will face serious challenges. The largest national gay rights organizations are sponsored by multibillion-dollar corporations and tied to the don't-rock-the-boat posture of the upper echelons of the Democratic Party. In the midst of massive layoffs and severe economic crisis some will advocate a go-slow, back-of-the-bus approach for LGBT issues. This can and should be challenged. In addition to social equality and legitimizing LGBT sexuality, the fight for equal marriage rights is for much-needed material benefits—health care, Social Security, inheritance, and the other rights and benefits of marriage that working-class people want and need. In other words, it is part of the class struggle. Also, the same-sex marriage battle lends itself to broader organizing and questions about everything from the origins of LGBT oppression to the history of the movement and the various theoretical and political challenges in understanding and overcoming divisions among us to win liberation.

There are positive indicators regarding social attitudes toward gays and lesbians. *Newsweek*'s latest national poll numbers show a marked increase in pro-gay attitudes nationally. Not only do 52 percent currently oppose the federal marriage ban (up from 45 percent in 2004), but decisive majorities are for ending all sorts of discrimination against LGBT people— 73 percent approve extending health care to gay partners, 86 percent are for equal hospital visitation rights, and so on.[12] These are startlingly good numbers given the equivocation (at best) from politicians and the near-absence for many years of any activist movement until recently. Imagine the impact on consciousness if ordinary working peoples' opinions were shifting not just on the basis of lived experience alongside the rising ranks of out coworkers, classmates, and family members but also inside organizations and struggles where sexual stereotypes were confidently contested.

There is a groaning hunger among scholars and social justice activists for knowledge and debate about the history, politics, and theory of LGBT liberation. This work makes no pretense about the author's political leanings. Left-wing historians and scientists such as John D'Emilio, Estelle Freedman, Susan Stryker, and Anne Fausto-Sterling along with many others have shaped and influenced my understanding of LGBT politics and history enormously. As a lesbian Marxist who came of age in the neo–Cold War, AIDS-ravaged 1980s, I am part of the post-Stonewall generation. Many of my peers question the relevance or possibility of organization and struggle. But reality is forcing those alternatives. I would caution readers against narrowing their sights, presuming that LGBT battles will or should necessarily rise independent of wider outrage against expanding wars and a collapsing economy.

Sexual minorities, after all, are directly affected by these unfolding catastrophes and our demands can and must be brought into broader battles that will eventually erupt and can be shaped by socialist ideas.

The Chicago example above shows that as a new political era begins to take shape, immigrant and labor groups can and in some places already are calling upon LGBT groups to join with them in organizing a response to the current crises. For those of us too young to have participated in the upheavals of the 1960s and 1970s and who have lived with the aching suspicion that we may have missed out on the revolution, take heart. In a world that bears a striking resemblance to elements of both the 1960s and 1930s—yet where attitudes about race, women, sexuality, and gender have evolved tremendously—it appears we are in for some heady times of our own.

What's in a name?

Right from the get-go, I must admit that I cannot use what I perceive as an offensive epithet that was scrawled across my high school locker and spat at me from the mouths of innumerable bigots—the word "queer"—as a positive signifier in a book about the history, politics, and theory of sexual liberation. As a socialist who advocates sexual liberation for all, the modern conundrum of desiring to be all-inclusive and readable means that one must settle on how to refer to lesbian, gay, bisexual, and transgender people collectively. I have chosen to largely use LGBT in keeping with many current historians as well as student and labor activists. There are, however, many places in which the words gay or homosexual are used as they are both historically and culturally accurate in those instances. Hopefully, the content of my exposition and arguments will satisfy even those most adamant in their preference for queer.

I think a truce on the issue of LGBT nomenclature is in order. Language is ever evolving in tandem with the wider society we live in, and time along with future struggles will tell what terms emerge from the current babble. I know that many feel quite passionate about this issue; however, after all the Sturm und Drang over this rather narrow question I believe that we ought to move on and respect each others' linguistic choices. All oppressed people should have the right to call themselves whatever they choose, a right that must also extend to me.

Sherry Wolf
May 2009

CHAPTER ONE

The Roots of LGBT Oppression

The oppression of lesbian, gay, bisexual, and transgender (LGBT) people hasn't always existed, and neither have LGBT people as a distinct sector of the population. The oppression of all sexual minorities is one of modern capitalism's myriad contradictions. Capitalism creates the material conditions for men and women to lead autonomous sexual lives, yet it simultaneously seeks to impose heterosexual norms on society to secure the maintenance of the economic, social, and sexual order.

Famous lesbians such as Melissa Etheridge pack concert venues and out comedian Ellen DeGeneres hosts an Emmy Award–winning syndicated talk show, while homophobic laws defend discrimination on the job and in marriage. LGBT people such as Matthew Shepard are brutally beaten to death by bigots, while public opinion has radically shifted in favor of LGBT civil rights.[1] This apparently contradictory state of affairs in the United States can be explained.

LGBT oppression, like women's oppression, is tied to the centrality of the nuclear family as one of capitalism's means to both inculcate gender norms and outsource care for the current and future generations of workers at little cost to the state, as explained in detail below. In addition, the oppression of

LGBT people under capitalism, like racism and sexism, serves to divide working-class people from one another, especially in their battles for economic and social justice. While capitalist society attempts to pigeonhole people into certain gender roles and sexual behaviors, socialists reject these limitations. Instead, socialists fight for a world in which sexuality is a purely personal matter, without legal or material restrictions of any sort. The right of self-determination for individuals that socialists uphold must include individuals' freedom to choose their own sexual behavior, appearance, and erotic preferences.

Sexuality, like many other behaviors, is a fluid—not fixed—phenomenon. Homosexuality exists along a continuum. The modern expression of this can be found among the millions of men and women who identify as LGBT—often identifying themselves differently at different times in their lives. There are not two kinds of people in the world, gay and straight. As far as biologists can tell, there is only one human race with a multiplicity of sexual possibilities that can be either frustrated or liberated, depending on the way human society is organized.

Reams of historical evidence confirm that what we define today as homosexual behavior has existed for at least thousands of years, and it is logical to assume that homosexual acts have been occurring for as long as human beings have walked the Earth. But it took the Industrial Revolution of the late nineteenth century to create the potential for vast numbers of ordinary people to live outside the nuclear family, allowing for modern gay, lesbian, and bisexual identities to be born. Not until the late twentieth century did some gender-variant people begin to identify themselves as transgender, though people who have defied modern Western concepts of gender-appropriate behavior have existed throughout history in many different cultures. The systematic oppression of LGBT people as it is experienced in most contemporary Western societies, therefore, is also a fairly recent phenomenon in human history. This is not to argue, however, that prior to capitalism humans existed in a sexual paradise free of repression or restrictions of any kind. Rather, legal prohibitions and social taboos from antiquity through the precapitalist era existed in many cultures on the basis of sex acts, often denouncing non-procreative sex, without the condemnation or even the conception of sexual identity as an intrinsic or salient aspect of a person's being.

Contemporary industrial societies created the possibility for men and women to identify themselves and live as gays and lesbians, argues the collection *Hidden from History*.

> What we call "homosexuality" (in the sense of the distinguishing traits of "homosexuals"), for example, was not considered a unified set of acts, much less a set of qualities defining particular persons, in precapitalist societies.... Heterosexuals and homosexuals are involved in social "roles" and attitudes which pertain to a particular society, modern capitalism.[2]

It was capitalism, in fact, that gave rise to modern individuality and the conditions for people to have intimate lives based on personal desire, a historic break from the power of the feudal church and community that once arranged marriages. Under capitalism, a person's labor is converted into an individually owned commodity that is bought and sold on the market. Individuals are thrust into competition with each other for work, housing, education, etc., and individual citizens of states are counted in a census and register to vote, or, if they have the means, own property. All of these features of capitalist society establish individuality in ways unthinkable under earlier systems like feudalism, creating the potential for a flourishing of sexual autonomy as well. As Karl Marx put it, "In this society of free competition, the individual appears detached from the natural bonds, etc., which in earlier historical periods make him the accessory of a definite and limited human conglomerate."[3]

Historical evidence suggests that homosexual behavior was successfully integrated in many precapitalist cultures. The most famous example is ancient Greece, where sexual relationships between older men and teenage boys were heralded as one of the highest forms of love. These relationships, however, were encouraged between wealthier, older, and powerful "betters" and their subordinates who were younger, poorer, or conquered. For the early Greeks and Romans, status and power between lovers were central to their conception of same-sex relations and they held starkly different views of those who played the penetrative role in sex and those who were penetrated. Plutarch, the Greek-born historian of the first century explained, "We class those who enjoy the passive part as belonging to the lowest depth of vice and allow them not the least degree of confidence or respect or friendship."[4]

Many American Indian tribes embraced transvestite men and women, known as *berdaches*, who adopted the gender roles of the "opposite" sex and are sometimes referred to today as "two-spirited" people. A multiplicity of sexual and gender arrangements existed from tribe to tribe, according to anthropologists. Some male berdaches had sex exclusively with other men, though not other berdaches, while some remained celibate, had partners of both sexes, or had

exclusively heterosexual sex.[5] Gender variance, not sexual preference, defined the berdache, and rather than deriding them
for their gender nonconformity, American Indian tribes saw
berdaches as valuable members of their society. One Crow
elder explains: "We don't waste people the way white society
does. Every person has their gift."[6]

Even the Roman Catholic Church, until the twelfth century, celebrated love between men. When it ended priestly
marriage and enforced chastity, homosexuality was prohibited as well.[7] However, in these societies, it was homosexual
actions that were tolerated, lauded, or pilloried, not an identifiable category of people. Economic and social conditions had
not yet developed in ways that allowed for large numbers of
people to acknowledge, express, or explore same-sex desire
as a central feature of their lives or their identities.

The French philosopher Michel Foucault challenged modern society's attempts to superimpose its sexual outlook on
the ancients. He argues:

> The Greeks did not see love for one's own sex and love for
> the other sex as opposites, as two exclusive choices, two
> radically different types of behavior.... Were the Greeks bi-
> sexual then? Yes, if we mean by this that a Greek [free
> man] could, simultaneously or in turn, be enamored by a
> boy or a girl.... But if we wish to turn our attention to the
> way in which they conceived of this dual practice, we need
> to take note of the fact that they did not recognize two kinds
> of "desire".... Their way of thinking, what made it possible
> to desire a man or a woman was simply the appetite that na-
> ture had implanted in man's heart for "beautiful" human be-
> ings, whatever their sex.[8]

Whereas previous class societies prohibited certain sex
acts, the rising capitalist state and its defenders in the fields of

medicine, law, and academia stepped in to define and control human sexuality in ways previously unimagined. These nineteenth-century professionals—almost entirely white men—reflected the interests and prejudices of the rising middle class. With economic growth and development came the need for higher levels of education for more kinds of jobs, which extended adolescence and removed teenagers from many occupations, thus reducing social interaction between unrelated adults and children. Medical professionals aiming to legitimize their field pathologized masturbation, while legislators encouraged age-of-consent laws and pressed for higher minimum ages for marriage. Homosexual relations between adults and "innocent minors" were outlawed and juveniles were rendered asexual.[9] No less a figure than Sigmund Freud, the father of modern psychiatry at the turn of the twentieth century, theorized and popularized the "problem of homosexuality" while transforming heterosexuality into "the norm we all know without ever thinking much about it."[10]

Our conceptions about gender roles have changed radically from one society to another and from one historical period to the next. Even our bodies have been radically transformed by our changing material conditions. Modern female athletes such as forty-one-year-old Olympian and mother Dara Torres, whose lean and muscular body is capable of beating professional male and female swimmers half her age, would have been inconceivable a generation ago. Advances in nutrition, training, and civil rights for women created the potential not only for a middle-aged American woman to compete and win three silver medals at the 2008 Summer Olympics but for her androgynous appearance to be accepted and even valorized in the pages of the *New York Times*.[11] In contrast, the earlier onset of puberty among girls in the United States, particularly low-income African-American girls, is thought to be the result of diet, environmental chemicals, inactivity, and other factors that are features of modern industrial society.[12]

Medical science has long acknowledged the existence of millions of people whose bodies combine anatomical features that are conventionally associated with either men or women. These intersex individuals, estimated at one birth in every two thousand in the United States alone,[13] are legally operated on by pediatricians who force traditional norms of genital appearance on newborn infants, often rendering them incapable of experiencing sexual pleasure later in life. The physical reality of intersex people calls into question the fixed notions we are taught to accept about men and women. Intersex people challenge not only society's construction of gender roles, but compel us to examine the concept that sex itself is constructed, confined, and forced to fit into a tidy male/female binary. It appears that even our physical sex—not just how we comport ourselves—is far more ambiguous and fluid than previously imagined. The imposition of surgery on perfectly healthy infants in order to force their bodies to conform to societal sex norms is a blatant form of state-sanctioned physical abuse. These acts of sexual mutilation must be opposed by everyone who believes that self-determination should include the right of individuals to control and experience pleasure from their own bodies, as well as define themselves as whatever gender they choose.

Socialists argue that what humans have constructed they can also tear down. If the contention of this book is accurate—that capitalist society has transformed how people express themselves sexually yet simultaneously has aimed to restrict human sexuality as a means of social control—then a fundamentally different kind of society, based on human need and not profit, could put an end to modern sexual and gender definitions and limitations. A socialist society must be one in which people are sexually liberated—that is, all would have the freedom to choose whether, how, when, and with whom to engage in whatever sexual gratification they desired so long as no other person were harmed.

The changing family

The roots of homosexual identity and its subsequent repression can be found in the ever-changing role of the family. The family—that supposedly sacrosanct institution exalted by right-wingers and surreally depicted in countless laundry detergent commercials—has changed radically throughout human history. In fact, the family itself has not always existed.

Karl Marx's closest collaborator, Frederick Engels, employed the anthropological research of Lewis Henry Morgan in his groundbreaking nineteenth-century work *The Origin of the Family, Private Property and the State*. Anthropology was then a new science; nevertheless, Engels's theoretical conclusions have been substantiated by more recent anthropological research.[14]

Engels argued that although modern human beings have existed as a species for more than a hundred thousand years, people only began living in family units in the last several thousand years—when previously egalitarian societies divided into classes. Pre-class human social organization was based on large clans and collective production, distribution, and child-rearing. A division of labor often existed be-

tween men and women in pre-class societies, but there is no
evidence to suggest that women were systematically oppressed—and in some societies, women were afforded an
even higher status than men.[15]

Anthropologist Eleanor Burke Leacock provided detailed
studies on early societies, particularly the Montagnais-Naskapi
of the Labrador Peninsula, to argue, "With regard to the autonomy of women, nothing in the structure of egalitarian band societies necessitated special deference to men."[16] Women made
decisions alongside men on where and when to move, whether
to join or leave a mate, and about the distribution of food—all
central to daily life and survival. Even the sexual division of
labor is called into question by Leacock and other anthropologists who examined societies in which women did the hunting
and men took on roles like child-rearing as often as they performed tasks modern society conceives of as appropriate to
their genders.

The oppression of women corresponded with the rise of
the first class divisions in society and the creation of the
monogamous family unit. Prior to humans' ability to store food
and other goods as a surplus, there was no "wealth" to be
hoarded, precluding the possibility of class inequality between
different groups of people. Classes arose when human beings
found new ways of sustaining a livelihood. New methods of
production required that some people were needed to labor,
while others needed to be freed from that labor to coordinate
the organization of the group and ensure the storage of a surplus for times when crops failed or the group grew in size. As
socialist Chris Harman describes, "The 'leaders' could begin
to turn into 'rulers,' into people who came to see their control
over resources as in the interests of society as a whole.... For

the first time social development encouraged the development of the motive to exploit and oppress others."[17]

Since there was no surplus wealth prior to classes, there was nothing to be passed on from one generation to the next. But with the development of a surplus and classes came the impetus for those who had control over a surplus to hold onto it and pass it to their own children. With the appearance of social classes and the possibility of passing wealth in the form of inheritance from those who had it to their offspring arose the desire for monogamy, at least imposed on women, so that male leaders could ensure the veracity of their own bloodline. The rise of the patriarchal family was a consequence of these changes.

The initial meaning of the word "family" is a far cry from Norman Rockwell's images of domestic bliss. Early Romans used the term *famulus* to describe household slaves, and *familia* to refer to the "total number of slaves belonging to one man."[18] For the early feudal aristocracy, marriage was an economic, not emotional, relationship—a means to transfer land wealth or to secure peaceful relations between landed estates. Over time, men were increasingly drawn into production and women were increasingly isolated in the role of reproduction, or child-rearing.

Until the rise of capitalism, the peasant family was both a unit of production and reproduction. Peasant women were not only in charge of child-rearing, cooking, and cleaning, but they were also expected to make clothes, churn butter, milk the cows, make beer, spin cloth, etc.; unlike the modern nuclear family, which is purely a reproductive unit. Women were unequal to men and had gender-defined jobs in the feudal family, but with the rise of markets and industry that came to dominate Western societies in the nineteenth century, productive work like brewing and the manufacture of textiles was removed from the realm of the family.

The changing economic structure of society drastically altered attitudes toward both women and sexuality. Imposing monogamy—for women only—afforded the means through which wealthy men's property could be inherited by children whom the father could be certain were his own. Monogamous marriage, in essence, developed as the agency through which ruling-class men could establish undisputed paternity.[19] As Engels wrote,

> The first class opposition that appears in history coincides with the development of the antagonism between man and woman in monogamous marriage, and the first class oppression coincides with that of the female sex by the male. Monogamous marriage was a great historical step forward; nevertheless, together with slavery and private wealth, it opens the period that has lasted until today in which every step forward is also relatively a step backward, in which prosperity and development for some is won through the misery and frustration of others.[20]

Among the middle classes and landowning peasants under European feudalism, the patriarchal household dominated. Although landless peasants possessed no wealth of their own, the institution of the family was nevertheless legally established as the norm for all sectors of society. Feudal communities usually arranged marriages between poor peasants. Family life was filled with grinding work for all family members, and childbirth often ended in death for either mother or infant, or both.

In these societies, sexual repression took a form different from what we know today. Severe sanctions were enforced against all sexual behaviors that were non-procreative. In 1533, for example, Britain's King Henry VIII—whose obsession with producing a male heir led to six marriages—introduced the Buggery Act, which would put men to death for "buggery," the catchall term of the day for non-procreative sex that was considered a crime against nature.[21] The act coincided with other laws in the same period punishing "vagabonds," i.e., peasants forced off the land with nowhere to go. Buggery was included in the Articles of War beginning in the seventeenth century in Britain and was punished the same as mutiny and desertion.

The households of European colonists in the seventeenth and eighteenth centuries were independent units of both production and reproduction in which all family members worked together on a plot of land to supply virtually all of the family's needs. In the New England colonies, "solitary living" was forbidden. Servants and apprentices had to live with the households for which they worked, but even without legal constraints, economic survival in colonial times was inconceivable outside the family structure.[22]

The need for labor in the colonies fueled efforts by New England churches and courts to outlaw and punish adultery, sodomy, incest, and rape. Extramarital sex by women, who were considered incapable of controlling their passions, was punished more severely than extramarital sex by men. Sodomy could mean either sex between two people of the same gender or any "unnatural" acts such as anal or oral intercourse that couldn't result in procreation, even between married couples. In a society that prized productivity, to the Puritans sodomy was wasted time. Though officially punishable by death from 1607 to 1740, sodomy was more often punished by lashings. Some cases of "lewd behavior" between women were punished by whippings, though no one was executed for sodomy in the colonies during the eighteenth century, probably due to the legal requirement of proof of penetration and two eyewitnesses.[23] The dominance of the church and the lack of any means to care for children born out of wedlock drove neighbors' zealous watch over the sexual mores of their community.

As historian Jonathan Ned Katz explains, "The operative contrast in this society was between fruitfulness and barrenness, not between different-sex and same-sex eroticism…. In these colonies, erotic desire for members of a same sex was not construed as deviant because erotic desire for a different sex was not construed as a norm."[24]

With the rise of urban centers and industrial production methods in the late-nineteenth century in Western Europe and North America, wage labor became much more common. Compared with farm life, there was an increased separation of home from work so the family became much more exclusively a center for reproduction. Over the decades, the growth of industry created a new kind of family ideal, as a haven from a changing, often hostile world. But the relationship between the family and capitalism was fraught with contradictions from the beginning. John D'Emilio's groundbreaking essay, "Capitalism and Gay Identity," uses the historical materialist method developed by Marx and Engels to analyze these contradictions. He writes,

> On the one hand, capitalism continually weakens the material foundation of family life, making it possible for individuals to live outside the family, and for a lesbian and gay male identity to develop. On the other, it needs to push men and women into families, at least long enough to reproduce the

next generation of workers. The elevation of the family to ideological preeminence guarantees that a capitalist society will reproduce not just children, but heterosexism and homophobia. In the most profound sense, capitalism is the problem.[25]

The capitalist mode of production brought about the rise of an entrepreneurial class—and with it, the notion of personal achievement and individuality as a social ideal. At the same time, the increasing prosperity of a new middle class and the broader accumulation of personal wealth and transferable inheritances demanded strict sexual morality, especially for women. British historian Jeffrey Weeks describes the contradictions of this new family structure: The bourgeois family was "both the privileged location of emotionality and love...and simultaneously an effective policeman of sexual behavior."[26]

In contrast to the prosperous middle class, industrial life was literally killing the working class in mid-nineteenth century England. Middle-class men in the rural area of Rutland, England, lived to be fifty-two, while working-class "men" died at the average age of seventeen in industrial centers like Manchester, sixteen in Bethnal Green, and fifteen in Liverpool.[27] Textile mill owners employed mostly women and children at far less pay than men for long hours of arduous labor, which led to illness and mortality rates that threatened to cut into owners' profits.

Frederick Engels described the near-collapse of working-class family life in *The Condition of the Working Class in England*. He detailed the crowded and filthy conditions in working-class homes and quoted one report by the Ministry of Health: "In Leeds, brothers and sisters, and lodgers of both sexes, are found occupying the same sleeping-room with the parents, and consequences occur which humanity shudders to contemplate."[28]

A reinvention of the working-class family was urgently needed. Victorian reformers campaigned for changes in factory work and housing, which led to the creation of a "family wage" for men, an amount that was intended to sustain a family and allow women to stay at home to care for their children and clean their homes. This wage rarely did suffice and many working-class women continued to take in sewing and other piecework. Though the adaptation of the middle-class nuclear family to the working class had the impact of trapping working-class women, it also relieved them from exhausting hours of factory work. Children were sent to school, not only to educate them for future jobs, but also to instill in them the discipline of work. Middle-class sexual mores were propagated widely among the working class to drive down the rate of prostitution and the deadly diseases and out-of-wedlock births that were its consequences.

In *The Construction of Homosexuality*, David Greenberg makes a compelling case for why the rising capitalist order sharpened gender roles and strengthened the ideology of the family.[29] The agricultural societies of seventeenth- and eighteenth-century colonial North America required strict obedience in a world of rigorous labor where there was little social mobility. The priorities of the nineteenth-century market, however, drove shifts in what the new society treasured most of all in the male character—competitiveness and a desire for personal achievement. In this environment, emotional expressiveness, a nurturing attitude, and dependence on others translated into weakness and vulnerability. By 1860, men no longer embraced, cried, or kissed other men in public for fear of appearing effeminate.[30] As men left the home for employment in factories and offices, women's role in raising the children and running the household shaped the medical profession's new gender ideal of women as nurturers and dependent on men for material and social sustenance.

Capitalist society continues to grapple with the contradictions between the privatization of child-rearing and household maintenance and the countervailing forces that tear the family apart. The nuclear family today provides the ruling class with an inexpensive means for the feeding and preservation of the current workforce and the raising and disciplining of the next generation of workers.

The family also serves a sociological function. By training young people to accept traditional sex roles—men are the smart or strong breadwinners, while women are the nurturing companions and child-raisers—families are ideal incubators for rigid sex norms. Homosexual and transgender behaviors present a challenge to this ideological norm. After all, if women can look and act "like men" and men can look and act "like women" and/or if men and women can live in same-sex relationships and each embody attributes conventionally attributed exclusively to men *or* women, gender and familial norms are thrown into question. The behavior of sexual minorities and gender-benders weakens and even defies these sex and gender roles, thus undermining the attitudes most desirable to the smooth functioning of capitalist society.

Half of all American children live in a single-parent family at some point, and half of all marriages end in divorce. As women in industrialized societies have become thoroughly integrated—though unequally paid—in the workforce, women's ability to dissolve marriages and live independent of men has

strengthened. This has created tensions between the ideology of the family and the reality of people's lives. Even the
contentious abortion battle is an expression of this contradiction: as women have become central to the labor force, abortion is both economically necessary and socially desirable to
many. But despite capital's needs for women workers to have
fewer children and to control whether and when to get pregnant, the right wing continues to oppose legal abortion and to
bolster ideology that strengthens the nuclear family and the
ideal of women as mothers.

The American ruling class today is split on the question of
whether to legalize same-sex marriage, because while marriage serves to further legitimize traditional family values,
gay marriage would normalize homosexuality and break
down gender divisions in the working class. Thus, the Christian right sees no contradiction in heralding family values
while depicting the right to same-sex marriage as a harbinger
of an end to all that is sacred. George W. Bush's $1.5 billion
marriage initiative to goad poor (heterosexual) women into
getting and staying married was also fueled by the ruling
class's desire to offload any responsibility to care for their
workers' children, who have five times the chance of living in
poverty and twice the risk of two-parented kids of dropping
out of school.[31]

The battle for equal marriage rights—Massachusetts, Con-
necticut, Iowa, Vermont, and Maine are the only U.S. states
where same-sex marriage has been legalized[32]—is about more
than the 1,049 federal rights and benefits that accrue to those
who are married. Ruling-class bigots who oppose equal marriage rights understand that this civil rights battle could well
open the door to the end of all legal discrimination against

gays and lesbians, in the way that the 1947 California Supreme Court decision striking down the ban on interracial marriage in that state opened the way for further struggles. Gay marriage also challenges the traditional notion of what a family is supposed to look like. Its legalization creates an obvious confrontation with the very idea that there is anything natural about the heterosexual nuclear family.

The construction of homosexuality

Modern capitalism created the "social space" for a gay identity to emerge.[33] Industrial and financial centers concentrated people in huge numbers, thereby creating the potential for anonymity that had never before existed in human societies. Having created the possibility for individuals to live apart from their families and to experiment with alternative sexual practices away from the narrowness of rural life, capitalist society then sought to define and repress this new sexual "deviance." As D'Emilio explains,

> As wage labor spread and production became socialized, then, it became possible to release sexuality from the "imperative" to procreate…. In divesting the household of its economic independence and fostering the separation of sexuality from procreation, capitalism has created conditions that allow some men and women to organize a personal life around their erotic/emotional attraction to their own sex.[34]

Industrial capitalism's hostility to homosexuality is unique in comparison to previous societies' laws punishing alternative sex practices. Whereas old laws condemned homosexual acts that threatened procreation, new proscriptions were enacted against a small class of people whose behavior set them apart from the majority. As British socialist Noel Halifax puts it, "Under capitalism sexuality was now not a 'private affair regulated by...traditions and prejudices of the community' but become 'a public matter for the state.'"[35]

Gay and lesbian stigmatization became systematized as the "homosexual type" in the form of a small minority of men and women whose erotic interests in others of the same sex came to the attention of legal and medical authorities in big cities in the latter half of the nineteenth century. In Britain, laws began to distinguish between bestiality and homosexuality and, for the first time, to punish gay men caught seeking others like themselves in public venues. In 1861, the death penalty for buggery was ended and a sentence of ten years in prison, later amended to two years of hard labor, was enacted because authorities discerned that a sentence less harsh than death was likely to be applied more frequently.

There are some historians who oppose the social constructionist framework and instead argue that homosexuality is part of peoples' essence and has existed throughout history. This "essentialist" viewpoint contends, "queer desire is congenital and then constituted into a meaningful queer identity in childhood."[36] Chapter 7 will take up the biological determinist claims; however, it's important here to assert the centrality of economic and social forces in shaping the possibility for the existence of LGBT identities as we understand them today. It is one thing to argue that sex acts between individuals of the same sex have occurred since there were humans, and quite another to assume a suprahistorical homosexual *identity*.

Social constructionism for Marxists is both materialist and dialectical.[37] In other words, it is based upon an understanding of history that sees human beings both as products of the natural world and as able to interact with their natural surroundings; in the course of their actions humans change themselves and the world around them. Several processes developed over time to create the following: 1) the social spaces for same-sex desire to flourish; 2) the formation through repression, resistance, and accommodation of self-identified homosexuals with subcultures of their own; and 3) the legal regulation of these social spaces that authorities defined as "deviant." Because the development of sexual identity took place over many years as societal shifts enabled it to evolve, there were elements of the later homosexual subculture in the era that preceded the Industrial Revolution. For example, men who had sex with men in what were known as Molly houses in early eighteenth-century London and Paris usually had wives and children and abandoned all effeminate affectations and used quintessentially male mannerisms when they left those houses for work or home. When the Society for the Reformation of Manners worked to close these Molly houses in 1726 and shut down more than twenty, it was part of their campaign against sodomites, prostitutes, and those who didn't honor the Sabbath—not homosexuals.[38]

When essentialists like Rictor Norton challenge constructionists they argue that some Renaissance Italian artists and monks were gay men, yet this contention also serves to undermine his case. The economic and social organization of Florentine and monastic life made it possible for some men in these sections of the Old World to express their homosexual desire— precisely the case constructionists argue. Conditions, however, had not yet ripened for many outside of the arts or the monastery to express this desire or for those who did to see themselves or be seen by others as a separate sexual identity, distinct from heterosexuality. As one historian explains, "The homosexual, however, is not simply a 'sodomite' who has accidentally stumbled into new capitalist conditions."[39] The process of developing gay, lesbian, or bisexual identities occurred over time, with some elements of the new social relations in the old and vice versa. Without the ability to live autonomously, without society's efforts to limit the erotic potential of some human beings, and without the development of a subculture of these new social categories, those who engaged in what modern society refers to as gay sex are likely to have remained sodomites.

In Paris and Berlin, medical and legal experts in the 1870s examined a new kind of "degenerate" to determine whether or not these people should be held responsible for their actions. The word "homosexuality" was first coined in 1869 by a German-Hungarian physician named Karl Maria Benkert (he went by the surname Kertbeny after 1847). Benkert wrote an open letter in defiance of the developing illegality of homosexuality in some German states (unification of Germany did not occur until 1871). Benkert argued that homosexuality was "inborn, not acquired" and therefore should not be punished by the state.[40]

Homosexuality as a modern "type" evolved in scientific circles from a "sin against nature" to a mental illness. The first popular study of homosexuality, *Sexual Inversion* by Havelock Ellis in 1897, put forward the idea that homosexuality was a congenital illness not to be punished, but treated. Nineteenth-century sexologists developed ideas about homosexuality as a form of insanity. One famous theory held that gayness was the result of "urning"—the female mind was trapped in a male body (or vice versa). This widely disseminated theory of sexual "inversion" by Benkert's colleague and friend, Karl Heinrich Ulrichs, referred to homosexuals as a third sex.[41] Ulrichs was the first openly "inverted" man to speak favorably of homosexuality in public forums beginning in the 1860s.

In fact, it took more than two decades after the advent of the "homosexual" before medical doctors began to write about the "heterosexual." Modern bourgeois ideology assumes that we need not trace the genealogy of heterosexuality because it must be a timeless concept and practice. But just as homosexuality was invented, so too was heterosexuality.

The first recorded instance of the word "heterosexual" dates back to medical journals of the early 1890s. The English publication of the Viennese doctor Richard von Krafft-Ebing's *Psychopathia Sexualis* in 1893 actually introduces heterosexuals not as "normal" sexual beings, but as those with wide-ranging sexual appetites that included non-procreative sexual acts, though not with those of the same sex.[42] By 1905, the terms heterosexual and homosexual were in wide enough use for Sigmund Freud to employ them to refer to types of people and feelings, not simply sex acts. His sessions with various upper-class patients led him to conclude that homosexuals must be treated for their "fixation" on what he contended was an "immature" stage of their sexual development. Interestingly, Merriam-Webster's first dictionary entry for homosexuality in 1909 describes it as "morbid sexual passion for one of the same sex," while heterosexuality wasn't defined until 1923.[43]

As historical materialists who believe that peoples' behavior and attitudes are shaped by their material surroundings, it follows that socialists are constructionists when it comes to questions of gender and sexuality. In other words, sexuality is a fluid and not fixed behavior, and its various expressions have been historically determined.

Capitalist society depends on the nuclear family and the ideology that justifies it. Among those ideological tenets are reactionary sexual ideas—including gender norms—that not only reinforce the family but also are used to stoke divisions among workers and the oppressed, as well as to control our behavior. Capitalism's creation—and repression—of sexual identities has produced divisions that have often proved lethal. In a society where people were not oppressed, or even defined, by their sexual identity, people would be able to develop a fully liberated sexuality.

CHAPTER TWO

Repression, Resistance, and War: The Birth of Gay Identity

When the famous Irish-born writer Oscar Wilde was convicted of sodomy in 1895 and sentenced to two years of hard labor, newspapers around the world were filled with lurid descriptions of a form of sexuality few had previously acknowledged existed. The trial came to define gay men in the popular consciousness as effeminate aesthetes, but also raised awareness among latent homosexuals of the existence of others like them. Newspaper accounts allowed Londoners to discover where to go to find men looking to have sex with other men. But it was hardly an exuberant "coming out" moment. Wilde, who was married with two children, accepted the popular clinical thinking about his "condition." His writings of the period reflect the debate about whether homosexuality was a form of sickness or insanity, complaining of his "erotomania" while in prison.[1] For years Wilde remained the world's most famous gay man.

Early on, women who had sex with women were less visible than gay men. Men's greater financial independence and integration in the public spheres of work and community afforded them more opportunities to explore alternative sexual lifestyles. Wage-earning men could live in urban boarding houses where they could invite other men to their rooms, providing an outlet beyond familial controls, something far less available to working-class women. In addition, while most working-class women in the United States during the late-nineteenth and early-twentieth centuries were literate enough to read the Bible, few left records of their intimate lives. As lesbian historian Lillian Faderman concludes, "The possibility of a life as a lesbian had to be socially constructed in order for women to be able to choose such a life. Thus it was not until our century [twentieth] that such a choice became viable for significant numbers of women."[2]

In the mid-nineteenth century, a few working-class women who "passed" as men in order not only to seek employment but also in some instances to pursue romantic relationships with other women came to the attention of authorities. Stories appeared in newspapers about cross-dressing lesbian women such as "Bill" in Missouri who became the secretary of the International Brotherhood of Boilermakers. One report read: "She drank...she swore, she courted girls, she worked hard as her fellows, she fished and camped, she even chewed tobacco."[3] As it was virtually unheard of for women to wear trousers, especially in urban environments, almost nobody suspected the identity of an androgynous woman dressed as a man. Not all of these passing women were lesbians; some were seeking equality with men and freedom from raising children. Performing men's work for men's wages, owning property, holding bank accounts in their own names, and voting were among the many benefits these women accessed that were typically available to men only. But a fair number of these passing women did get married to other women, occasionally more than once, as newspaper headlines of the day announced: "A Gay Deceiver of the Feminine Gender," "Death

Proves 'Married Man' a Woman," and "Poses, Undetected, 60 Years as a Man."[4] Union Army doctors recorded at least four hundred women who served surreptitiously as men during the Civil War.[5]

It was not until the 1880s, when sexual relationships between women in the United States were more openly acknowledged, that they were repressed. Laws against "perversion" and "congenital inversion" were applied to women as well as men for the first time. In Britain, though, lesbianism was left out of the criminal code because Victorian prudery dictated that women had no desire for sex, and legal authorities feared that including sanctions against women having sex with others of their gender would actually promote homosexuality among them. Lord Desart, who had been the director of public prosecutions when Oscar Wilde was imprisoned for sodomy, said this about including lesbianism in the 1921 criminal code: "You are going to tell the whole world that there is such an offense, to bring it to the notice of women who have never heard of it, never thought of it. I think it is a very great mischief."[6]

For American women of the middle class, access to higher education provided the first opportunity to break free from their families and experience life surrounded by other young single women, especially for those attending all-female institutions. Between 1880 and 1900, 50 percent of college women remained single, as opposed to 10 percent of non-student women their age.[7] For those college graduates who sought professional careers, which usually meant eschewing marriage, the phenomenon of cohabitating "spinsters" or "Boston marriages" developed. These same-sex relationships, often referred to at the time as "romantic friendships," were not always sexual, but letters, novels, and occasionally even shared beds indicate they often were. The statistics that sexologist Alfred Kinsey gathered among women born in the late nineteenth century show that 12 percent of them had had orgasms from sexual contact with another woman.[8]

However, some of these women, including radicals like Emma Goldman, didn't always perceive their intimate relationships with other women as lesbian relationships. Despite erotic correspondence between Goldman and Almeda Sperry, a woman with whom she'd reputedly had a sexual affair, Goldman expressed the common notion that lesbians were manhaters, and since she was not antagonistic toward men she didn't categorize herself that way. In one letter, Goldman expressed her dismay about a woman friend who ran off with another woman: "Really, the Lesbians are a crazy lot. Their antagonism to the male is almost a disease with them. I simply can't bear such narrowness."[9] What's striking is that this negative perception of lesbians was echoed by a woman who campaigned on behalf of gays and lesbians and who denounced all legal punishment against homosexuality.

The number of women entering the U.S. labor force between 1870 and 1900 tripled from 1.8 million to 5.3 million, double the rate of increase of women in the population overall.[10] For many of these women leaving their families in rural areas for urban industrial centers, it was the first time they would have an opportunity to live independently, and often they shared housing to save costs. Not all or even most of them experimented with lesbian sex, but anecdotal accounts from some of these women along with the popularity of novels and proliferation of articles about female "inverts" and their "disorders," reveal that lesbianism was on the rise. Prior to 1895, only one article on lesbianism existed in the *Index*

Catalogue of the Library of the Surgeon General's Office, which covered the previous 150 years. By 1916, there were nearly 100 books and 566 articles covering women's sexual "perversions."[11] With social mores hovering between Victorian sexual stultification and the urban lesbian chic of the roaring twenties, early twentieth-century lesbians were construed as gender-bending and even hypersexualized. As Faderman explains, "Lesbianism and masculinity became so closely tied in the public imagination that it was believed that only a masculine woman could be the genuine article."[12]

As industry grew, so did the gap between the lives of the wealthy classes and the impoverished working class. In the late nineteenth century, upper- and middle-class men often sought out casual encounters with younger working-class men whom, they believed, were indifferent to anti-homosexual mores. Aside from bourgeois prejudice, this belief was also based on the real-life conditions of working-class people, who were crowded into one-room tenements and slums where middle-class social rules against sexual promiscuity and alternative sexual activities often did not apply.

The bourgeois family and its moral codes of sexual control and hard work held the upper classes to strict rules of conduct—at least outwardly. They believed that sexual purity among women was essential for them to carry out their domestic roles as teachers and disciplinarians of their children, and sexual control among men allowed them to be successful in business. Men were allowed their occasional discreet trysts, unlike women, but stepping over the line was harshly punished. Oscar Wilde, whose writings were widely read and respected by the middle class, may not have been convicted if he hadn't publicly flaunted his sexual activities with much younger men, amid loud outcries over the corruption of youth and the importance of the family to the maintenance of the British Empire. Lust and sexual perversion were cited by social-purity advocates as enemies of the empire. "Rome fell; other nations have fallen; and if England falls it will be this sin, and her unbelief in God, that will have been her ruin," wrote one advocate of sexual purity.[13]

New patterns of living, however, defied the puritanical calls to abstain from homosexuality. Gays and lesbians invented ways of meeting, and by the early twentieth century virtually every major American and European city—and some small towns—had bars or public places where gays could find one another. Berlin was the global center of a gay subculture, with hundreds of bars and cafés that catered to a largely homosexual clientele until the early thirties rise of the Nazis that laid waste to gay lives and culture. The revolutionary legacy of France made it the only industrial country without laws against homosexuality, and Paris became a magnet for expatriate American lesbian literary figures fleeing repression. Riverside Drive and the Bowery in New York City, Lafayette Park in Washington, D.C., YMCAs and public bathhouses in St. Louis and Chicago all served as gathering spots and cruising spaces for gays. Poet Walt Whitman, the most famous nineteenth-century American homosexual, called Manhattan the "city of orgies, walks and joys" and bragged of New York's "frequent and swift flash of eyes offering me love."[14]

Popular songs among Blacks in the 1920s and 1930s with lesbian and gay themes and titles such as "Sissy Man Blues" and "Fairey Blues" provide evidence of an African-American gay community.[15] Black lesbian butch/femme couples even married in large wedding ceremonies in Harlem during the

1920s. By altering the first name of the butch lesbian, these couples actually obtained legal licenses from the city.[16] Writer Sherwood Anderson popularized these post–First World War marriages in his collection of short stories, *Winesburg, Ohio*. The annual Harlem Hamilton Lodge Ball, or what Blacks in the neighborhood called The Faggots Ball, drew thousands of Black and white men and women to watch and participate in the country's most celebrated and flamboyant drag queen event. Harlem resident Abram Will described what must have been the biggest event to transgress gender and racial norms of that era:

> There were corn-fed "pansies" from the Deep South break-ing traditional folds mixing irrespective of race. There were the sophisticated "things" from Park Avenue and Broadway. There were the big black strapping "darlings" from the heart of Harlem. The Continent, Africa and even Asia had their due share of "ambassadors." The ball was a melting pot, different, exotic and unorthodox, but acceptable.[17]

Gay historian George Chauncey presents a fascinating chal-lenge to the assumption that all early gays were closeted, par-ticularly those in big American cities like New York. Using police records, newspaper accounts, novels, letters, and diaries between 1890 and 1940, Chauncey counters "the myth of invisi-bility" and focuses on a thriving gay male scene in Harlem, Greenwich Village, the Lower East Side, and Times Square neighborhoods in *Gay New York*.[18] But only those men who as-sumed the sexual role and effeminate dress and mannerisms of women conceived of themselves as gay, or called themselves by the popular terms of the day: "fairy," "pansy," or "queer." In that sense, gender identity was what determined sexual iden-tity, including for those partaking in homosexual sex. As

Chauncey argues, "The heterosexual-homosexual binarism that governs our thinking about sexuality today, and that, as we shall see, was already becoming hegemonic in middle-class sexual ideology, did not yet constitute the common sense of working-class sexual ideology."[19] In a sense, the campy femininity of those who identified as gay often acted to reconfirm the masculinity of "normal" men who had sex with them. Gay men wanting to attract suitors dressed and spoke in ways that were known to be gay, and hung out in parks, bathhouses, and pubs where they could attract others like themselves or working men and sailors on leave looking for sex.

Gays in working-class districts were accepted in some circles as part of city life, if not always respected or welcomed. They made easy targets for those looking to steal from or rough up someone whose outlaw status made it unlikely that they would go to the police, as hundreds of those suspected of being homosexual were arrested on charges of "indecency" every year. While it is difficult to speculate on how people attracted to those of the same sex perceived themselves in the era prior to the Second World War, evidence from diaries and novels seems to indicate that "'Coming out'…was a lonely, difficult, and sometimes excruciatingly painful experience."[20] Even for those able to enjoy the urban gay subculture in their leisure time, coming out to families and coworkers most often meant risking social ostracism at least and the loss of a job in most cases. No wonder then that some of the liveliest gay American scenes were in places where men lived apart from the families and communities in which they were raised.

With the exception of Jewish immigrants fleeing pogroms in Eastern Europe, most of the millions of immigrants arriving in New York from Ireland, Italy, and elsewhere around the turn of the twentieth century did not come with their families. For example, 80 percent of Italians who came to the United States between 1880 and 1910 were men, most of them between fourteen and forty years old. By contrast, 42 percent of immigrant Jews were women and 25 percent were under fourteen years of age.[21] The huge influx of single working men often settled in tenements and rooming houses, far from wives and family, if they had any. The *New York Times Magazine* referred to its hometown as the "City of the Single," where during the first third of the twentieth century, 40 percent of the male population over fourteen was unmarried.[22] The social, work, and home lives of working-class men were conducted in largely sex-segregated environments. Even most popular after-work entertainment in pubs was largely male, since aside from prostitutes women rarely frequented pubs in that era. The lack of available women, as well as the camaraderie of the workplace, the military, and the bars, led some of these men to experiment sexually with other men. During the gold rush of the late nineteenth century, a vast migration of miners and speculators streamed into San Francisco, already California's biggest port city, creating huge concentrations of single migrant men passing through that city's boarding houses. "In 1890, there was one saloon for every ninety-six residents, the highest proportion in the United States—double that of New York or Chicago," explains one historian.[23] In San Francisco as in New York, this large transient population was less likely to feel the constraints of social norms and rules.

Fear of public exposure and middle-class social convention drove thousands of professional men, often married with children, to have sex with working men in secret, on the "down low." They went "slumming" on the Bowery, in Greenwich

Village cafés, in San Francisco's North Beach, and at the massive Harlem balls. Tragically, many of them blamed the more flamboyant gays and "mannish" lesbians for the hostility and fear mainstream society heaped on them. One gay man in the 1930s summed up the contempt of many "assimilated" middle-class gays this way: "As the cultured, distinguished, conservative Jew or Negro loathes and deplores his vulgar, socially unacceptable stereotype…so does their homosexual counterpart resent his caricature in the flaming faggot…. The general public [makes no distinction], and the one is penalized and ostracized for the grossness and excesses of the other."[24]

The new openness of urban gay subcultures gave way to new theories of homosexual behavior. Doctors and sexologists advanced the notion that homosexuality was inherent in a person who had no power to change his or her nature. The widespread conception of gays as butch women and effeminate men ran so counter to the feminine and masculine ideals put forward in popular culture that ruling-class ideology embraced the unscientific conclusion that gays were suffering from a condition that set them apart from "normal" people. Gender-based biological explanations only served to confirm the inevitability of bourgeois gender norms and the nuclear family.

Many gays and lesbians themselves thought that their erotic urges and desires made them fundamentally different from heterosexual society. Writers such as Radclyffe Hall, who successfully fought the banning in the United States of her lesbian novel *The Well of Loneliness* in 1928 (it was, however, banned in Britain), popularized the medical definition of homosexuality as an inescapable, emotionally tormenting, natural deviance. *The Well of Lonliness* remains today one of the most widely read lesbian works of fiction, despite its anachronistic portrayal of sexual inversion. It was for years the only lesbian novel that demanded of the world, "Give us also the right to our existence!"[25]

The development of a visible and identifiable gay minority not only led to gay oppression but also to the possibility of organized resistance to it. Socialist Eleanor Marx, daughter of Karl Marx and a close friend of sexologist Havelock Ellis, wrote and spoke frequently to large crowds on women's liberation and the rights of homosexuals. In Germany, Social Democratic Party (SPD) member Magnus Hirschfeld started the first gay organization, the Scientific-Humanitarian Committee, in 1897. Hirschfeld, with the support of the SPD, campaigned to repeal a law against men having consensual sex.[26] During the failed German Revolution of 1918–1923, dozens of gay organizations and periodicals appeared calling for the liberation of homosexuals. Following the Russian Revolution of 1917, when all laws against gays were struck from the books, the German Communist Party argued, "The class-conscious proletariat...approaches the question of sex life and also the problem of homosexuality with a lack of prejudice.... [T]he proletariat...demands the same freedom from restrictions for those forms of sex life as for intercourse between the sexes."[27] The anarchist Emma Goldman went on a speaking tour throughout the United States in 1915 and defended homosexuality. Goldman commented to friends about the numbers of men and women who would approach her afterward to say that it was the first time they had ever heard about others like themselves.[28]

But for most gays and lesbians through the early twentieth century, life was filled with self-hatred and public condemnation. Few had the luxury of coming out for fear of losing jobs or the risk of becoming a social pariah. Pervasive legal and religious hostility and social restrictions sent many to seek a "cure" from doctors or to find a release from emotional strain and internalized self-loathing through alcohol and drugs. In a pattern that was to repeat itself later in the twenti- eth century, gay life in the United States was forced out of the public sphere by the end of the twenties as authorities and their ideology reasserted control over the sex lives of work- ers and the poor. As Chauncey argues, "the state built a closet in the 1930s and forced gay people to hide in it."[29]

"Do you like girls?"

Sixteen million young American men and women enlisted or were drafted for duty during the Second World War. Almost as many millions more—mostly young women—left home for military or industrial jobs in new cities, often living in board- ing houses and dorms, as part of the war effort. Never before had there been this many young people mobilized into sex- segregated living situations, often under life-and-death condi- tions in which bonds between people can be intense and long lasting. The impact on sexuality overall, and on homosexual- ity in particular, was astonishing.

Among the famous gays who served were actors Tyrone Power and Rock Hudson and writers Gore Vidal and John Cheever. But a wealth of evidence exists to prove that the war created conditions for sexual experimentation and the devel- opment of a gay identity among hundreds of thousands, if not more. If researcher Alfred Kinsey's wartime studies are accu- rate and can be applied to the U.S. military population, then at least 650,000 and as many as 1.6 million male soldiers were gay.[30] D'Emilio writes,

In releasing large numbers of Americans from their homes and neighborhoods, World War II created a substantially new "erotic situation" conducive both to the articulation of a homosexual identity and to the more rapid evolution of a gay subculture. For some gay men and women, the war years simply strengthened a way of living they had previously chosen.... At the same time, those who experienced strong same-sex attraction but felt inhibited from acting upon it suddenly possessed relatively more freedom to enter into homosexual relationships. The unusual conditions of a mobilized society allowed homosexual desire to be expressed more easily in action. For many gay Americans, World War II created something of a nationwide coming out experience.[31]

The First World War, by comparison, only mobilized 4.7 million Americans over a nineteen-month period.[32] However, its cataclysmic impact on European life translated into a similar phenomenon there. Books referring to sexual trysts in the trenches, homoerotic relationships between comrades in arms, poetic exchanges, and long nights in fear- and lust-induced embraces are chronicled in collections such as *Lads: Love Poetry of the Trenches*.[33] Of the homosexually-tinged poetry between soldiers, one writer explains, "No one turning from the poetry of the Second World War to that of the First can fail to notice there the unique physical tenderness, the readiness to admire openly the bodily beauty of young men, the unapologetic recognition that men may be in love with each other."[34] In the twenties, a largely underground subculture for gay men and lesbian women expanded in London, Paris, and Berlin in particular. The successful prosecution in Britain of Radclyffe Hall's *The Well of Loneliness* in 1928 was evidence of the continued state repression of any open expression of same-sex love, even in popular literature.

One major, if indirect, impact that the First World War had on gays in the U.S. military was the $1 billion cost incurred for the care of psychiatric casualties—half of all veterans' hospital beds were still filled with psychiatric inpatients at the start of the Second World War.[35] This enormous cost was used as an incentive by the emerging psychiatric profession to promote the necessity of psychiatric screening for the millions of military inductees in the lead-up to the new war.

One of the chief advocates for psychiatric screening, Harry Stack Sullivan, was a psychologist who lived discreetly with his male lover in Bethesda, Maryland. Sullivan did not believe that gays should be banned from military service or discriminated against in any way and had no intention of including any reference to homosexuality in the screening. But in May 1941, the Army Surgeon General's office for the first time included "homosexual proclivities in their lists of disqualifying deviations."[36] There were—of course—no scientific means of determining who was gay; therefore, crude guidelines called for excluding any man who displayed "feminine bodily characteristics," "effeminacy in dress and manner," or "a patulous (expanded) rectum." As historian Allan Bérubé notes, "All three of these markers linked homosexuality with effeminacy or sexually 'passive' anal intercourse and ignored gay men who were masculine or 'active' in anal intercourse."[37]

What this amounted to in practice was hardly scientific. Millions of young men were forced to stand naked in front of physicians, or their assistants, and were asked—often to their great embarrassment—"Do you like girls?"[38] Given the years of propaganda for a coming war against the Nazis, the stigma of being deemed unfit for service, and the fact that nearly a whole generation was being mobilized to fight, ample incentive existed for those who knew they were gay to lie and go to war with their peers.

Coming out in close quarters

The armed forces segregated men in crowded barracks or in close ship quarters. The fear of death in a war that killed more than four hundred thousand Americans was ever present and created harsh and extraordinary circumstances in which the norms of civilian life were often suspended. Men on leave in port cities danced together, an offense that would have brought arrest during peacetime; soldiers performed in popular drag shows with explicit homosexual themes to rapturous applause in Europe and the Pacific; GIs shared beds in crowded YMCAs and slept wrapped in each others' arms in public parks while waiting to be shipped overseas; and intense emotional bonds were formed between soldiers who were often physically demonstrative in ways that American male culture in peacetime condemns.[39] This created an atmosphere in which homosexuality was often ignored or accepted by peers. Gay veterans, such as Long Island native Bob Ruffing, recall how easy it was to cruise other men in the military. Said Ruffing, "When I first got into the navy—in the recreation hall, for instance—there'd be eye contact, and pretty soon you'd get to know one or two people and kept branching out. All of a sudden you had a vast network of friends, usually through this eye contact thing, some through outright cruising. They could get away with it in that atmosphere."[40]

Nearly 250,000 women served in the armed forces, most of them in the Women's Army Corps (WAC), and few, if any,

were rejected for lesbianism. Working as mechanics, drill in-
structors, and motor vehicle operators, women in the armed
services were recruited with posters showing muscular, short-
haired women wearing tight-fitting, tailored uniforms. Training manuals praised the female comradeship and close bonds
between recruits, two-thirds of whom were single women
under the age of twenty-five. There is evidence to suggest that
a disproportionate number of women who joined the WAC
were lesbians looking to meet other women and to get the opportunity to do "men's work."[41] Even a popular Fleischmann's
Yeast advertisement during the war showed a uniformed WAC
riding a motorcycle beneath the heading: "This is no time to
be FRAIL."[42] More than a few WAC veterans recall women
showing up for their inductions wearing men's clothing with
their hair slicked back in the classic butch style of out lesbians
of the day.

The realities of the war and the dire need for servicemen
and women trumped all other concerns of the War Department. Despite the official hostility to homosexuality in the
military, very few gays were actually rejected. Out of eighteen
million men examined for service, only four thousand to five
thousand were officially nixed for being homosexual.[43]

The most famous example of how central many gays and
lesbians were to the war effort and the impact that had on
forcing an unofficial wartime suspension of the witch hunt is
recounted by historian Randy Shilts. General Dwight Eisenhower, acting on a rumor, ordered a member of his staff,
WAC sergeant Johnnie Phelps, to draw up a list of all lesbians
serving in the WAC battalion for him to dismiss from service.
After informing him of the medal-winning service of the battalion and the vast number of lesbians in it, Phelps said, "I'll

make your list, but you've got to know that when you get the list back, my name's going to be first." The secretary of the battalion then interrupted to say, "Sir, if the General pleases, Sergeant Phelps will have to be second on the list. I'm going to type it. My name will be first."[44] General Eisenhower promptly tore up the order.

With millions of men gone from the workforce, jobs in aircraft and shipbuilding, as well as in clerical and consumer industries, opened up to women for the first time. Many women had to relocate in order to take these jobs and found housing in same-sex dormitories, boarding houses, and trailers. Aside from working and living in close proximity with other women, many had a chance to socialize in all-female environments. Despite persistent anti-homosexual bias in society, the unprecedented mobility afforded to many working-class women during the war loosened previous sexual constraints. As D'Emilio argues,

> The war temporarily weakened the patterns of daily life that channeled men and women toward heterosexuality and inhibited homosexual expression.... For men and women conscious of a strong attraction to their own sex but constrained by their milieu from acting upon it, the war years eased the coming out process and facilitated entry into the gay world.[45]

The social upheaval created by the Second World War has had a long-lasting impact on gay life in the United States. Some men and women who had been pulled from small-town life at an early age were attracted to port cities, such as San Francisco, which presented the opportunity to be openly gay among a community of others like themselves. San Francisco in particular became a gay mecca toward the end of the war, when fighting was most intense in the Pacific, and official military policy turned up the heat on gays, discharging gay men by the hundreds into the picturesque port town. Denver, Kansas City, Buffalo, and San Jose, California, among other cities, opened their first gay bars after the war and developed the beginnings of gay enclaves. During the postwar period, there was a flood of new gay- and lesbian-themed books in which, unlike past works, gay characters accepted their sexuality, even if these books still portrayed gay and lesbian characters as tragic figures. Like many Black soldiers who were emboldened to fight against racial segregation at home after their participation in a war they were told was about fighting for democracy, gays returned from the war with a greater sense of entitlement to rights and benefits.

Tellingly, while the U.S. government attacked the barbarism of the Nazis, it managed to avoid any discussion of Adolf Hitler's treatment of homosexuals. While gays were "coming out under fire" in the American armed forces, the Nazis went on a campaign of terror against homosexuals in Germany. Beginning in 1938, gays and lesbians were sent to concentration camps and were forced to wear pink triangles. Berlin, which had been home to one of the world's largest gay subcultures, became a nightmare for gays. "Indecent activities" between two men or two women—a touch, a kiss, or handholding—were enough to be sent to the camps. The head of Hitler's storm troopers, Heinrich Himmler, said, "We must exterminate these people root and branch...the homosexual must be entirely eliminated."[46] The Nazis claimed to be doing all of this in the name of the sanctity of the family and motherhood. In Germany, a country wracked by unemployment and destitution and gearing up for war, Hitler imposed a complete lockdown on dissent of every kind, including implied dissent of homosexuality.

Among the many crimes of the United States in that war, one crime that has remained largely hidden from history is the decision by the U.S. occupying forces to continue the imprisonment after the war of gays and lesbians who were found in Hitler's concentration camps.[47] Of the estimated fifteen thousand gays sent to the camps, one-third survived, many of whom were forced to remain in prison in American-occupied West Germany through the 1960s, when the Nazi-era anti-homosexual law, Paragraph 175, was finally stricken from the books.[48]

While the number of homosexuals thrown into Hitler's camps is far outnumbered by other targeted groups, accounts from survivors leave no doubt of the universality of barbarism meted out to all of the Third Reich's victims. Of the non-Jewish prisoners in the camps, homosexuals had the highest death rates, 53 percent, three-quarters of whom died within a year of their imprisonment.[49] Pierre Seel's memoir of his experiences in the camps describes vividly the recollection that decades later still awakens him shrieking into the night. He was ordered along with others of his barracks to watch in indescribable horror as his eighteen-year-old lover was stripped naked and torn to shreds by German shepherds while his lover's final screams echoed inside a tin pail placed over his head.[50]

Cold War crackdown

Nothing shook up the sexual consciousness of postwar American society like the release of the 1948 and 1953 Kinsey Reports on American male and female sexual behavior. Fifty percent of ten thousand men surveyed admitted erotic feelings at some point toward other men; 37 percent had had sex with men; 4 percent claimed to be gay. Of the women surveyed, 28 percent admitted erotic feelings toward other women, while 13 percent said they'd had sex with women; about 2 percent said they were lesbians.[51] Alfred Kinsey commented at the time that, given the predominance of homophobia, his results indicated "such activity would appear in the histories of a much larger portion of the population if there were no social constraints."[52] Kinsey's studies gave public expression to the reality of a growing gay minority in the United States. This was to have a profound impact on gays' ability to mobilize for their rights. In the immediate postwar period gays in the United States went from complete isolation to developing an awareness of themselves as an oppressed class of people.

As groundbreaking as these studies were in revealing the widespread presence of lesbian, gay, and bisexual people in U.S. society after the war, it is important not to take Kinsey's figures as permanent and suprahistorical. Instead, what Kinsey's studies and others since suggest is that LGBT people are not a fixed proportion of any society, but instead their ability to come out or for anyone to explore alternative sexual possibilities are largely shaped by fluctuating social and economic conditions. D'Emilio again sums up well the implications of this perspective:

> I have argued that lesbian and gay identity and communities are historically created, the result of a process of capitalist development that has spanned many generations. A corollary of this argument is that we are not a fixed social minority composed for all time of a certain percentage of the population. There are more of us than one hundred

years ago, more of us than forty years ago. And there may very well be more gay men and lesbians in the future.[53]

If the war opened up a vast space for the development of a gay community, the postwar period witnessed concerted attempts to close that space. The shifting needs of the American Empire, which emerged from the war a superpower, did in fact create both the conditions for heightened repression and sowed the seeds of opposition.

There were strong economic and social incentives for ratcheting up harassment and legal discrimination against gays after the war. With U.S. industry churning out more than 60 percent of all manufactured goods in the world, the need for a higher birth rate to staff the labor force and military raised the idealization of the nuclear family to new levels. America's new industrial prowess brought household appliances and a marketing blitz unknown to previous generations of workers.

Women were driven out of the industrial jobs they held during the war. White women were told to go back home, put on housedresses, and make babies, while Black women were meant to return to their prewar jobs as low-wage domestic servants. Gone were women's practical, square-shouldered, androgynous fashions of the 1940s; in came the frilly dresses with exaggerated busts and hyperfeminine lines of the 1950s.

Unlike the previous image of the working-class male—who in the thirties and late forties unionized, took political action, and went on strike—a new masculine domesticity was encouraged. Sociologists like C. Wright Mills dissected Corporate America's drive to create "organization man," an obedient team player who assiduously followed the rules of the corporate structure, bowed to authority, and sought domestic security while eschewing confrontation and struggle. The new medium of television was used to help promote a suburban family man and avid consumer in shows like *Father Knows Best*, *Leave It to Beaver*, and *The Adventures of Ozzie and Harriet*. As one historian put it, "Cold War political discourse tended to position Americans who protested the rise of 'organization man' or who rejected the postwar American dream of owning a home in the suburbs as homosexuals and lesbians who threatened the nation's security."[54]

This heightened emphasis on the nuclear family was part and parcel of an era of political reaction in the United States. The launching of the Cold War with the Soviet Union brought with it an anticommunist witch hunt at home, led by Senator Joseph McCarthy. Gays were among McCarthyism's many targets. Liberal historian Arthur Schlesinger, both reflecting and promoting the twisted conflation of communism and homosexuality of the time, equated the way secret members of the Communist Party supposedly recognized each other to gay men cruising for sex in public places in his 1949 work, *The Vital Center*.[55]

The U.S. Senate launched an investigation into allegations of homosexuals "and other perverts" in federal government jobs in 1950. According to the Senate report, gays "lack the emotional stability of normal persons"; "sex perversion weakens the individual"; and "espionage agents could blackmail them."[56] This led to President Eisenhower's executive order calling for the dismissal of homosexuals from government service. Disbarment from the military of gays, or suspected gays, went from a trickle to two thousand every year during the 1950s, and up to three thousand or more per year into the 1960s.[57] D'Emilio situates the crackdown on gays and lesbians within the wider social context:

The anti-homosexual campaigns of the 1950s represented but one front in a widespread effort to reconstruct patterns of sexuality and gender relations shaken by depression and war. The targeting of homosexuals and lesbians itself testified to the depths of the changes that had occurred in the 1940s since, without the growth of a gay subculture, it is difficult to imagine the homosexual issue carrying much weight. The labeling of sexual deviants helped to define the norm for men and women.... There was a congruence between anti-Communism in the sphere of politics and social concern over homosexuality. The attempt to suppress sexual deviance paralleled and reinforced the efforts to quash political dissent.[58]

Though both gays and Communist Party (CP) members were persecuted by the anticommunist witch hunt, gays could not look to the CP for solidarity. After Stalin took power in the Soviet Union, he reversed all the gains made by the 1917 Revolution by the early 1930s, including the revolution's laws decriminalizing gay sexuality. The CP in the 1950s adopted Stalin's hostility to homosexuality, denouncing it as a "bourgeois deviation."[59]

Nonetheless, the first U.S. movement to organize against gay discrimination on the job and police harassment in the bars and cruising spots was initiated by former members of the CP. The broader critique of economic injustice and racism that initially attracted many people to the CP, despite its many failings, not surprisingly compelled these communists to take up the fight against antigay bigotry. Harry Hay left the CP—and his wife—to help found the Mattachine Society in Southern California in 1950. Named after an ancient masked secret fraternity that told truth to power, the Society's "Statement of Purpose" claimed the group's goals were to unify, educate, and lead the homophile—meaning pro-homosexual—movement. Shaped by the reactionary atmosphere and isolation that defined the lives of most gay and lesbian people, the statement called for the creation of a feeling of "belonging," to develop "a homosexual ethic...disciplined, moral, and socially responsible," and to "provide leadership to the whole mass of social deviants."[60] Yet, these "pioneers in a hostile society,"[61] began to develop a theoretical understanding of their oppression rooted in the structure of capitalist society, solidarized with Latinos assaulted by police, and experienced rapid growth in organizing efforts after waging a successful campaign against the police entrapment of one of their members. By 1953, they estimated that more than two thousand men and women had participated in Mattachine's activities.[62] In an era of racial segregation, Mattachine was open to all. A Black member of the organization, Guy Rousseau, provided the name for the monthly magazine, *One*, whose editorial board members were in Mattachine. The title's allusion to Second World War jargon, "He's one," was recognizable to gay men of that era.[63]

But the gay movement was not immune to the McCarthy crusade. A red-baiting article attacking the group's secrecy and insinuating communist influences inside Mattachine appeared in 1953 in the Los Angeles *Mirror*, stoking suspicion and division within the group, with profound ramifications for Mattachine's structure and political organizing thereafter. With the House Un-American Activities Committee (HUAC) in full swing against communists and dissenters of every sort, anticommunist gays took over the leadership of the group, banned communists like Hay, and turned away from challenging the government jobs ban to focus on urging its members to "try to get cured."[64]

Hay stayed active in gay politics throughout his life and remained committed to struggles against oppression and exploitation. When film director Elia Kazan—who had cooperated with the McCarthyite HUAC hearings in 1952 by providing names of communists—was given an Honorary Academy Award in 1999, an elderly Hay and his lover John Burnside joined hundreds in protesting Kazan's duplicity. The eighty-seven-year-old Hay proudly marched wearing his signature love beads and long mane of gray hair, saying he was an unrepentant communist who had no regrets for having helped launch a movement that changed his own life and affected millions of others.[65]

In San Francisco in 1955, lovers Del Martin and Phyllis Lyon founded the Daughters of Bilitis (DOB), naming the lesbian advocacy group after an erotic poem. More than fifty years later, this couple was the first in San Francisco to marry after the California Supreme Court found the illegality of same-sex marriage to be unconstitutional, though notably the corporate media made almost no mention of their historic contribution to lesbian rights.

Given the much lower visibility and numbers of lesbian activists, the group of mostly white-collar women workers focused on lesbian self-help and tried to provide a social space outside the bar scene, as limited as it was. An estimated thirty lesbian bars existed throughout the country by 1963, whereas there were that many gay male bars in San Francisco alone.

The Cold War atmosphere and constant police harassment helped to nudge both the Mattachine Society and the DOB in a conservative political direction. Both organizations sought to "stress conformity" in order to "diffuse social hostility as a prelude to changes in the law and social policy."[66] Del

Martin's "President's Message" that appeared in the first issue of the DOB's publication, the *Ladder*, argued, "Membership is open to anyone who is interested in the minority problems of the sexual variant.... Why not discard the hermitage for the heritage that awaits any red-blooded American woman who dares to claim it?"[67] The one big victory of that era came in 1958 when the Supreme Court ruled unanimously in an un-written decision to allow the circulation of the gay publication *One* through the mail.

The continued repression of gays and lesbians in American society served to keep most of them closeted. Hollywood films portrayed gays as tragic and suicidal figures. *Time* magazine ran a story on homosexuality in 1966 in which the author character-ized it as "a pathetic little second-rate substitute for reality...no pretense that it is a pernicious sickness."[68] The American Psy-chiatric Association kept homosexuality on the books as a mental illness until 1973, when the struggles of the late 1960s and early 1970s forced a change in medical thinking.

The battle over LGBT people in the military

Despite the fact that, in 2008, 75 percent of all Americans supported the right of LGBT people to serve openly in the military—including majorities of both major political parties and 50 percent of military personnel—the "don't ask, don't tell" policy signed into law by Bill Clinton remains in place.[69] There has been rising support for un-closeted LGBT mili-tary servicepeople over the years since the policy was en-acted in 1993, when 44 percent of the overall population supported the right of gays to serve openly in the military.[70] Any notion that this policy overturned the antigay witch hunt is misguided, even though it technically allows lesbians and gays to serve so long as they remain closeted. According to the Servicemembers Legal Defense Network, the Pentagon fires two LGBT people each day, which is actually fewer than the number hounded out of the military prior to the wars inspired by the events of September 11, 2001.[71]

In late August 2008, the first-ever study was done on transgender military personnel and their treatment. More than one-third of the 827 people surveyed said they had experienced discrimination and 10 percent had been turned away by the Veterans Administration due to their sexual nonconformity.[72] In defiance of the actual policy, one in five transgender military personnel had been asked about their sexual orientation. In keeping with military social mores that value masculinity over femininity, pre-transition transwomen (men who are physically transitioning into women) had been discriminated against more than pre-transition transmen (women who are physically transitioning into men).[73]

Any suggestion that lifting such a ban would amount to a wild social experiment is easily put to rest by the facts. Twenty-four nations, including those with recent histories of fascist or apartheid regimes, such as Spain and South Africa, currently have LGBT people serving openly in their military forces with no serious internal strife reported. This is not a new development. Back in 1992, when the ban on gays in the military was being debated during an election year, the *Washington Monthly* weighed in decisively on the question:

> But with our policy stuck in hypotheticals, the strongest argument for gays in the military is quietly made elsewhere—in countries such as Holland, Denmark, Sweden, Israel, and to a lesser extent France, where gays have already been in-

tegrated into the armed forces. While the Pentagon pursues a policy that every year hounds 1,000 able-bodied gay men and women out of the service—wasting $27 million in training costs annually—other countries demonstrate that with the right mix of education and cajoling, a military with gays can work.[74]

Why then was a policy that institutionalizes discrimination and advances reactionary gender norms enacted in the first place? While the 1992 election campaign was marked by rabid homophobia from the podium of the Republican National Convention, the party leadership was not immune to the social upheavals taking place on the streets. As will be discussed in greater detail in later chapters, the AIDS (acquired immune deficiency syndrome) crisis sparked a rise in LGBT activism from 1988 to 1992, to a level not seen since the early 1970s. Then-Secretary of Defense Dick Cheney had even argued that excluding gays from the military on the basis of them being a security risk was an "old chestnut."[75] When activists outed President George H. W. Bush's Pentagon spokesman Pete Williams as gay, Bush responded, "Who cares?"[76]

Yet the leadership of the Democratic Party under the rising star of Arkansas governor Bill Clinton adopted an approach that has become familiar to millions of Americans since. They "compromised" with the far right while equivocating and insisting that their deal was both pragmatic and just. Clinton expressed sympathy and hosted an unprecedented personal meeting with gay and lesbian leaders in the White House to promise lifting the ban on gays in the military—as well as promising to pass gay civil rights legislation—all the while betraying his base. Exactly four days after his inauguration, Bill Clinton's administration "declared defeat and unconditionally surrendered on the issue" on *Face the Nation*.[77] In a posture that was to become the standard on virtually every social and economic policy, the Clinton administration—with both houses of Congress in Democrats' hands—insisted that if his base didn't support a crappy deal, a worse one was sure to pass instead. The politics of lesser-evilism, that is, the presumption that accepting a bad deal is the best way to prevent something worse, became the political justification for many of Clinton's most conservative and pro-corporate policies. As one gay Democratic Party activist put it at the time, "we elected a president and got a barometer."[78]

Some political responsibility for the "don't ask, don't tell" legislation must be laid at the door of the leadership of many of the LGBT groups as well, in particular Human Rights Campaign (HRC). In 1993, an estimated one million people marched on Washington for LGBT rights, yet the movement leaders diverted an estimated $3 million into the Democratic Party coffers and deflated the demands of activists hungry for change.[79] Urvashi Vaid, a former leading member of the National Gay and Lesbian Task Force (NGLTF), is refreshingly honest and reflective on the decisions taken at that time when she writes:

> Electoral politics is extremely seductive to all movements for social change; it seems the shortest distance to liberation. The theory is invitingly simple: elect people who support you, and they will do the right thing. But the fact is that when broad-based protest movements—like the black civil rights movement and the women's liberation movement—shifted their major focus from community organizing to electing our own, the movements lost momentum even as they gained mainstream acceptability.[80]

In the run-up to the 2008 presidential election, all the major Democratic candidates—including Hillary Clinton and Barack Obama—called for the repeal of "don't ask, don't tell" in their primary campaigns. Former secretary of state and retired general Colin Powell, who helped craft the policy under Bill Clinton, called for "reevaluating" the policy in December 2008 given the shifts in public attitudes over the years since it was implemented.[81] It remains to be seen what will come of this, though with wars spreading and quagmires deepening it's quite possible that this anachronistic nod to bigotry may be swept aside out of sheer desperation for more "boots on the ground." But if history is a teacher, without activists putting pressure on politicians, it is possible that we could see the end of "don't ask, don't tell" and the creation of some other "compromise" to appease homophobes in the military and government. Nonetheless, if LGBT people are eventually deemed qualified to kill or be killed for the empire, then other legal and social restrictions would only be amplified.

Some progressives who oppose U.S. military operations around the world ask whether the left ought to support the right of sexual minorities to serve openly in the military. What is the point, they argue, of challenging legal restrictions to the bulwark of American imperialism if one doesn't agree with its methods and aims? While hostility to the military is certainly understandable, this approach raises the question too narrowly and ignores the wider implications of social policies advanced by the federal government in its hiring practices. In essence, allowing the U.S. government to continue to discriminate on the basis of sexual and gender behavior in its military workforce of nearly three million people[82] gives a green light to persistent social and legal restrictions on LGBT people and continued bigotry. There is nothing incompatible with demanding an end to draconian laws barring open LGBT folks from serving in the military while opposing armed forces recruitment and U.S. imperial actions all over the world. The demand for equal access not only exposes the hypocrisy of an institution that claims to expand democracy while advancing its antithesis, but it can also have a direct impact on the lives and consciousness of millions of people who are compelled by economic circumstance or social conditioning to turn to the military for employment. In addition, it can create yet another chink in the system's ideological armor. As with war itself, demands for equality, even inside a reactionary institution, can have unintended consequences.

CHAPTER THREE

The Myth of Marxist Homophobia

The argument that Marxism either ignores or relegates issues of oppression to the back burner because it "privileges" class has become pervasive in recent decades. These ideas are put forward by those who want to separate class from oppression and see the two as running on different, parallel tracks. It has created a mythology of Marxism's supposed blind spot—or even hostility—when it comes to attitudes and practices regarding homosexuality. At best, we are told, Marxists put off the question of sexual liberation until after the dilemma of workers' power is resolved. At worst, the argument goes, Marxists are indifferent or unsympathetic to the oppression of sexual minorities.

One typical criticism is cited from the *Journal of Homosexuality* in the widely read online encyclopedia, Wikipedia:

> [S]exuality and the problematic of femininity/masculinity were disowned as legitimate issues as Marxism came to dominate. Utopian socialism's methods...were narrowed by Marxism to class struggle; utopian socialism's goal—new social relationships between people—was restricted to a new economic order and redistribution of material goods.[1]

Lenin and Leninism are subjected to particular criticism. "Leninism, which dominated left political discourse, 'rejected many of the feminist and sex-radical traditions' of the pre-war left,"[2] write anarchist historians on the Bolsheviks after the First World War. "The Communist Party was—especially when compared to the pre-war anarchists—a redoubt of heteronormative attitudes."[3] As with similar historiographies, the anarchist history of homosexuality in the United States in which these quotes are cited, *Free Comrades*, completely ignores the radical sexual gains of the revolution in which Lenin played a leading role (detailed below), while repeating well-worn hearsay and conflating the Stalinist legacy with that of Marxism.

The treatment of LGBT people in Stalinist and Maoist states in the twentieth century has served to mask the earlier record of the socialist movement regarding sexual freedom. Sexual minorities under Stalin and later Mao and Castro were imprisoned, tormented, and generally targeted for abuse in states that falsely claimed the mantle of socialism. Tragically, many Westerners on the far left—though not all—defended these abuses or rationalized attitudes and behaviors that are anathema to the commitment to human liberation that lies at heart of Marxism. In addition, the legacy of McCarthyite anticommunism in the United States in particular, combined with the middle-class outlook that often dominates in academia and modern gay movements, serve to discredit, dismiss, and distort the contributions of socialists and the liberating potential of the Marxist tradition on this question. Let us set the record straight, so to speak.

Marxism and oppression

Because the ruling class under capitalism is a small minority of the population, it must use the institutional and ideological tools at its disposal to divide the mass of the population against itself in order to prevent the majority of exploited peoples of the world from uniting and rising in unison to take back what is rightfully theirs. Homophobic, sexist, racist, nationalist, and other divisions in modern society reflect the needs of the class that owns and controls capital. The Black abolitionist Frederick Douglass put it aptly when he said of the slaveholders, "They divided both to conquer each."[4]

Contrary to the dominant myth of socialism prevalent in the academy, Marxists do not reduce the oppression of sexual minorities—or anyone else—to the issue of class. Rather, Marxists locate the source of racial, gender, sexual, and all other oppressions within the framework of capitalist class relations. As the earlier discussion of the nuclear family showed, women's oppression derives from the structure of the family, in which the reproduction and maintenance (child care, housework, cooking, etc.) of the current and future generations of workers are foisted upon individual families rather than being the responsibility of society. Capitalism depends on privatized reproduction to raise the next generation of workers at little expense to itself. Likewise, the oppression of LGBT people stems from the implicit challenge that sexual minorities pose to the nuclear family and its gender norms.

Far from subordinating the issue of fighting homophobia and transphobia to the class struggle, Marxists cannot conceive of the liberation of the exploited without the liberation of the oppressed. As any cursory look at the modern working class will show, class unity is inconceivable so long as these divisions are allowed to fester among working-class people who are themselves Black, transgender, immigrant, and members of every other oppressed group. Even straight, white, male workers under capitalism experience oppression in the form of the denial of decent health care, affordable housing, good education, adequate leisure time, and any number of grievous conditions imposed on them by the class that owns and controls the means of production—that is, the ruling class.

LGBT people—like women and Blacks—experience a special oppression in that they can be denied jobs and housing (often legally), are subject to verbal and physical harassment, and are treated as second-class citizens when it comes to marriage and health care. They experience daily humiliations like being accosted in public toilets for appearing to be the "wrong" gender.

Socialists oppose oppression of every sort, no matter who is affected. As Russian revolutionary leader Lenin wrote in *What Is to Be Done?*:

> Working-class consciousness cannot be genuine political consciousness unless the workers are trained to respond to *all* cases of tyranny, oppression, violence, and abuse, no matter *what class* is affected…. The [socialist's] ideal should not be the trade union secretary, but the tribune of the people, who is able to react to every manifestation of tyranny and oppression, no matter where it appears, no matter what stratum or class of the people it affects.[5]

It is for this reason that socialists have been found in the forefront of struggles for sexual liberation from the nineteenth century to the present day. The absence of freedoms for LGBT people in countries such as the former Soviet

Union, Cuba, and China is not, as will be shown, an example of socialism's blind spot to the oppression of gays but an indication of the distance that separates these societies from genuine socialism.

Marxism, if it's about anything at all, is about the oppressed and exploited taking control of society and running it in their own interests. To argue, as do some academics, anarchists, and a few on the broad left, that those who are sexually oppressed are theoretically and organizationally left outside of socialists' vision for a new society is a serious charge. The facts, however, tell a different story.

"The queer Marx loved to hate"

There is an argument that the original sin of socialism lies with the authors of *The Communist Manifesto* themselves, Karl Marx and Frederick Engels. The most frequently cited evidence for this comes from a brief exchange of personal communication between Marx and Engels in 1869. The letters concern a text by the sexologist Karl Heinrich Ulrichs that Marx passed on to Engels for comment about the rights of Uranians (the supposed "third sex"). These letters have been popularized online[6] and snippets appear in queer theory texts today. On June 22, 1869, Engels wrote Marx:

> The Urning [title of Ulrichs's work and his term for 'a female psyche in a male body,' whose attraction is to other men] you sent me is a very curious thing. These are extremely unnatural revelations. The pederasts [homosexual pedophiles] are beginning to count themselves, and discover that they are a power in the state. Only organization was lacking, but according to this source it apparently already exists in secret. And since they have such important men in all the old par-

ties and even in the new ones, from Rosing to Schweitzer, they cannot fail to triumph. *Guerre aux cons, paix aus trous-de-cul* [war on the cunts, peace to the assholes] will now be the slogan. It is a bit of luck that we, personally, are too old to have to fear that, when this party wins, we shall have to pay physical tribute to the victors. But the younger generation! Incidentally it is only in Germany that a fellow like this can possibly come forward, convert this smut into a theory, and offer the invitation: *introite* [enter], etc.[7]

Marx replied regarding the aforementioned von Schweitzer, "You must arrange for a few jokes about him to reach Siebel, for him to hawk around to the various papers."[8]

There is no sense in attempting to polish a turd here, as there is nothing politically enlightened or progressive about these comments between the two leading figures of the International Workingmens' Association. Though it might be asserted that neither man ever intended his personal letters to become a matter of public record—most of us would cringe at the exposure of the modern equivalent of our correspondence, e-mails, and iChats—it is worth considering both the historical context and actual behavior of these two architects of revolutionary socialism.

It is insufficient, however, to argue that Marx and Engels were merely prisoners of the era in which they lived, though they were undoubtedly influenced by the dominant Victorian morals of the early Industrial Revolution. These two men eschewed the racial, gender, and ethnic stereotypes of their day to champion Black and women's liberation, and they spent their lives exposing and organizing against oppression and exploitation.

During the American Civil War, Marx and Engels unequivocally sided with the North against the slave-holding South, arguing, "Labor cannot emancipate itself in the white skin where in the black it is branded."[9] In Marx's opus on economics, *Capital*, he skewered capitalism for creating the horrors of slavery and racism:

> The discovery of gold and silver in America, the extirpation, enslavement and entombment in mines of the indigenous population of that continent, the beginning of the conquest and plunder of India, and the conversion of Africa into a preserve for the commercial hunting of black skins.... Capital comes dripping from head to toe, from every pore, with blood and dirt.[10]

Even anti-Irish racism, central to the nineteenth-century British Empire, came under fierce attack by Marx and Engels, who argued for British workers to side with Irish independence as a precondition for unified class struggle among the ethnically divided workforce. Engels's *Origins of the Family, State and Private Property* laid the essential groundwork for a Marxist understanding of the roots of women's oppression. By applying a materialist analysis to the family, Marx and Engels showed how women's oppression arises out of historically specific phenomena—the shift from classless, communal societies without states to the rise of elaborate divisions of labor and states to safeguard the accumulation of wealth by a newly developing ruling class. *Origins of the Family* explained how with the rise of capitalism women's unpaid labor in the home became central, and with that, women's labor outside the home became devalued. As Dana Cloud, a Marxist professor of communications, notes, "The ideology of domesticity not only burdens women with the tasks of reproduction and nurturance, but also justifies wage differentials in the productive economy, according to which women can be paid less than men."[11]

All this refutes definitively the argument that Marxism is interested only in questions of class. Marx and Engels's body of writings and life's pursuit have influenced generations of revolutionaries who have fought for a better world, including a sexually liberated one. Yet there is no reason to defend every utterance and act as if they were infallible gods instead of living men, warts and all. Nonetheless, why were Marx and Engels essentially un-Marxist in their approach to the situation of gays?

The year of this exchange is noteworthy, since 1869 is the date when the word "homosexual" was first coined by Austrian-Hungarian writer Karl-Maria Kertbeny at the start of his campaign against the Prussian law criminalizing those with—in his words—"abnormal tastes." This was the Victorian era when the dominant medical texts still argued that masturbation caused idiocy and even death, and it was more than twenty-five years before the Oscar Wilde trial, which brought the concept of homosexuality into international news for the first time in history. This period marked the dawn of industrializing countries' creation of the social space for autonomous living outside the nuclear family that allowed for a self-identified gay community to develop. In addition, there are the sticky facts regarding the ways that gays thought of and referred to their own sexuality, as well as the historical record regarding the target of the letters, German politician and poet Johann Baptiste von Schweitzer.

Modern historians and activists who attack the language used by Marx and Engels apply contemporary sensitivities to an era one century before the modern gay movement exploded onto the scene. For example, the flamboyant Wilde described himself as "sick" and "abnormal." It was he who popularized homosexuality as "the love that dare not speak its name."[12] Even in France, where the Napoleonic Code of 1810 wiped away all laws against sodomy, gay men called themselves the French terms for "fag" or "queer," while lesbians referred to themselves as "amazon," "dyke," or "tribad," in the rare instances they'd speak of their sexual proclivities at all.[13]

Though von Schweitzer is referred to by historian Hubert Kennedy as "the queer Marx loved to hate,"[14] the facts surrounding the case tell a different story. For one, von Schweitzer was in fact a convicted pederast, as Engels called him—that is, a man who seduces boys. More than once he was arrested for soliciting sex with a boy under the age of fourteen. Whatever the wrongs of age-of-consent legislation that carry over into the modern era, it should stand as a basic socialist principle that sex between two people must be consensual. It is incompatible for genuine consent devoid of the inequality of power to be given by a child to a man of thirty.

The most glaring aspect of the characterization of Marx's enmity toward von Schweitzer is the confusion of Marx's political hostility with personal contempt. Von Schweitzer was a right-wing social democrat who identified with the Lassallean current of social democracy that aimed to reform and not overthrow the state, as Marx and his adherents advocated. Despite these differences, Marx was happy to collaborate with von Schweitzer after Lassalle's death. Regarding a popular account of Marx's *Capital* that von Schweitzer wrote, Marx told Engels in 1868: "[H]e is unquestionably the most intelligent and most energetic of all the present workers' leaders in Germany." And Marx goes on to say he will argue with von Schweitzer that "he must choose between a 'sect' and a 'class.'"[15] At the time of the reactionary epistolary exchange between Marx and Engels, von Schweitzer was openly advocating collaboration with the aristocratic prime minister of Prussia who went on to become the first chancellor of Germany, Otto von Bismarck, known as the "iron chancellor." In 1870, according to Kennedy, von Schweitzer veered decisively away from any claim to pro-working-class politics by voting for war with France. By 1878, Bismarck had outlawed all socialist activity in Germany.

None of this evidence is to forgive the decidedly backward slurs from Marx and Engels about von Schweitzer. After all, socialists must oppose oppression no matter what class it affects and no matter what the political bent of the advocate. But reducing the dispute between them to a snarky private exchange of homophobic bigotry ignores the historical record of political collaboration with von Schweitzer that ended with an ideological split. Whatever Victorian notions Marx and Engels may have held toward homosexuality, historians present no evidence that this affected their political practice.

In fact, it is quite striking how dismissive many modern-day queer academics often are of some of the earliest attempts at theorizing the history of human sexual and class relations, put forth in 1884 in *The Origin of the Family, Private Property and the State*. In one oft-quoted passage, Engels refers to "the abominable practice of sodomy,"[16] of which gay historian Jeffrey Weeks has accurately surmised, "It would have been extraordinary in the early 1880s if Engels had thought otherwise."[16] But in another one that is generally ignored, Engels speculates about what human sexual relations might be like in a future socialist society:

> What we can now conjecture about the way in which sexual relations will be ordered after the impending overthrow of

capitalist production is mainly of a negative character, limited for the most part to what will disappear. But what will there be new? That will be answered when a new generation has grown up: a generation of men who never in their lives have known what it is to buy a woman's surrender with money or any other social instrument of power; a generation of women who have never known what it is to give themselves to a man from any other considerations than real love or to refuse to give themselves to their lover from fear of the economic consequences. When these people are in the world, they will care precious little what anybody today thinks they ought to do; they will make their own practice and their corresponding public opinion of their practice of each individual—and that will be the end of it.[18]

While here Engels is explicit about how heterosexual relations would undoubtedly be transformed by a socialist revolution, his broader point is that by removing the material obstacles to sexual freedom the ideological barriers can fall. This raises far-reaching possibilities for a genuine sexual revolution on all fronts.

Sexuality and early socialists

Far more revealing of the attitude and practice of Marxists toward gays is the position that organized socialists took once industrial states accelerated their attacks on the earliest visible LGBT populations in urban centers. The first politician anywhere in the world to speak on record on the floor of a national legislature for the rights of gays was August Bebel, leader of the Social Democratic Party (SPD), who addressed the German Reichstag on January 13, 1898.[19] Though many socialists broke with this mass workers' party fifteen years later when they voted for German entry into the First World War, there is no denying the political significance of the openly pro-gay attitude of many members of the world's largest socialist party up to that time. Not only did leading SPD members such as Karl Kautsky and Finance Minister Rudolf Hilferding sign a petition demanding the repeal of the German anti-sodomy law, Paragraph 175, but they also helped circulate the petition and encouraged thousands to add their names. Bebel argued:

> The number of these persons [gays] is so great and reaches so deeply into all social circles, from the lowest to the highest, that if the police dutifully did what they were supposed to, the Prussian state would immediately be obliged to build two new penitentiaries just to handle the number of violations against Paragraph 175 committed within the confines of Berlin alone.[20]

Even earlier, the most prominent socialist journal, *Die Neue Zeit*, defended the Irish writer Oscar Wilde in his 1895 trial for sexual relations with the son of a well-known aristocrat. Eduard Bernstein wrote in the journal that bourgeois attacks on homosexual acts as "unnatural" were reactionary. Instead, he argued for sympathetic language such as "not the norm" since *"moral attitudes are historical phenomena."*[21] Wilde himself was drawn to socialism and describes the potential for sexual liberation in his essay, "The Soul of Man Under Socialism."[22]

The SPD's newspaper, *Vorwärts*, popularized gay issues in its pages. In preparation for a 1905 parliamentary debate on gay issues, SPD member August Thiele did research using works from the library of the first openly gay movement, the Scientific Humanitarian Committee. Included in his thirty-four pages of speeches in the Reichstag is this insightful nugget that many members of today's U.S. Congress would never admit: Anti-gay legislation is the legacy of "priestly cruelty and intolerance" that "reminds one of the period of the Middle Ages, of that time when witches were burned, heretics were tortured, and proceedings against the dissenters were conducted with the wheel and gallows."[23]

Some leading SPD figures, however, used the unpardonable tactic of attempting to slur the Nazis as promoters of homosexuality. This was partially an expression of the SPD's heterogeneous character—it had a right wing that supported German imperialism and a focus on winning elections, which renders its members' advocacy for homosexual rights that much more impressive given the unpopularity of the cause. The prominent Nazi storm trooper, Captain Ernst Röhm, was a gay man, as were several of the elite Nazi SS of the early 1930s. Before Röhm's downfall, led by Hitler in the Night of the Long Knives, some leftists engaged in outing members of his fascist Nazi Party. This backward strategy of exposing closeted gays who advocated a right-wing agenda only fed the atmosphere of witch hunts and calumny against lesbians and gays. One radical courageously took on his comrades in a lengthy attack on gay-baiting in 1932: "We are fighting against the infamous Paragraph 175 in whatever way we can, but we have no right to join in with the chorus of those who would prefer to outlaw a man simply because he is homosexual."[24] Jokes and denunciations of Röhm helped stoke the danger of blowback on the very same sexual minorities who were targeted by the Nazis and thrown into concentration camps by the thousands during the Second World War. It is one thing to expose the hypocrisy of right-wingers for acting in defiance of their own codes, but the left can never defend itself by using the reactionary ideas of the right.

One of the earliest openly gay men, Edward Carpenter lived with his lover George Merrill in England and was an influential socialist from the 1870s till his death in 1928. He was perhaps the world's first hippie socialist—a socialist bohemian (and avid sandal-wearer) influenced as much by Walt Whitman as by Karl Marx. His radical rejection of Victorian capitalism, sexism, and sexual repression drove him to a life of writing and organizing alongside William Morris, Eleanor Marx (Karl's daughter), and other leading British socialists of his day.[25]

Finding "civilization" oppressive and soulless, Carpenter's politics veered at times toward the Utopian or anarchist wings of early British socialism. His vegetarianism and advocacy for nudity would have placed him in happy company with modern hippies, though his activities organizing the unemployed and writings advocating women's liberation through the dismantling of class society kept him in the socialist camp throughout much of his life.

At the height of his popularity, in the early twentieth century, Carpenter spoke before audiences of thousands. Writing and speaking in a society where not only was homosexuality illegal but the Oscar Wilde trial of the mid-1890s had also raised hackles against same-sex love, Carpenter unabashedly drew the connections between a system based on economic competition and the breeding of a culture of sexual repression. He argued that an intermediate-sex spirit—or as he put it, "Uranian" spirit—was possible in everyone and that socialism's vanguard might even be a gay movement.[26]

Alfred Kinsey, the mid-twentieth-century American sexologist, acknowledged Carpenter along with his contemporary social-democratic ally Havelock Ellis as forerunners in the theorization of the natural variety of human sexuality.

Ellis was an early advocate for birth control, legal abortion, and women's sexual liberation. He married a lesbian who was as free as he was in their relationship to engage in open affairs with women.[27]

The illegality of publishing explicit material about homosexuality in Britain forced Ellis to publish his seven-volume *Studies in the Psychology of Sex* (the first volume on homosexuality was entitled *Sexual Inversion*) in the United States. His aim in studying sexual variation and "anomalies" was not only to prove that all human sexuality is natural, found elsewhere in nature, but also to undermine the scientific pretexts used to legally persecute those who deviate in any way from the sexual norm. While he rejected Carpenter's assertion of homosexuality as a "third sex," he contended that sexual "inversion" was a "quirk of nature."[28]

Despite Ellis's ardent defense of the naturalness of human sexual variation and his open discussion about and defense of lesbianism and masturbation under the tyrannical moral code of Victorian England, some of his arguments were tenuous and even led to reactionary conclusions. For example, he defended eugenics, the science of biological engineering, though Ellis died before the Nazis put selective breeding into horrific practice. As a middle-class reformer who remained outside the socialist movement—though he influenced a range of activists from the socialist Carpenter to the anarchist Emma Goldman—Ellis's sexual radicalism was limited by his biological determinism. As historian Jeffrey Weeks argues, Ellis's ideological "weakness was [his] inability to ask *why* societies have continued to control sexuality and persecute sexual minorities throughout the ages; and as a result [his] eventual absorption into capitalist value structures."[29]

This theoretical inquiry went largely unexplored until workers took control for the first time in history in 1917.

The sexual revolution in Russia

The Russian Revolution of October 1917 was a mass struggle of ordinary people led by workers in a largely peasant society. American journalist John Reed reported on the revolution from Russia: "This is the revolution, the class struggle, with the proletariat, the soldiers and peasants lined up against the bourgeoisie. Last February was only the preliminary revolution.... The extraordinary and immense power of the Bolsheviki lies in the fact that the Kerensky government absolutely ignored the desires of the masses as expressed in the Bolsheviki program of peace, land and workers' control of industry."[30] Russian peasants were steeped in religious superstition and society was a mix of semifeudal relations amid booming industrialism. Yet, the revolution achieved reforms that most modern LGBT people still fight for. The Russian Revolution upended all previous structures of society, including the most intimate relations between people. When that revolution was overturned by economic isolation, war, and reaction those gains were jettisoned.

There are some who try denigrate the enormity of advances for LGBT people in the aftermath of the Russian Revolution.[31] Russian historian Igor Kon, for example, writes, "Bolshevism abolished, on the one hand, God, ecclesiastical marriage, and absolute moral values, and, on the other, the individual's right to personal self-determination and love that might stand higher than all social duties."[32] But facts are stubborn things. In 1917, all laws against homosexuality were struck down by the new revolutionary government along with the rest of the tsarist criminal code. Consensual sex was deemed a private matter and not only were gays free to live as they chose without state intervention, but the Soviet courts also approved of marriage between homosexuals and, extraordinarily, there are even recorded instances of sex change operations in the 1920s. In other words, the revolution accomplished this grandiose social-sexual leap three years before American women achieved the right to vote and nearly ninety years before the Supreme Court of the United States finally struck down all sodomy laws.[33]

In defending the record of extraordinary improvements for sexual minorities in the early Soviet Union, it is important to grasp the context in which these gains were achieved. Russia was a semifeudal, culturally backward, and predominantly rural society upon which capitalist industry was grafted in a few industrial centers like St. Petersburg. Only vulgar Marxists dare assert that under such conditions could a society leap in a seamless, unwavering line from repression to liberation. Social progress is more complicated and dialectical than linear evolution suggests. Russian revolutionary leader Leon Trotsky accurately summed up the state of prerevolutionary Russia:

> Russia's development is first of all notable for its backwardness. But historical backwardness does not mean a mere retracing of the course of the advanced countries a hundred or two hundred years later. Rather it gives rise to an utterly different "combined" social formation, in which the most highly developed achievements of capitalist technique and structure are integrated into the social relations of feudal and pre-feudal barbarism, transforming and dominating them, fashioning a unique relationship of classes.[34]

This character of "combined and uneven development" that Trotsky describes as existing in Russia necessitated the Bolsheviks' call for spreading the revolution internationally, to more industrially and culturally advanced nations. The international character of a successful revolution was central to Lenin's and Trotsky's understanding of how the initial advances could be expanded, lest the first shoots of a new order be destroyed by civil war, isolation, and privation. In the end, it was not the Bolsheviks' bad politics but the strangling of the revolution by imperialism that led to the impasse and rise of Stalin.

A groundbreaking history by Dan Healey of sex and sexuality in Russia before, during, and after the revolutionary period provides fresh evidence of the enormous societal shifts on questions of sexuality that the revolution engendered.[35] Legal, political, and medical records of that era strike down the antisex image of Bolshevism popularized by Hollywood films such as the 1939 classic *Ninotchka*, in which the dour and humorless Soviet apparatchik portrayed by Greta Garbo is wooed by the charm and wit of a dashing American. Given the depth of historical distortion and outright lies, it is worth quoting at length from the 1923 pamphlet *The Sexual Revolution in Russia*, written by Dr. Grigorii Batkis, director of the Moscow Institute of Social Hygiene:

> The present sexual legislation in the Soviet Union is the work of the October Revolution. This revolution is important not only as a political phenomenon, which secures the political rule of the working class. But also for the revolutions which emanating from it reach out into all areas of life…
>
> The social legislation of the Russian communist revolution does not intend to be a product of pure theoretical knowledge, but rather represents the outcome of experience. After the successful revolution, after the triumph of practice over

theory, people first strove for new, firm regulations along economic lines. Along with this were created models governing family life and forms of sexual relations responding to the needs and natural demands of the people....

The war set in motion the broad masses, the 100 million peasants. New circumstances brought with them a new life and new outlook. In the first period of the war, women won economic independence both in the factory and in the country—but the October Revolution first cut the Gordian knot, and instead of mere reform, it completely revolutionized the laws. The revolution let nothing remain of the old despotic and infinitely unscientific laws; it did not tread the path of reformist bourgeois legislation which, with juristic subtlety, still hangs onto the concept of property in the sexual sphere, and ultimately demands that the double standard hold sway over sexual life. These laws always come about by disregarding science.

The Soviet legislation proceeded along a new and previously untrodden path, in order to satisfy the new goals and tasks of the social revolution...

Now by taking into account all these aspects of the transition period, Soviet legislation bases itself on the following principle:

It declares the absolute noninterference of the state and society into sexual matters, so long as nobody is injured, and no one's interests are encroached upon. [Emphasis in original.]

Concerning homosexuality, sodomy, and various other forms of sexual gratification, which are set down in European legislation as offenses against public morality—Soviet legislation treats these exactly the same as so-called "natural" intercourse. All forms of sexual intercourse are private matters. Only when there's use of force or duress, as in general when there's an injury or encroachment upon the rights of another person, is there a question of criminal prosecution.[36] [Emphasis author's.]

This is a rather extraordinary statement of principles for any society, no less for one that in the midst of a global conflagration undertook revolution and endured civil war in which millions died, starvation was rampant, and industrialization was catapulted back to the level of the eighteenth century.

Prior to the revolution, a weak bourgeoisie that owned and ran industry under the tsar largely outlawed, yet tolerated, a commercial sex trade of various sorts in the bathhouses and brothels of major cities, according to Healey.[37] An illegal gay subculture emerged in the latter years of the nineteenth century in St. Petersburg and Moscow after the emancipation of the serfs in 1861 brought vast numbers of mostly young men to these cities for employment in industry, where they lived in same-sex housing away from family and largely segregated from women.[37] Most recorded instances of lesbianism occured among women in Russian brothels who served the cities' male population, though a tiny number of wealthy women also purchased sex from women for hire.[39] But outside of rare couplings between upper-class men who lived together, homosexuality in prerevolutionary Russia was generally a closeted affair and sex was most often purchased by older or wealthier men from younger and poorer ones. However, even consensual sodomy between men was punishable by exile to Siberia, including hard labor if a minor were involved. Misogynistic conceptions of women's sexuality, as in Europe, left lesbianism unlegislated; the constraints of nuclear family life rendered it nearly inconceivable.

The revolution changed all that. Dr. Batkis's pamphlet was not merely a toothless statement of intent: genuine changes in sexual attitudes and behavior—beyond the elimination of the penal code—did take place as a result of the Bolshevik Revolution in 1917. One indication was in the choice of individuals to represent the revolution internationally—the openly gay commissar of public affairs was Grigorii Chicherin, who served at this post from 1918 till illness forced his retirement in 1930.[40] This was not some back room bean-counter but a man who worked alongside Red Army leader Leon Trotsky in negotiating peace with Germany at Brest-Litovsk and was entrusted to be a prominent face of the revolution abroad. Chicherin was an aristocratic-born diplomat who was lifelong friends with the most prominent Russian gay poet, Mikhail Alekseevich Kuzmin, the flamboyantly campy author of the first known gay-positive novel in any language, *Wings*.[41]

Much is often made of the supposed debate on the importance of sex and sexual freedom between revolutionary leader Lenin and Commissar for Social Welfare Alexandra Kollontai, who advocated "free love." Even Healey joins in the opprobrium in his remarks: "The implication of his [Lenin's] remarks for a politics of homosexual emancipation under socialism was that this particular 'freedom of love' should wait (as would all sexuality) until a proletarian revolution reconstructed the material order."[42] This seems a rather stilted reading of Lenin's thoughts that conforms to the Cold War—and Stalinist—caricature of Lenin as a teetotalling ascetic, despite his enjoyment of wine, sport, and, yes, even the intimate company of women. In Lenin's 1915 letters to the woman with whom he was having an affair, Inessa Armand, he wrote that the revolution would free love from "the constraints of religious prejudice, patriarchal and social strictures, the law, police, and courts."[43] When he argues against privileging the organizing of female prostitutes above other women, his critics presume Victorian rigidity on his part.

Socialist Duncan Hallas describes the conditions in the years following the revolution:

> By May 1919 Russian industry was reduced to 10 percent of its normal fuel supply. By the end of that year 79 percent of the total railway track mileage was out of action—and this in a huge country where motor transport was practically nonexistent. By the end of 1920 the output of all manufactured goods had fallen to 12.9 percent of the 1913 level.
>
> The effect on the working class was catastrophic. As early as December 1918 the number of workers in Petrograd had fallen to half the level of two years earlier. By December 1920 that city had lost 57.5 percent of its *total* population. In the same three years Moscow lost 44.5 percent…. War, famine, typhus, forced requisitioning by red and white alike, the disappearance of even such manufactured goods as matches, paraffin and thread—this was the reality in the Russia of 1920–21. According to Trotsky even cannibalism was reported from several provinces.[44]

In context, Lenin's sentiments appear reasonable.

Lenin's infamous 1920 letter to revolutionary leader Clara Zetkin decries some of the chaos of adolescent sex lives under the revolution. He wrote that sexual gratification should not be "as simple and inconsequential as drinking a glass of water."[45] Lenin argued that Marxists should strive instead for social responsibility and honesty in intimate relations. In a stark rebuke to his detractors, Lenin commented, "Communism is not supposed to bring asceticism but joy in life and vitality by means of a gratified love life."[46] Wilhelm Reich, an early twentieth-century psychoanalyst who was an advocate of sexual liberation and Marxism at the beginning of his career, challenged the notion that Lenin's ideas were prudish. Reich described the eruption under the Bolsheviks of debate about issues concerning

sexuality and writes about the frustrations expressed by workers and Bolshevik leaders alike at not being able to put theoretical questions of the sexual revolution to the test due to material
limitations imposed by Russia's isolation and poverty.[47]

Even if Lenin's critics were accurate about his personal
opinions, and I believe they are not, it doesn't erase the enormous progress the revolution brought. In fact if the charges
are correct, they only give further credence to the reality that
the revolution was not some coup by Lenin and a small
cabal—as is often claimed—but a mass phenomenon, in which
debates and open disagreements about how to run a new society dominated all political life.

When a new criminal code was written in 1922, sodomy,
incest, and age-of-consent laws were left out entirely. "Sexual
maturity" was to be determined on a case-by-case basis according to medical opinion.[48] Prostitution became a matter of
public health, not a crime, and a health commission was insti-
tuted to combat sexually transmitted diseases; policies of social assistance were enacted to provide women and young
men with alternatives to the sex trade in terms of employe-
ment and living arrangements.

Contrast the treatment of Lenin and the Bolsheviks with
that of the anarchist Emma Goldman, who is regularly lion-
ized as the uncompromising sex radical of her day. In a letter
to Havelock Ellis in 1924, Goldman attacked the "narrowness" of some of the lesbians she encountered, whom she
called a "'crazy lot' whose fixation on the conditions of their
own oppression to the exclusion of all other matters grated on
her."[49] Those quick to condemn every critical utterance of
Lenin—often snagged out of historical context—readily provide justification for what may have been Goldman's perfectly

reasonable critique in the context of wider forces engaging in revolutionary upheavals in her day.

Typical of the commentary about the revolutionary leaders' supposed ascetic ideal that dominates most historians' work is Aileen Kelly's comment that "The revolutionary was to turn himself into a flawless monolith by suppressing all private emotions, interests, and aspirations.... Not only art, literature, and personal relations, but all intellectual enquiry, when not directly relevant to the cause, were prohibited as the futile pastimes of superfluous men."[50] How does this square with the fact that Red Army leader Leon Trotsky, Lenin's closest collaborator during the revolution, wrote essays on art and literature published by the Soviet government in 1924, later released as the book *Literature and Revolution*? In this work Trotsky, a full-time revolutionary, expresses startling familiarity with poetry, literature, and all manner of artistic expression. Trotsky assesses the writings of openly gay poets like Nicolai Kliuev without ever commenting one way or the other on their sexuality. Is not the right to be judged on the content of one's work and not on one's sexuality a definitive and positive break from long-standing bourgeois tradition?

Revolutionary Russia also sought to break out of the narrowness of its feudal traditions by engaging with those outside the country who had studied and agitated around questions of sexual freedom for years. A delegation of Soviet physicians and researchers traveled to Berlin in 1923 for a visit with sex reformer Dr. Magnus Hirschfeld at his Institute for Sex Research. There they requested a screening of a documentary about same-sex love, which the Russians were surprised to discover had been banned. Hirschfeld's journal records the impressions of health commissar Samashko: "[He] stated how pleased he was that in the new Russia, the former penalty against homosexuals has been completely abolished."[51]

Cross-dressing women who served in the Red Army, often passing as men, were given positions of authority. The director of the Institute of Neuro-psychiatric Prophylaxis in Moscow in the 1920s, Lev Rozenstein, invited "Lesbians, militiawomen and Red Armyists" to provide him with their life stories, and he claimed that "women [in Soviet Russia] may legally take men's names and live as men."[52] Rozenstein thought it was his job as a psychologist to help his patients accept their same-sex desire, a position way ahead of its day—in contrast, the American Psychiatric Association maintained homosexuality on its books as a mental disorder until 1973.

Soviet officials appear to have looked more favorably upon women who dressed as men and acted in stereotypically masculine ways than they did upon men who dressed as women and mimicked "feminine" behavior; nonetheless, same-sex marriage was approved in the courts. Male femininity was seen as socially backward by some, but the law did not intervene to stifle those who expressed themselves in that manner.[53] Clinical psychologists openly discussed some physicians' practices of performing sex-change operations. The Moscow health department in 1928 discovered a "huge quantity of cases" of one doctor who "changed sex and made women of men and vice versa, using rather primitive surgical operations."[54] They seem to have been mostly concerned with the ethical and physiological ramifications of this practice, but did not pursue the issue as a legal matter.

Bolshevik leader Alexandra Kollontai described the explosive changes in sexual relationships in 1921: "History has never seen such a variety of personal relationships—indissoluble marriage with its 'stable family,' 'free unions,' secret adultery; a girl living quite openly with her lover in so-called 'wild marriage'; pair marriage, marriage in threes and even the complicated marriage of four people—not to talk of the various forms of commercial prostitution."[55]

Within weeks of the Bolsheviks taking power in 1917, they abrogated patriarchal power in family life through edicts such as "On the Dissolution of Family Life," which "took away the man's right to a dominating position in the family, gave the woman full economic and sexual self-determination, and declared it to be self-evident that the woman could freely determine her name, domicile, and citizenship."[56] Abolishing the family in law was relatively simple, but it could only go so far without a wider and longer-term struggle to change the culture and material conditions. Some communal kitchens and childcare centers to free women from the home were established by the revolutionary state, but many women whose lives had previously centered on taking care of children and the home were left feeling inconsolable, their lives empty of purpose.[57]

Wilhelm Reich argued that part of the sexual revolution in Russia was stunted by the limited time and material conditions necessary to restructure "the mass psyche" because "the subjective factor is not just a product of economic forces" but also "their motor force."[58] In other words, there is a dynamic relationship between ideas and reality and neither time nor conditions existed to fully realize revolutionary aspirations. Attempts to remake family life under a new economic and social order were not limited by the Bolsheviks' Marxist vision, but by prevailing material and social realities. Trotsky reflected on the family in revolutionary Russia in *Problems of Everyday Life*: "You cannot 'abolish' the family; you have to replace it. The actual liberation of women is unrealizable on the basis of 'generalized want.'"[59] The alternatives to the traditional family were inadequate because they lacked the resources to provide the kind of public child care, kitchens, laundries, and other means necessary to construct a new society.

The degeneration of the revolution from its original goals—including sexual liberation—was not due to some original sin of Leninist or Bolshevik ideology, but rather to the impossible conditions that revolutionaries faced. Years of isolation from any other successful socialist revolution in an advanced industrial state and the backwardness of Soviet industry combined to deteriorate all gains of the revolution by the 1930s. All the original leading Bolsheviks were either dead, executed, in exile, or in prison, with the sole exception of Joseph Stalin, who gave political expression and leadership to what was effectively a counterrevolution in the USSR. Mass deindustrialization due to war, famine, homelessness, and deprivation marked daily life for most working people.

Along with the reaffirmation of the sanctity of the nuclear family and conventional gender norms came the reintroduction of anti-sodomy legislation in 1934. Stalin looked to his cultural spokesman Maxim Gorky to provide written justification for the reversal in the daily *Pravda*. Justifying the recriminalization of homosexuality as "a form of bourgeois degeneracy," Gorky argued, "Destroy the homosexuals—Fascism will disappear."[60]

The rise of Stalinism heralded the end of workers' power and along with it the reversal of material gains that allowed for sexual minorities and women to lead free lives. Because the USSR was in competition with the West militarily and industrially, it needed more labor power, which required higher birth rates and, therefore, a return to the nuclear family. Women were given medals for having more children and along with this came the inevitable reversal of sexual freedoms that challenged the procreative sexual function that implies enforced heterosexuality. All workers' lives were diminished and constrained and gays were sent back into the closet.

Because of the internal degeneration of debate and democracy inside the world's communist parties (CPs), which increasingly saw their role as defending the interests of Moscow and not that of the working class, the CPs around the world, including in the United States, promoted the same narrow-minded and reactionary policies that the Soviet regime practiced. To oppose the Communist Party's antigay policies from this period on is *not* to go against Marxism, but rather to oppose its bloody antithesis, state capitalism—that is, a state-controlled economy where workers do not control the state.

Stalinism, Maoism, and homophobia

While the genuine Marxist tradition has stood squarely in favor of sexual liberation, most states claiming the socialist moniker in the twentieth century have failed to deliver any real alternative to the sexual repression of capitalist societies. These states—and the political organizations that have supported them—used the language of socialism to justify practices that are its opposite.

In the new political climate of the 1930s under Stalin, Soviet social policies promoted "compulsory motherhood, compulsory families, [and] compulsory heterosexuality."[61] Women were needed in the factories and on the land to help Russia industrialize and compete more effectively with the West, and

Soviet legislation simultaneously drove women into the work-force in unprecedented numbers, while banning abortion and curbing access to birth control. The late-thirties' drive toward war necessitated both higher production levels and a reversal of low birth rates. As Healey recounts, "a cult of motherhood was celebrated, reaching proportions critical observers found grotesque, as the lives of mothers of seven, eight, or ten children were vaunted as examples of patriotism," and the pages of "*Pravda* condemned 'so-called free love and all disorderly sex life.'"[62]

The homophobic policies of the American CP, like its other policy decisions, toed the line of the central authority in Moscow. There were official purges of LGBT people in the American CP, whose ideological impact cannot be underestimated. It was the nation's largest left-wing party, which at its height in the thirties had tens of thousands of members, many of whom played key roles organizing unions and fighting racial segregation. But rather than exposing the antisocialist political underpinnings of a party that defended the pact between Stalin and Hitler, the gulag work camps for dissidents, the crushing of workers' rebellions, most famously in Hungary in 1956 and Prague in 1968; gave support for the internment of U.S. citizens of Japanese descent during World War II; and openly embraced the bourgeois Democratic Party, the purges of LGBT members have been conflated with somehow representing a socialist perspective on sexuality. With the notable exception of the American CP's seventy-year alliance with the Democrats, however, both the left and the right have equated the CP's reactionary practices with socialism over the decades. For critics on the right, the oppression and unenviable living standards of most workers in the USSR and its satellite empire in Eastern Europe exposed the unde-sirability of revolution; for those on the left, the rise of Stalin-ism led to the conclusion that revolutions inevitably fail. Either way, the experience of the so-called socialist states gave rise to the notion that workers' liberation—and sexual liberation by extension—could not be won through revolu-tion, discrediting the project of revolutionary socialism for generations of left-wing militants. The inability of states like China, Cuba, and the former Soviet Union to deliver on their promises also led a generation of leftists to reject the working class as the agent of change in society (the topic of chapter 6 on postmodernism, identity politics, and queer theory).

In the summer 2008 issue of *New Politics*, Bettina Aptheker, the lesbian daughter of former American CP leader Herbert Aptheker, writes about how through the Second World War and the fifties and sixties gays and lesbians were driven out of the CP as security risks, especially during the height of the McCarthy period of the fifties. She corroborates her own recollections of the purges with an account by sociologist Ellen Kay Trimberger:

> The Party leadership made a decision to drop all homosex-uals from the Party because of their presumed openness to blackmail as state repression increased. A local organizer was asked to speak to several known lesbians to request their resignations. These lesbians were friends of the or-ganizer, although she never discussed their sexual prefer-ence with them. When she met them, they all cried, but the lesbians "obeyed" and resigned. Looking back on this inci-dent this activist says that neither she nor the lesbians, al-though some may have questioned the assumption, ever considered opposing the Party decision.[63]

Decades later, Aptheker's own position paper for the party's Women's Commission was rejected due to her inclusion of lesbian women in a historical account of early twentieth-century organizing of the International Ladies Garment Workers Union. Bettina Aptheker describes an unstated "don't ask, don't tell" policy in the party by the late seventies, and the pervasive hostility to open discussion of the nature of sexuality under capitalism continued under the guise that it would be a "diversion" from class politics.[64]

While Mao's China never officially banned homosexuality, there is no doubt that sexual and gender conformity and hostility toward and imprisonment of lesbians and gays were the norm there and as a result sexual minorities were driven underground. During the Cultural Revolution (1966–76), homosexuals faced what is estimated to have been the worst period of persecution in Chinese history. Police regularly rounded up gays and lesbians, who were charged with "hooliganism" or disturbing public order, and threw them into prisons where some were tortured and disappeared for years. Up until 2001, the Chinese CP considered homosexuality a mental disorder— it's now been upgraded to a possible cause of depression—and some Chinese officials continue to deny the existence of gays in that society and even, despite obvious scientific evidence, the existence of AIDS.[65]

Integration in the world capitalist market for the last three decades and widespread access to international communications and travel have led to the possibility of hundreds of millions of Chinese living independently of families and expressing their sexuality openly. Today middle-class Chinese can socialize at dozens of gay and lesbian venues in major urban centers.[66] This is not because embracing the capitalist market has been sexually liberating; rather, in China as in the United States, middle-class gays and lesbians are treated as a market niche where profit can be made. As with the Soviet bloc, China's totalitarian regime brooks no official independent political initiative by workers gay or straight—undermining any claims to having established a "worker's state." The most glaring example of its intolerance of democratic demands was projected on television sets around the world with the massacre of workers and students at Beijing's Tiananmen Square in 1989.

Cuba: island of freedom?

In Cuba, though the 1959 revolution ushered in a number of positive educational and land reforms, homosexuality was banned. Homosexuality in Cuba was not illegal prior to the revolution, but afterward LGBT people were openly repressed and even sent to concentration camps from 1965–68 or forced into exile with other "criminals" and "scum" in the Mariel Boat exodus of 125,000 Cubans in 1980. It is estimated that up to 60,000 LGBT people, mostly gay men, were sent to the Military Units to Aid Production (UMAPs) where, surrounded by barbed wire, they were forced to cut sugarcane or marble under a tropical sun for twelve to sixteen hours a day in order to meet unrealistic production levels.[67] While the UMAPs were a temporary phenomenon, the ongoing arrests and torments of artists such as Renaldo Areinas, author of *Before Night Falls*, and others led to the "ever-present fear that at any moment there might be a knock on the door to report for an interrogation, or simply to be perfunctorily shipped out by truck-load to the countryside."[68]

Under the American-backed dictator Fulgencio Batista, Havana was turned into a sexual playground for wealthy

Cubans and American tourists; this was used by revolutionary leader Fidel Castro to justify the repression of anyone who did not conform to gender norms in dress and manner or who partook in same-sex activities, whether in private or public. In a taped interview with American journalist Lee Lockwood in 1965, Castro defends barring "deviant" homosexuals from jobs where they could influence young people and argues, "we would never come to believe that a homosexual could embody the conditions and requirements of conduct that would enable us to consider him a true Revolutionary, a true Communist militant."[69] In 1971, the First National Congress on Education and Culture reiterated the state's position on "the social pathological character of homosexual deviations" and resolved "that all manifestations of homosexual deviations are to be firmly rejected and prevented from spreading."[70]

Cuba's sexual policies, more so than any of the other so-called socialist states, have had an enormous impact on the American left and left-wing LGBT people in the United States. The American Empire's five-decade embargo and its attempts to overthrow and discredit the Castro regime for having the temerity to nationalize former U.S. properties in Cuba and to thumb its nose at imperial arrogance rightly earned Cuba the support and respect of anti-imperialists. However, it is one thing to oppose imperialist aggression toward Cuba—as any leftist must—and quite another to paint its economic and social policies as socialist. Cuba is a one-party state in which independent political activity—even by defenders of the revolution—as well as independent unions and strikes are barred and the governing party claims to rule *in the name of* the working class.

Left-wing organizations in the United States that worshiped the Cuban Revolution as socialist, despite the lack of workers' control and social policies they would have raged against at home, defended Cuba's earlier record of abuse against sexual minorities or simply ignored it. Similarly, regarding the Eastern Bloc countries, these leftists turned their backs not only on the struggle for gay liberation, but on the essence of Marxism—the self-emancipation of the working class. From the Maoist Revolutionary Communist Party (RCP), which until 2001 held that gays were counterrevolutionary by nature, to the American Socialist Workers Party (SWP), which for a time banned not only gays but also transvestites from its membership, many leftists jettisoned the liberatory core of socialism and engaged in torturous verbal calisthenics to defend repression in the name of Marxism. In order to argue that Cuba or China or the Eastern Bloc was somehow socialist, they had to either deny the repression of gays or defend it, and many groups vacillated between these two practices.

The Workers World Party (WWP)—one current spinoff group is the Party for Socialism and Liberation (PSL)—has been quite active and vocal in LGBT struggles from the seventies to the current day. Award-winning novelist and transgender activist Leslie Feinberg is one of WWP's most prominent members. But WWP/PSL's uncompromising defense of virtually every country claiming to be socialist—from Saddam Hussein's Iraq and Kim il-Sung's North Korea to modern China (including a hearty defense of the Tiananmen Square massacre)[71] and Castro's Cuba—leads to a bafflingly simplistic gauge of these societies' sexual policies and attitudes. To raise criticisms in any way of these bureaucratic and often tyrannical regimes, in WWP/PSL's philosophically dualistic view, is to place oneself at the service of empire. This has left them in the curious position of promoting countries as workers' states that would imprison or torment some of the very members organizing within the United States to defend them! Workers World's paper explains:

> There is no country in the world today that has an adequate position with regard to ending the oppression of homosexually inclined people. But to single out any of the socialist countries for special attack, as some leaders of the gay movement in the U.S. have done, is to cover over the important fact and, in addition, it lets the U.S. imperialists, the ones who have a real stake in the maintenance of racism, sexism, and anti-homosexual attitudes, off the hook.[72]

Following three years of heated internal party debate over the question of homosexuality, a 1975 pamphlet on gay liberation by the SWP first makes the case for gay rights on the basis of civil liberties, but then argues that it would be "cultural imperialism" to impose those expectations on Cuba,[73] as if sexual liberation were somehow an imperialist value not to be imposed on so-called macho Latinos. Aside from its obvious analytical sleight of hand, there is a subtle racism in expecting Latinos to be heterosexuals who inherently embrace bourgeois gender stereotypes. Documentation, including popular films like the 1994 Oscar-nominated *Strawberry and Chocolate*, explores same-sex relations in Cuba, provides ample evidence of sexual variation in Cuban society as rich as anywhere.

Historian and activist David Thorstad, who was an SWP member for six years before resigning over their politics regarding sexuality and the gay movement, collected the internal documents from the debate that raged from 1970–73. At the time the SWP was America's largest Trotskyist organization, though its adherence to notions that the Eastern Bloc was made up of "degenerated workers' states" and their starry-eyed enthusiasm for Cuban "socialism" expressed their own conflation of state ownership with Marxism, akin to the outlook of Stalinism. Shockingly, just after the 1969 Stonewall Riots in Greenwich Village provided the opening shot of the modern gay liberation movement, they "unofficially" banned gays from the party, and their youth group, the Young Socialist Alliance (YSA), did in fact officially ban gays and lesbians in August 1970.[74] While the ban ended soon afterward—party leader Jack Barnes insisted it was "unenforceable"[75] and it alienated them from radicalizing youth—the debate around the nature of homosexuality was shelved by the leadership and a sort of don't-step-on-the-grass-policy perspective was put forward. Fears of alienating workers by projecting an "exotic" or "far-out"[76] image through cross-dressing or same-sex canoodling at party gatherings took hold and drove internal policing measures around party members' behavior. At the same time, internal critics argued that if a revolutionary party were to gauge its other positions and behavior according to what conservative workers thought, then fighting racism or even engaging in any of the countercultural behaviors of the day would be nixed as well. Despite the SWP's initial reaction against gay and lesbian organizing and politics, the group undertook a three-year internal debate that expressed members' regular involvement in the various gay movement struggles.

Few groups were as crude as the RCP's precursor, the Revolutionary Union, in its rejection of homosexuality in the late sixties. Its 1969 position paper is mind-bogglingly backward, illogical, and, to put it bluntly, insensitively stupid. While opposing the criminalization of homosexuality, the Rev-

olutionary Union argued against the nascent gay rights movement on the basis that:

1) Because homosexuality is rooted in individualism it is a feature of petty bourgeois ideology which puts forth the idea
   that there are individual solutions to social problems.
2) Because homosexuality is based on petty bourgeois ideology and deals with the contradictions between men and
   women by turning its back to it (at least in intimate personal relationships), homosexuals cannot be Communists,
   that is, belong to communist organizations where people
   are committed to struggle against *all* forms of individualism, in *all* aspects of their lives.
3) Gay liberation in its putting forth of gayness as a strategy
   for revolution in this country is a reactionary ideology and can
   lead us only down the road of demoralization and defeat.[77]

The impact of Cuba on New Leftists of the late sixties and
early seventies, at the start of the explosion of the modern
LGBT movement, was profound. Despite the travel ban to
Cuba, many American radicals organized young people to go
on work trips to cut sugarcane and pick fruit on the island to
help meet export quotas from Cuba to the USSR. The Venceremos Brigades began in 1969 and included hundreds of former activists from Students for a Democratic Society and
others, including gay militants Allen Young and Leslie Cagan,
a leading figure in today's liberal antiwar movement. Stories
of the bitterly homophobic treatment meted out to many lesbians and gays by other *brigadistas*, as well as by some
Cubans, made their way into the newly emergent gay press in
the United States. Gays who protested the homophobia of the
Cuban government were claimed to have taken part in a "cultural imperialist offensive" against the revolution, according
to Young.[78] Though Cagan and well-known lesbian folk singer

Holly Near were barred along with other LGBT folks from returning on future trips, many militants continued to defend the Cubans' policies, arguing there was no "material basis for the oppression of homosexuals."[79]

Much has changed in the last few years regarding sexuality in Cuba, though it is hardly a bastion of sexual freedom. Raúl Castro's daughter, Mariela Castro Espín, who directs the Cuban National Center for Sex Education (CENESEX), explained in 2004, "Yes, I believe that people are a little more relaxed about a homosexual presence, both in public and in the privacy of the family, but only a little bit relaxed, not more tolerant. We have much more work to do in our society for this 'relaxation' to mean real respect toward diversity."[80] In 1988 homosexuality was decriminalized, though enforced AIDS testing led to the compulsory quarantining of those who were HIV-positive, most of whom were gay men. A society in which people were free to express their sexual preferences would have approached the crisis with a massive education campaign and open discussion and debate about how to proceed, rather than impose coercive measures. Although Havana celebrated its first International Day Against Homophobia in May 2008, one month later the first-ever unofficial Cuban Gay Pride March was cancelled minutes before it was to start and organizers were arrested for demanding an official apology for the past criminalization and poor treatment of gender and sex rebels in Cuba. This is in keeping with the crackdown on unofficial organizations and initiatives in Cuba. The 2009 "Diversity Is Natural" campaign launched by CENESEX is both a step forward and an open acknowledgment that discrimination and repression persist. Mariela Castro Espín says of the campaign's reform efforts to include gender identity and the rights of sexual minorities in Cuba's Family Code, "The work that we are doing will help to ease the prejudices behind these processes."[81]

While Cubaphiles of the left argue that the progress that has occurred is the fruit of revolutionary developments, this explanation is incompatible with the facts. Fifty years have passed since the revolution initiated the open repression of LGBT people and decades later its worst aspects have been mitigated, but the state's denial of the democratic right to organize any independent movement for sexual liberation persists. As socialist Paul D'Amato argues, "Oppression is not the product of an unfinished revolution; oppression continues to exist in Cuba because exploitation continues…. A society that has not liberated the working class is incapable of achieving the full liberation of the oppressed either. The condition of one is the condition of the other."[82]

The anti-Stalinist left and LGBT liberation

Narrowing the scope of the Marxist left to encompass only those groups that styled their politics after Stalinist or Maoist states, however, would negate the existence and organizing efforts of revolutionaries who stood apart from those traditions that distorted and debased Marxism. In the historiography of the left and LGBT liberation, this practice has served not only to erase the radical and liberatory core of Marxism and its early German and Bolshevik traditions, but also to deny the existence of a large swath of the postwar left that retained the commitment of Marxism to fighting gay and lesbian oppression.

Christopher Phelps recently uncovered a long-out-of-print document issued by members of the anti-Stalinist Young Peoples Socialist League (YPSL), originally published in *Young*

Socialist, "Socialism and Sex."[83] It was issued at the height of the McCarthy period in 1952, a time when, writer James Baldwin explained, "You weren't just in the closet, you were in the basement. Under the basement."[84] In his preface to the piece, Phelps recounts a conversation with the YPSL national chairperson at that time, who was asked to formulate a platform on the rights of sexual minorities. The author of "Socialism and Sex" wrote under the pseudonym, H. L. Small, because he or she would have surely lost his/her job in those years for writing a piece calling for "the freedom of the legally of-age adult of both sexes to have sexual relations with whomever he or she wishes of the same or opposite sex."[85] The author is careful to place the derogatory term "deviant" in quotes and explains that socialism can be a "constructive force in the transformation of America into a truly happy country where the individual rights of all its people (regardless of their departure from the Puritan 'norm') are both observed and respected."[86]

The early seventies internal bulletin documents of the American revolutionary group, the International Socialists, show an evolution from the basic civil libertarian live-and-let-live sexual values they'd held prior to the 1969 rebellion. This group of several hundred revolutionary socialists cut their teeth in the Freedom Summer desegregation battles, Berkeley Free Speech Movement, anti–Vietnam War protests, and industrial workplace organizing struggles of that era. The debates in these documents take on the nature of sexual repression of heterosexuals as well as homosexuals under capitalism: "The struggle for homosexual liberation is in part a critique of the socialization characteristic of our society, with its rigid definitions of sex roles and prerogatives, and its rigid linking of these to social roles—a socialization which is as limiting to all people as it is oppressive to homosexuals in particular."[87] They argue strategies for taking on homophobia in the working class as well as confronting a nascent gay separatism— later known as queer nationalism—within the movements in which they were involved. They explicitly reject the argument that LGBT politics should be placed on the back burner in deference to the class struggle: "The gay struggle…cannot afford to 'wait' for the new society and its promise of liberation…. Thus we are for an independent gay movement, as well as for a commitment to gay liberation by the revolutionary organization."[88] These blunt discussions reflect the experiences of LGBT members of the group as they plotted a path toward deeper engagement with the movements around them.

Among the most prominent Marxist gay circles in the English-speaking world was the Gay Left Collective (GLC) in London, whose most well-known member was historian Jeffrey Weeks. Their journal, *Gay Left*, which published from 1975–80, attempted to theorize how Marxists should approach questions and debates raised by the movement as well as how to correct the real failings of revolutionary groups on these issues. They go after leftists' attempts to whitewash Cuban homophobia, resurrect Engels's and Edward Carpenter's writings, and rightly take on the British SWP for its 1950s-style backwardness on sexuality—"homosexuality will disappear naturally"[89] under socialism, a position the SWP soon nixed—while foreseeing certain developments, like the attempt to co-opt the movement into a market niche: "Indeed the present requirements of capitalism are for privatized hedonism to maintain the extensive consumerism on which the system rests, and here homosexuals represent an attractive market rather than a social threat."[90] While some of their writings appear to cave in to the developing gay separatism and identity politics that came into full bloom in later years, the GLC was adamant in their attempt to wed gay liberation with Marxism both in theory and practice.

In assessing the left's political orientation around LGBT politics, it is worth asserting that radicals too are impacted by developments in their midst, unless of course they operate as a sect. "It is not consciousness that determines life," Marx famously wrote, "but life that determines consciousness."[91] By this, Marx meant that human society is shaped by neither some abstract system of morals nor the ideas of a few great women or men—but, on the contrary, that material conditions shape people's ideas and conceptions. Socialists too are shaped by the conditions and struggles around them and fashion their understanding of the world and how to change it by engaging with shifting forces and new phenomena.

For this reason it is hardly surprising that small groups of radicals facing the eruption of a new social movement would have to learn from the emerging struggles and think through new possibilities and ways of thinking and acting. No socialist, regardless of how brilliant or perceptive, can possibly think through all the implications of questions that inevitably arise as society changes and contradictions intensify. However, it is one thing for leftists to reflect aspects of conservatism prior to the eruption of struggles of the oppressed; it is quite another to disregard or belittle these political movements when they arise—or worse, to attack their legitimate demands, as many Stalinists and Maoists did. In recent decades, however, virtually the entire organized U.S. left has abandoned their old positions and taken up the fight for LGBT civil rights, regardless of their varying analyses of pseudo-socialist societies.

The explosion of AIDS and queer activism in the late eighties and early nineties was a period of high involvement by sections of the far left in the United States, most visibly the International Socialist Organization (ISO). Founded in 1977, after much of the left began its decline, the ISO from its inception has stood for the liberation of lesbians and gays and continued to grow in size and youthful participation throughout the eighties and nineties and through the present period. Advocating a worldview of "Neither Washington nor Moscow, but Workers' Power East and West" enabled the ISO to weather the political storms that swept through much of the American left—that segment looked to Eastern Europe or other self-declared socialist states—in the aftermath of the fall of the Berlin Wall and collapse of the USSR.

As the economic crisis in U.S. society unravels alongside the right wing's old culture wars against sexual minorities, socialism is reemerging as a political touchstone for many students and workers. Marxism's real history and emancipatory potential can play a role not just in advancing LGBT civil rights in the modern era, but in advocating a broader vision for sexual liberation for all in the future.

CHAPTER FOUR

The Birth of Gay Power

The sixties are often perceived as an era of social upheaval and orgiastic revelry. But for LGBT folks in America, the efflorescence of sexual expression did not begin until the waning months of that decade in the heart of the nation's then-largest bohemian enclave and gay ghetto, New York City's Greenwich Village. The Stonewall Riots that began in the wee hours of June 28, 1969,[1] lasted six nights and catapulted the issue of sexual liberation out of the Dark Ages and into a new era.

The relative freedoms and social acceptance experienced today by millions of American LGBT people, in particular urban residents, would have seemed as surreal to that generation as the prospect of electing an African-American president. On the heels of the U.S. military's postwar purge of gays, President Eisenhower signed a 1953 executive order that established "sexual perversion" as grounds for being fired from government jobs. And since employment records were shared with private industry, exposure or suspicion of homosexuality could render a person unemployable and destitute. "Loitering in a public toilet" was an offense that could blacklist a man from work and social networks, as lists of arrestees were often printed in newspapers and other public records. Most states had laws barring homosexuals from receiving professional licenses, which could also be revoked upon discovery. Sex between consenting adults of the same sex, even in a private home, could be punished by up to life in prison, confinement in a mental institution, or, in seven states, castration.[2]

Since 1917, foreign LGBT people were barred from legally immigrating to the United States on the grounds that they suffered from "psychopathic personality disorder."[3] Illinois was the only state in the country, since 1961, where homosexuality was not explicitly outlawed. New York's penal code called for the arrest of anyone in public wearing fewer than three items of clothing "appropriate" to their gender. And California's Atascadero State Hospital was compared with a Nazi concentration camp and known as a "Dachau for queers" for performing electroshock and other draconian "therapies" on gays and lesbians. One legal expert argues that in the 1960s, "The homosexual...was smothered by law."[4]

This repression existed alongside a growing acknowledgement of the existence of lesbians and gays in literature, theater, movies, and newspapers. Cultural outlets exposed an expanding gay world to people who may never have known of its existence, including those who would finally discover affirmation and a name for their desires. In an interview with NPR's Terry Gross, Daughters of Bilitis (DOB) cofounder Phyllis Lyon recounts how when she met her lover and the group's cofounder Del Martin in 1949 she had no idea there was such a possibility as lesbianism.[5] By the 1960s, that would no longer be possible for an adult woman in urban America. Bestsellers like James Baldwin's *Another Country* and Mary McCarthy's *The Group* included lesbian characters in their plots. And the *New York Times* ran a front-page story on the city's gay male scene as "the most sensitive open secret," leading to a spate of feature articles—ranging from hostile to sympathetic—in *Life, Look, Newsweek*, and *Time*.[6]

The groups that formed to organize gays and lesbians in the 1950s remained small, largely disconnected from one another, and conflicted in their political agendas well into the 1960s. Seven years after its New York City launch, the Mattachine Society's local chapter had fewer than one hundred members in 1963, while New York's DOB chapter had twenty-two voting members in 1965.[7] The continued insistence on referring to their movement as "homophile" to avoid any explicitly sexual connotations betrayed their groups' conservatism. Most telling was the internalized homophobia that dominated the homophile movement's leadership, which looked to medical professionals who deemed their sexuality "deviant" and requiring a "cure." DOB's publication, the *Ladder*, was still urging its members "to stop the breeding of defiance toward society" and to exhibit "outward conformity."[8] Donald Webster Cory, a pseudonym for a leading Mattachine activist, took on a handful of younger militants for advocating public protests and their rejection of the medical pathologizing of gays for "alienating [the movement] from scientific thinking...by its constant, defensive, neurotic, disturbed denial" that homosexuals were sick.[9] It was a milestone, therefore, when militants like Frank Kameny won over the Washington, D.C., Mattachine chapter in 1965 to approve a resolution proclaiming that "homosexuality is not a sickness...but is merely a preference, an orientation, or propensity, on par with, and not different in kind from, heterosexuality."[10] Another signpost on the road ahead appeared in 1967 when students at New York's Columbia University founded the first university-chartered gay organization, the Student Homophile League, declaring equality among all sexual orientations.[11] Imagine the Black civil rights movement of that era having to challenge white supremacist ideas within its ranks and one begins to grasp the enormous ideological obstacles that permeated the thinking of many LGBT people.

But the involvement of many mostly closeted gays and lesbians in the civil rights, women's, and anti–Vietnam War movements shaped a new generation of budding radicals chafing at their own oppression. Influenced by the Black Power militants who had made slogans like "Black is beautiful" and "Black power" the argot of the radical movements, by 1968 the homophile movement adopted "gay is good" and "gay power" as their rallying cries. A glimpse of things to come was perceptible at the formation of the East Coast Homophile Organizations (ECHO) in 1963, where militants adopted plans to picket openly against legislation barring gays from federal employment. Wearing suits and ties, dresses and heels, on July 4, 1965, handfuls of picketers began an annual tradition of protesting outside Philadelphia's Independence Hall to remind the nation that there remained a group of Americans who had yet to receive humane treatment and rights. In San Francisco's Tenderloin district there had even been a Stonewall dress rehearsal of sorts in the summer of 1966, when a cop's manhandling of a transvestite at a local eatery frequented by drag queens and gay street youth led to "general havoc," including smashed windows and the burning of a newsstand.[12] This event, known as the Compton's Cafeteria Riot, not only forced the police and restaurant management to stop harassing transvestites and other LGBT people, but also led to the formation of Vanguard, the first known organization of transgender people and gay street hustlers.[13] But nothing as dramatic or far-reaching as what occurred in New York in 1969 took off from that fierce expression of rage.

Out of the bars and into the streets!

In a society filled with hatred, fear, and ignorance of homosexuality there was at least one public venue for socializing where gays and lesbians in most major towns and cities could go—the bars. But as with all public life for LGBT people, the bars also provided a place for police and authorities to harass and humiliate their victims. From police entrapment in public cruising spots and raids on bars for perceived "disorderly" conduct within, the cultural openings and nascent activism of gays and lesbians was frustrated by state repression from California to New York. Despite there being no explicit laws against serving gays, many bars refused to do so, and there was no legal recourse since kissing or dancing with a member of the same sex and cross-dressing were considered disorderly. It was in this context that the Mafia came to run many of the drinking establishments that catered to gays, lesbians, and transgendered people in New York City. The Stonewall Inn was no exception.

Located at the crossroads of Christopher Street and Seventh Avenue South, near a major subway station, and steps away from the former offices of the nation's largest independent weekly, the *Village Voice*, the Stonewall Inn was dark, with two bars, a jukebox, and an eclectic crowd of drag queens, gay street youth, cruising men, and a smattering of lesbians. There was no running water to wash the glasses of watered-down booze and beer that were rinsed in a murky tub behind the main bar, leading to at least one known outbreak of hepatitis among customers.[14] Black, Latino, and white LGBT folks mixed and mingled there, one of the few joints around with dancing. Film historian and author of *The Celluloid Closet*, Vito Russo, described the place as "a bar for the people who were too young, too poor or just too much to get in anywhere else. The Stonewall was a street queen hangout in the heart of the ghetto."[15]

As with most drinking establishments that catered to gays, the Mob owner, Fat Tony, paid off the cops to keep the place from being shut down for city code violations. For a bar that took in between $5,000 and $6,000 on an average Friday night, Fat Tony had little problem skimming off $1,200 a month to assuage New York's Finest in the local Sixth Precinct.[16] Yet raids were still commonplace at bars like the Stonewall—one had occurred there just days before the riots—but a choreographed kabuki routine was established between mobsters and cops, each of whom played out their roles to keep up appearances while never threatening their mutual access to easy cash at the expense of the LGBT clientele. Bars generally reopened the night after a raid, as happened at the Stonewall the last week of June 1969. To this day rumors and speculation swirl around the reasoning for people's response to the police raid on the night of June 28. Police asserted that gay Wall Street brokers, who could not be legally bonded by brokerage houses due to their homosexuality, were being blackmailed there, exposure that would have destroyed the lives of those men. Others suggest that it was the shocking death earlier that week of forty-seven-year-old gay icon Judy Garland that exacerbated anger that night.

Whatever the immediate catalyst for the unprecedented response to a routine raid, the fact is that lives immersed in shame and secrecy in a world rocked by social upheaval and defiance could not have remained untouched much longer by the ferment that surrounded them. It was, after all, 1969.

Under the pretext of the Stonewall Inn's operating without a liquor license, a handful of police, led by Deputy Inspector Seymour Pine, figured they'd make quick work of shutting down the bar and rounding up its patrons that night. Sexist and homophobic stereotypes of gays and lesbians certainly reassured the cops that resistance was unlikely at best, irrelevant at worst. Initially, when the cops forced the men and women inside to line up, show identity papers, and prepare to be arrested, everyone did as they were told, despite some cheeky back talk. But as crowds gathered outside and the harassment built, a once buoyant, even carnivalesque mood was transformed into active rage. This snippet from the *Daily News* article "Homo Nest Raided, Queen Bees Are Stinging Mad" provides a distressing glimpse of the smug contempt toward LGBT people at that time. The article begins: "She sat there with her legs crossed, the lashes of her mascara-coated eyes beating like the wings of a hummingbird. She was angry. She was so upset she hadn't bothered to shave. A day old [*sic*] stubble was beginning to push through the pancake makeup. She was a he. A queen of Christopher Street."[17]

The *Village Voice* coverage of events of the first night of rioting captures not only the spirit of the fight but also the open disdain that even progressive writers had for gay people. Keep in mind, this account was written by two journalists twenty years before anyone ever thought to openly invoke words like "fag" and "dyke" as ironically empowering—in 1969, these were insensitive, nasty slurs.

[A]s the patrons trapped inside were released one by one, a crowd started to gather on the street...initially a festive gathering, composed mostly of Stonewall boys who were waiting around for friends still inside or to see what was going to happen. Cheers would go up as favorites would emerge from the door, strike a pose, and swish by the detective with a "Hello there, fella." The stars were in their element. Wrists were limp, hair was primped, and reactions to the applause were classic....

Suddenly the paddywagon arrived and the mood of the crowd changed. Three of the more blatant queens—in full drag—were loaded inside, along with the bartender and doorman, to a chorus of catcalls and boos from the crowd. A cry went up to push the paddywagon over, but it drove away before anything could happen. With its exit, the action waned momentarily. The next person to come out was a dyke, and she put up a struggle—from car to door to car again....

Pine ordered the three cars and paddywagon to leave with the prisoners before the crowd became more of a mob. "Hurry back," he added, realizing he and his force of eight detectives, two of them women, would be easily overwhelmed if the temper broke....

It was at that moment that the scene became explosive. Limp wrists were forgotten....

..."Pigs!" "Faggot cops!" Pennies and dimes flew. I stood against the door. The detectives held at most a 10-foot clearing. Escalate to nickels and quarters. A bottle. Another bottle. Pine says, "Let's get inside. Lock ourselves inside, it's safer."...

The door crashes open, beer cans and bottles hurtle in. Pine and his troop [sic] rush to shut it. At that point, the only uniformed cop among them gets hit with something under his eye. He hollers, and his hand comes away scarlet. It looks a lot more serious than it really is. They are suddenly furious. Three run out in front to see if they can scare the mob from the door. A hail of coins. A beer can glances off Deputy Inspector Smyth's head.

...The cop who is cut is incensed, yells something like, "So, you're the one who hit me!" And while the other cops help, he slaps the prisoner five or six times very hard and finishes with a punch to the mouth. They handcuff the guy as he almost passes out....

...The exit left no cops on the street, and almost by signal the crowd erupted into cobblestone and bottle heaving [*sic*]. The reaction was solid: they were pissed. The trashcan I was standing on was nearly yanked out from under me as a kid tried to grab it for use in the window-smashing melee. From nowhere came an uprooted parking meter—used as a battering ram on the Stonewall door....

By now the mind's eye has forgotten the character of the mob; the sound filtering in doesn't suggest dancing faggots any more [*sic*]. It sounds like a powerful rage bent on vendetta....

...One detective arms himself in addition with a sawed-off baseball bat he has found. I hear, "We'll shoot the first motherfucker that comes through that door."...

I can only see the arm at the window. It squirts liquid into the room, and a flaring match follows. Pine is not more than 10 feet away. He aims his gun at the figures.

He doesn't fire. The sound of sirens coincides with the whoosh of flames where the lighter fluid was thrown....It was that close....[18]

After this initial forty-five-minute confrontation, the riot squad arrived, and for hours a cat-and mouse game ensued between groups of police and groups of rioters, numbering around two thousand in all. In a decade punctuated by riots in most major cities, it was a rare victory for the rioters over the police. The fact that it had been "faggots," "trannies," "dykes," and street kids who delivered a decisive blow to the police was lost on nobody. News of the first night's rebellion spread widely, and by the following evening organized leftists and more gays, lesbians, transvestites, and transgendered people came out to see what would happen, catch a glimpse of the previous night's detritus, and snag their own opportunity for revenge against police who had humiliated and beaten them all for years. The violence resumed each evening through Wednesday night, July 2, with taunts from young gays and chants by experienced activists stoking police violence through the labyrinthine streets of Greenwich Village. Mortified that they had been disgraced by a bunch of "queers," the cops returned in force each night to try and recapture Christopher Street. They never did.

Most eyewitness reports recount the leading role played by some of the most despised and oppressed groupings within the LGBT community. A multiracial lot of poor gay teens, many living on the streets because they had been tossed out of homes or had run away from abuse, taunted the cops with abandon. Transvestites who camped and mocked the cops while striking blows with spiked heels showed that defiance and humor could be complementary. And some reports credited at least one butch lesbian with a furious display of resistance that shamed some of the men present into shedding their passivity and fighting back that first night. Deputy Inspector Pine, who had fought in the Second World War and was injured in the Battle of the Bulge, where nineteen thousand American soldiers died, said of the first night of rioting, "There was never any time that I felt more scared than I felt that night."[19] Beat poet Allen Ginsburg walked through the Village that weekend and poignantly summed up the atmosphere: "You know, the guys there were so beautiful—they've lost that wounded look that fags all had 10 years ago."[20]

From a riot to a movement

What separated the Stonewall Riots from all previous gay activism was not merely the unexpected nights-long defiance in the streets, but the conscious mobilization in the riot's wake of new and seasoned activists who gave expression to this more militant mood. Like a dam bursting, Stonewall was the eruption after twenty years of trickling progress by small handfuls of men and women whose conscious organizing gave way to the spontaneous wave of fury. The riots alone would not be remembered today for transforming gay politics and life had they not been followed by organizations that transformed the raw outrage into an ongoing social force.

A clash between the old-guard organizers and newly rising militants was apparent from the Sunday of the riots, when Mattachine activists who'd met with the mayor's office and police posted this sign on the front of the Stonewall: "We homosexuals plead with our people to please help maintain peaceful and quiet conduct on the streets of the Village—Mattachine."[21] Their pleas were ignored. Each night thereafter through Wednesday, more and more gays and straight leftists, from socialists and Black Panthers to the Yippies[22] and Puerto Rican Young Lords, arrived on the scene to participate in the latest confrontation with police.

By the time the riots subsided, activists began distributing leaflets that read, "Do You Think Homosexuals Are Revolting? You Bet Your Sweet Ass We Are,"[23] and announced a meeting at a Village leftist venue known as Alternative U. What began as an ad hoc committee of Mattachine–New York to organize a march in commemoration of the riots evolved into a full-blown organization, the Gay Liberation

Front (GLF). In conscious tribute to the South Vietnamese National Liberation Front then fighting the U.S. government in Southeast Asia, these activists wanted to confront not just the stifling homophobia of U.S. society but the entire oppressive and exploitative imperial edifice. From the earliest gathering of the GLF, disputes about the political perspective of the movement were framed in terms of whether to focus exclusively on LGBT issues and consciousness-raising or to embrace a broader revolutionary agenda and solidarity with other oppressed minorities.

But almost all the newly radicalizing activists agreed that the old guard's approach needed to be upended. Looking back years later on the debates between the DOB and Mattachine leaderships and new radicals, one prominent militant, Jim Fouratt, summarized the tensions of that time: "We wanted to *end* the homophile movement. We wanted them to join us in making the gay revolution. We were a nightmare to them. They were committed to being nice, acceptable status quo Americans, and we were not; we had no interest at all in being acceptable."[24]

One agenda key to all the new gay liberationists was the act of coming out, since most gays remained publicly closeted. As D'Emilio notes, this cathartic act of coming out publicly—to one's family and friends, at work, and on the streets—"quintessentially expressed the fusion of the personal and political that the radicalism of the late 1960s exalted."[25] Shedding their internalized homophobia may have opened gays and lesbians to occasional attacks, but it also allowed them to claim a sense of self-respect that was incompatible with life in the closet. "Coming out," D'Emilio explains, "provided gay liberation with an army of permanent enlistees."[26] Ironically, the right wing's fears that gay visibility would encourage others to either experiment with homosexuality or at least be tolerant of it turned out to be accurate. While the right may shudder at that fact, the widening visibility and confidence of a gay movement did pave the way for others to come out and has transformed public consciousness ever since. Gallup polls taken over thirty years on questions regarding homosexuality show enormous advances. Since 1977, public support for legalization of "homosexual relations between consenting adults" has risen from 43 percent to a record 59 percent in 2007. In that same poll, 89 percent of Americans today believe that "homosexuals should have equal rights in terms of job opportunities."[27] Stonewall's wake created the conditions for this rise in social consciousness.

The influence of small radical groups in the GLF was evident in its statement to one underground newspaper, the *Rat*:

> We are a revolutionary homosexual group of men and women formed with the realization that complete sexual liberation for all people cannot come about unless existing social institutions are abolished. We reject society's attempt to impose sexual roles and definitions of our nature. We are stepping outside these roles and simplistic myths. We are going to be who we are. At the same time, we are creating new social forms and relations, that is, relations based upon brotherhood, cooperation, human love, and uninhibited sexuality. Babylon has forced us to commit ourselves to one thing...revolution.[28]

In response to the *Rat*'s question, "What makes you revolutionaries?" GLF members wrote,

"We identify ourselves with all the oppressed: the Vietnamese struggle, the third world, the blacks, the workers...

all those oppressed by this rotten, dirty, vile, fucked-up capitalist conspiracy."[29]

One of the earliest protests launched by the GLF was against the *Village Voice*, the very newspaper whose account of the Stonewall Riots (above) was circulated and cited in periodicals throughout the world. To raise money through dances and to publicize its activities, the GLF tried to advertise in the *Voice*, which refused to print the word "gay." Considering the word to be offensive and "equitable with 'fuck' and other four-letter words,"[30] the *Voice*'s offices were soon deluged with petitions carrying thousands of signatures demanding they alter their policy, forcing them to concede. As dozens of chapters of the GLF spread across the country, even to Britain, similar protests converged on newspapers, demanding respect and representation. The *Los Angeles Times* had even refused to print the word "homosexual" in its advertising, despite less flattering references to gays in cultural revues in the "family newspaper."[31] The *San Francisco Examiner* was picketed that fall for referring to gays and lesbians as "semi-males" and "women who aren't exactly women."[32] Even the right to put up flyers and distribute gay newspapers in the bars catering to LGBT people had to be fought for and won through protest. The GLF launched its own newspaper, *Come Out!* in the fall of 1969, which became a popular means of disseminating ideas and movement information. *Gay Power* and *Gay* also premiered that year, each selling twenty-five thousand copies per issue, expressing the hunger for an independent LGBT press.[33]

Later that year, a group of activists split from the GLF and formed a new single-issue group, the Gay Activist Alliance (GAA), with a constitution that defined its agenda as "exclusively devoted to the liberation of homosexuals and avoids involvement in any program of action not obviously relevant to homosexuals."[34] Right from the get-go they aimed their sights on getting rid of discrimination against LGBT people in the workplace and putting heat on local politicians to change bigoted laws. GLF and GAA collaborated on many efforts, including protests against further police raids and the annual Stonewall commemoration march.

Perhaps one of the greatest movement victories of that era came out of protests against the American Psychiatric Association's (APA) designation of homosexuality as a mental illness. So long as LGBT people were pathologized as sick, social and legal constraints would remain. Angry protests disrupted the usually placid APA gatherings in the early 1970s. Militants Barbara Gittings and Frank Kameny demanded and took seats at the table to discuss the damage psychiatrists' "therapies" were doing to the lives of gays and lesbians. One gay psychiatrist appeared on an APA panel wearing a mask and disguising his voice to plead for an alteration of that body's policy. In 1973, the APA's board of trustees removed homosexuality from its list of mental illnesses.[35] Five years later, gay and lesbian psychiatrists formed a caucus within the APA—never again would a gay psychiatrist have to hide from his colleagues behind a grotesque mask.

It was a major breakthrough when on August 21, 1970, Black Panther Party cofounder Huey Newton wrote the first openly pro-gay statement by a major heterosexual movement activist of any race, which was printed in the pages of the *Black Panther*, the party's newspaper. In "A Letter from Huey to the Revolutionary Brothers and Sisters About the Women's Liberation and Gay Liberation Movements," Newton admitted that the Black Panther Party had been inconsiderate concerning gays and lesbians. He argued, "Homosexuals are not given freedom and liberty by anyone in the society. Maybe they might be the most oppressed people in the society." Newton also accepted the criticism of gay activists, "The terms 'faggot' and 'punk' should be deleted from our vocabulary, and especially we should not attach names normally designed for homosexuals to men who are enemies of the people."[36] The radical transformation taking place in the minds of many gay activists was reflected in the following excerpt from the *Gay Flames* pamphlet, written by the Chicago chapter of the GLF.

> [B]ecause of the rampant oppression we see—of black, third world people, women, workers—in addition to our own; because of the corrupt values, because of the injustices, we no longer want to "make it" in Amerika....
>
> Our particular struggle is for sexual self-determination, the abolition of sex-role stereotypes and the human right to the use of one's body without interference from the legal and social institutions of the state. Many of us have understood that our struggle cannot succeed without a fundamental change in society which will put the source of power (means of production) in the hands of the people who at present have nothing....
>
> But as our struggle grows it will be made clear by the changing objective conditions that our liberation is inextricably bound to the liberation of all oppressed people.[37]

Splits In the movement

But as with any new movement that encompasses a wide range of people and perspectives, the GLF's meetings were often filled with tumultuous and heated debate. The participation of some Maoists and Stalinists whose politics, as discussed in the

previous chapter, were openly hostile to homosexuality complicated things even more. Alongside the newly radicalized inde-
pendents, the group attracted many radicals from far left
organizations who brought with them the baggage—both good
and bad—of their political tendencies' perspectives on gays
and lesbians. These ideas ranged from notions that homosexuality was a "bourgeois deviation" to liberatory concepts
about how sexuality is shaped by class society. The dominant
leftist influence in the GLF, as in the rest of the far left, was
Maoist—often calling itself "Marxist-Leninist"—which formally barred gays and lesbians from its organization. The
Stalinist Communist Party's official ideology taught that "homosexuality is part of the problem of a decaying society."[38]
Members of the largest Trotskyist group, the Socialist Workers Party (SWP), were often perceived as "notorious Puritans,"[39] though they advocated civil rights for gays and
lesbians while remaining standoffish at times to the movement. This stance set off a three-year internal party debate on
the nature of gay oppression and the organization's posture
toward gay movement work.[40] The analytical framework of
the Maoists and Stalinists therefore rendered them dubious
allies and participants in the movement, whereas the civil libertarian approach of most socialists from Trotskyist and social-democratic traditions placed them in unequivocal
solidarity with the aims of most LGBT activists and opened
the door to theoretical evolution on questions of sexuality.

Complicating this political cocktail was the fact that nations
claiming to be socialist, like China and Cuba, were defended by
Maoists, often uncritically. Mao's Cultural Revolution[41] under
way in China at that time led to castrations of "sexual degener-
ates," which further confused gay activists listening to move-

ment leaders quoting from his Little Red Book of aphorisms. Leftists like Allen Young in the GLF who clamored to join the Venceremos Brigades to cut sugarcane in Cuba—where gays were sent to concentration camps—were barred from the country due to claims they would try to influence Cuban gays, even as Young and others defended the revolution at the time.

Maoists also held the analysis that the most oppressed in society, the poorest African Americans in particular, must lead every struggle. As a result, debates in the GLF over whether to donate money to the Black Panthers' bail fund degenerated into charges of racism against those offended by some of the Panthers' overt homophobia and sexism. Panther leader Eldridge Cleaver's best-selling 1968 book *Soul on Ice* includes lines such as, "homosexuality is a sickness, just as are baby-rape or wanting to become the head of General Motors."[42] Black radical poet and playwright Leroi Jones (who later changed his name to Amiri Baraka) warned Blacks in the *New York Times* against the "vague integrated, plastic, homosexual 'rEVolUTioN.'"[43] The Panthers' and Yippies' pervasive use of the word "faggot" to denigrate their opponents was rationalized away by movement leaders like Fouratt, whose enthusiasm for the Black and countercultural struggles, he later admitted, blotted out all criticism of those with whom he wanted to struggle alongside.[44] The Maoist penchant for public acts of self-criticism to root out "counterrevolutionary" individuals amounted in GLF meetings at times to "little more than character assassinations."[45] Disagreements in this atmosphere easily degenerated into charges that the person in question was insufficiently radical. This kind of moralism was mixed with the anarchistic impulses of many activists wary of authority of any sort, including elected movement leaders. As a result, the GLF had no formal structure and decisions were generally made by consensus, meaning that any single individual or small minority in the room could derail all decision-making or drag out a discussion for hours, and that decisions made one week would at times be overturned the next. In the name of autonomy, democratic decision-making was subverted. For example, despite a decision taken at a GLF meeting not to print an article critical of the underground newspaper *Gay Power*, members went ahead and printed it anyway.[46] In practice, those with the most confidence and time, which often correlated with those who had more education and financial resources, wound up dominating the group. Feminist activist Jo Freeman laid out her criticisms of this common method in social movements in her essay "The Tyranny of Structurelessness," written in 1971:

> Contrary to what we would like to believe, there is no such thing as a structureless group. Any group of people of whatever nature that comes together for any length of time for any purpose will inevitably structure itself in some fashion....
>
> Thus structurelessness becomes a way of masking power, and within the women's movement is usually most strongly advocated by those who are the most powerful (whether they are conscious of their power or not). As long as the structure of the group is informal, the rules of how decisions are made are known only to a few and awareness of power is limited to those who know the rules.[47]

Only four months after its inception, the movement encountered its first stumbling blocks over political perspective and organizational methods. At a New York GLF meeting in mid-November 1969, this structurelessness and finger-pointing came to a head, leading several members to form the GAA, described above. As Carter explains, "Given the freewheeling style of GLF meetings, it could take a very long time to reach consensus on any matter. Understandably, it tried the patience of many to see matters that had been painstakingly discussed and decided reconsidered over and over at meeting after meeting."[48] It was the Panther bail contribution debate that finally led to a walkout and the launch of the GAA. The initial vote ended in a refusal to donate funds on the basis of some Panthers' frequent usage of homophobic language, but when GLF members reraised the issue for a vote the next week, which passed, several people walked out in frustration and started the new group.

This was the context in which a Revolutionary Peoples' Constitutional Convention took place in Philadelphia in September 1970. Thirteen thousand radicals participated.[49] The conference itself expressed many of the strengths and weaknesses of an evolving movement with a political leadership that was fraught with contradictions. Leading Yippies who attended, like Jerry Rubin and Abbie Hoffman, denigrated their enemies as "faggots." Many of the Panthers snickered at gay men and were dismissive of demands by women's groups, particularly the lesbian activists who asked for, but never received, a workshop to discuss their oppression. Some white LGBT radicals were confused about how to deal with a Black movement demanding leadership of the revolution, while FBI and police continued to arrest, frame, and even kill members of the Black Panther Party. White antiracists often allowed the moral authority of Black militants to silence any criticisms. The fierce desire to unite all oppressed groups against a racist and repressive society ran up against confusion about how to develop that unity on an honest and genuine footing. One organizer of the Transvestite-transsexual Action Organization explained why her group withdrew support and how at the convention she "felt like a complete fool facing 100 tactical police armed with magnums after hearing a Panther woman read a poem which included derogatory statements about 'white fags.'"[50]

Many liberal groups and individuals were caught flat-footed in the face of the nascent LGBT movement. Lesbians in the movement met with an often hostile response from women's organizations, gay men, and straight allies. National Organization for Women (NOW) president, Betty Friedan, famously attacked "mannish" lesbians for discrediting the women's movement and referred to them in 1969 as the "lavender menace."[51] NOW sought to distance itself from out lesbians they thought would jeopardize their progress, despite the fact that many lesbians, such as author Rita Mae Brown, had been active in the women's movement for years and that even then, as today, straight women who expressed defiance were regularly attacked as "dykes" by male chauvinists. Some lesbians formed separate organizations, such as Lavender Menace—a sassy nod to Ms. Friedan's slur—and Radicalesbians in New York, the Furies Collective in Washington, D.C., and Gay Women's Liberation in San Francisco. They developed a theory of lesbian separatism—"A lesbian is the rage of all women condensed to the point of explosion,"[52] Radicalesbians wrote in "The Woman-Identified Woman"— and advocated separating their political and personal lives from all men, who were collectively perceived as oppressors. They raised sex with women to a point of political principle and a means of rejecting women's "second-class status."[53]

One group of Maoist gays in the GLF split off to form the Red Butterfly cell, "an association of gay men and women who as revolutionary socialists see their liberation linked to the class struggle."[54] Latina and Black transvestites Sylvia Rivera and Marsha P. Johnson, who survived as prostitutes and both of whom had participated in the riots, remained active in GLF and GAA and started a new group to help young street gays and transvestites living on the margins. However, their precarious lives posed a serious obstacle to Street Transvestite Action Revolutionaries becoming a stable organization. A Black Lesbian Caucus developed to take on racism within the gay movement. Some GLFers formed a Radical Study Group that read and discussed Marxist classics such as Engels' *Origin of the Family, Private Property and the State*. Gay historian John D'Emilio, a student at Columbia University in the late 1960s, joined with others to organize the Gay Academic Union, many of whose participants became leading gay and lesbian scholars.

Although much of the left, influenced by Maoism and Stalinism, had a bad position on the question of sexual liberation, the actual trajectory of radicalization in this period meant that many gays and lesbians were drawing revolutionary conclusions, connecting issues, and presenting liberation as something that was not possible without the overthrow of capitalism. Splits in a movement of this character appear to have been the only way individuals with radically different worldviews and experiences could continue to be active. Many groups did not last long in the absence of ongoing mass struggle, a unifying goal, and the political maturity to sort out disagreements in tactics from disagreements in principle. A fractured far left, which in the case of the Panthers was being decimated by state violence, and revolutionary groups that often defended homophobic pseudo-socialist states abroad could not win leadership. Some gays and lesbians went in different directions—toward separatism, toward rejection of revolution, or toward the pull of bourgeois party politics.

CHAPTER FIVE

Whatever Happened to Gay Liberation?

The recession of 1973 was the beginning of the end of the postwar boom. This had major repercussions throughout U.S. society. Labor strikes from 1968 to 1974 had helped lessen the gap between rich and poor and the expansion of welfare programs during the Johnson administration, known as the "Great Society," had helped alleviate some of the worst poverty in rural and urban America.[1] Bosses launched an all-out assault on working-class living standards known as the "employers' offensive" to reverse these gains, which was accompanied by an ideological offensive to justify privatization, strike-breaking, and budget cuts. As socialist author Sharon Smith explains, "The employers' offensive could not succeed in its aims without an ideological assault on the social movements that had shifted the political climate so far to the left in the late 1960s and early 1970s."[2] From cuts in abortion funding for poor women to attacks on affirmative action as "reverse racism" under Democratic president Jimmy Carter, CEOs and right-wing ideologues kicked off a campaign to turn back the clock on social movements years before Republican Ronald Reagan took office in January 1981.

New Right groups such as Reverend Jerry Falwell's Moral Majority and former Florida orange juice spokesperson Anita

Bryant's Save Our Children aggressively promoted anti-abortion, racist, anti-woman, and antigay legislation under the rubric of family values. The right argued that state funding and legislation for women's, Blacks', and gays' rights were potential threats to the family and overall social order. Bryant posed her successful 1977 campaign to repeal Dade County's human rights ordinance that protected gays and lesbians from discrimination this way: "As a mother, I know that homosexuals cannot biologically reproduce children; therefore, they must recruit our children. If gays are granted rights, next we'll have to give rights to prostitutes and to people who sleep with St. Bernards and to nail biters."[3]

These attacks had an enormous impact on the trade unions and social movements. With Chrysler teetering on the edge of bankruptcy, Congress demanded and received hundreds of millions of dollars in concessions from autoworkers in exchange for a company bailout.[4] The Vietnam War ended in 1975, and the massive and radical opposition movements it had spawned were over by then. In the face of an ideological attack from the far right and with a splintered and weakened left, many activists began to look to the Democratic Party for relief.

The relationship between LGBT activists and the Democratic Party has been a dysfunctional one—the Democrats court gays' and lesbians' votes and money but offer few gains and a fair share of abuse in exchange. For those LGBT activists wooed by the Democrats, ditching the more militant strategy that won a hearing in the first place for a "don't rock the boat" one is the price to play.

That the last national gay and lesbian march on Washington, in 1993,[5] was scheduled *after* the 1992 presidential election, rather than as a show of force beforehand to pressure candidate

Bill Clinton, was a concession to the notion that LGBT activists ought not expose the Democrats to scrutiny or force them to stand before gays in public lest their broader appeal be tarnished. This approach is self-defeating, as the longer "support" for gays from politicians remains the purview of attorneys in backrooms, the longer homophobia is afforded an official pass.

Thirty-five years have passed since gay civil rights legislation was first proposed in Congress, yet LGBT people remain an unprotected class of citizens by the U.S. Constitution. Whereas, for example, the denial of rights for gays to work for the federal government was enacted with the stroke of a president's pen in Executive Order 10450 in 1953, no such swift action has been taken to overturn decades of institutional discrimination. Nearly six years into his presidency, Bill Clinton signed Executive Order 11478 providing partial relief for lesbian and gay federal employees—not including three million military personnel. But the fact that his action left intact sodomy laws, anti-same-sex marriage legislation (which he signed), and the military's unequal status for LGBT people (which he introduced!) and never mentions the rights of those who are transgender exposes the bankruptcy of the electoral route for winning civil rights for sexual minorities.

Since the Stonewall Riots in 1969, the Democrats have controlled the White House for twelve years under one Carter and two Clinton administrations. Most of that time both houses of Congress were controlled by the Democrats as well. Yet while the so-called party of the people has often looked to LGBT folks for votes and money, the Democrats have been opportunistic at best and hostile at worst.

In the aftermath of the 2008 election, expectations for the Obama administration are astronomical, not simply because eight years of George W. Bush were characterized by social reaction, but because the new president has openly embraced LGBT people in his speeches, despite his opposition to gay marriage. But social justice advocates have much to learn from the history of collaboration between LGBT people and the Democrats.[6] It's worth examining in some detail how a movement that exploded into action out of a popular rebellion on the streets wound up throwing its energy, money, and hopes into the Democratic Party.

Out of the streets and into the party

The Democratic Party has been, at best, a fair-weather to friend LGBT people, and at worst, an obstacle to their progress. Even the party's defenders and advocates have been equivocal in their willingness to carry through positive legislation. New York Representatives Bella Abzug and Ed Koch (who later became New York City's mayor) introduced the Equality Act of 1974 to expand the civil rights of women along with gays, lesbians, and unmarried people.[7] The bill would have made it illegal to discriminate on the basis of sex, sexual orientation, and marital status in housing, public facilities, and federally assisted programs. It never got out of committee. Each year after that, Koch or Abzug—a brash feminist who was a mainstay of progressive New York politics throughout the seventies and eighties—introduced some form of gay civil rights legislation that picked up small numbers of endorsers but mostly languished in the pages of the *Congressional Record*. The current incarnation that's been whittled down and bastardized since the nineties is the Employment Non-Discrimination Act (ENDA), which we'll get to as the story unfolds.

It is noteworthy that even these two historic congressional gay "allies," Abzug and Koch, have been unreliable
friends to LGBT people from the start. The account of one
lesbian attorney attempting to become a Democratic National Convention delegate in 1976 would be funny if the
stakes didn't render it tragic. Jean O'Leary describes Abzug
attempting to physically force her out the door to prevent a
gay plank or openly lesbian delegate from making it to the
floor of that year's convention.[8]

In the early sixties, Ed Koch ran for local office in New
York City promising to legalize sodomy, yet when the Greenwich Village legislator made it into office years later, he
launched a campaign against gay bars and met with the chief
of police to "rid the area" of homosexuals "and other undesir-
ables."[9] These were early signs that for politicians representing districts with vocal and visible numbers of LGBT people,
it is politically pragmatic to do just enough to corral their
votes into a campaign by promising support, but when the
rubber hits the road the Democrats are willing to toss gays
under a bus.

Many of the earlier generation of committed and active
LGBT Democratic Party activists came out of the Gay Activist
Alliance, despite GAA's formal adherence to independence
from the two major parties. As political divisions in the movement led to splits, many of those who had already jettisoned a
liberationist strategy, deeming it impractical and unwinnable,
felt the attraction of electoral politics most of all. O'Leary (the
lesbian Democrat who had the kerfuffle with Abzug) began in
GAA, split off to help found the separatist Lesbian Feminist
Liberation group, and, despite concerns about "selling out"
the struggle, wound up as chair of the Gay and Lesbian caucus

of the Democratic National Committee.[10] As O'Leary explains, "Harvey Milk was assassinated, and there was rioting in the streets of San Francisco after the Dan White [Milk's assassin] trial. But many had also realized it was time to take our battles from the streets to the corridors of power."[11] Socialist author Lance Selfa explains this dynamic:

> Developing during a period of widespread social agitation, these new social movements faced many of the same choices that the civil rights and anti–Vietnam War movements faced. These choices were manifested by divisions within these movements between militant grassroots campaigns and those that were more oriented toward lobbying and electoral activity. The latter group inevitably found itself feeling the gravitational pull of the Democratic Party.[12]

The focus of some activists in the early 1970s on defeating the sodomy laws on the books in most states led many to lobby legislators and vie for political parties to take up the issue of gay civil rights on their platforms. This was during an era when the major party platforms were actually fought out at the parties' conventions, as opposed to the highly choreographed puff performances of today. Along with a plank on abortion rights (this was one year before *Roe v. Wade* guaranteed women's right to choose), the gay and lesbian plank went down to defeat after presidential candidate George McGovern reversed his earlier support.[13] In fact, after the unprecedented event of a gay speaker addressing the convention—at 2 a.m.—the campaign ensured that he was followed by an antigay speaker who linked the gay movement to "child molestation, white slavery, and pandering."[14]

What stands out about participants' accounts of the 1972 Democratic National Convention is how quickly radical demands yielded to acceptance of a tepid hearing from those in power. Some activists literally went from demanding liberation one year to settling for "a seat at the table" a year or so on, even if all they were offered was the political equivalent of the kids' table, far from the ornate dining room with its crystal and silver. Unwilling to organize independent of the Democrats led good activists down the path of endless accommodation and capitulation. While not all or even most of the erstwhile militants threw themselves into the Democratic Party, those who pursued power from inside electoral confines wound up in some of the most visible and dominant positions within a slackening movement. David Mixner, for example, went from building solidarity for unionizing garbage workers in Arizona in the 1960s to mobilizing against the Vietnam War, and then entered the White House in 1993 as Clinton's adviser to the gay and lesbian community after helping to organize that year's march on Washington.[15]

During the Democratic primaries for the 1976 election, Georgia governor Jimmy Carter stated that he opposed "all forms of discrimination against individuals including discrimination on the basis of sexual orientation."[16] By the time he won the Democratic Party's nomination he was already hedging his bets in an interview with the national gay magazine, the *Advocate*, saying that he wasn't sure "how we could deal with the issue of blackmail in federal security jobs."[17] Somehow the notion of ending all legal restraints on LGBT people, rendering blackmail ineffective and irrelevant, never crossed his mind. Nor did such legislation ever cross his desk. In fact, under his administration more gays and lesbians were booted from the military than under the previous postwar Republican administrations.

The Supreme Court came down with a shocking verdict upholding Georgia's sodomy law in the 1986 *Bowers v. Hardwick* case, stating that adults had no constitutionally protected right to engage in anal or oral sex in the privacy of their own homes. Michael Hardwick brought this case to court after having been literally dragged out of his bed by Atlanta police and thrown into jail for having sex in his bedroom with a male lover. Rendering sodomy punishable by no less than one year in jail and no more than twenty, this decision was a devastating blow to civil rights.[18] At a time when AIDS was documented as the biggest killer of young men in New York City,[19] it is particularly notable how pathetic the response was from leading Democrats. Aside from Jesse Jackson, most prominent Democrats, including the party's 1988 presidential nominee, Michael Dukakis, remained aloof from LGBT issues—with Dukakis even coming out against the right of gays to become foster parents and opposing a gay caucus inside the convention.[20]

But little compares to the treachery of the Clinton administration. A masterful public speaker capable of Academy Award–style performances of empathy, Clinton could famously "feel your pain," but apparently could not alleviate any of it. As detailed in chapter 2, he came into office promising an end to draconian laws against gays in the military, caved after four days, and signed into law what is perhaps the only known order by a commander in chief for gays and lesbians to march back into the closet. While initially perceived as a more benign form of discrimination, his policy, officially known as "Don't Ask, Don't Tell, Don't Pursue," has allowed for the witch hunt against LGBT people in the military to continue. The Servicemembers Legal Defense Network summarizes:

Since the law's 1994 implementation, more than 12,500 women and men have been discharged. According to a 2005 Government Accountability Office report, nearly 800 of those discharged were "mission-critical" specialists—including pilots, intelligence analysts, medics and linguists. A Blue Ribbon Commission Report found that the cost to replace and train service members discharged from fiscal years 1994 through 2003 exceeded $363.8 million.[21]

Though Clinton hired out gays to serve in his administration and held an unprecedented White House meeting with gay leaders, aside from enriching some of these individual gays and lesbians, public policy and the lives of millions of LGBT people were not significantly improved. (In fact, even that White House visit caused a flap over his Secret Service personnel frisking gay entrants while wearing rubber gloves so as not to contract AIDS, a physiological impossibility.)[22] This highly publicized meeting certainly bought the White House enormous good will from many of these leading figures, as former National Gay and Lesbian Task Force leader Urvashi Vaid puts it, "It co-opted gay leadership into silence at the instant it needed to be strident."[23]

Human Rights Campaign (HRC) leaders, among those who had met with Clinton, played a significant role in watering down what was once a broad civil rights bill for gays and lesbians (but not transgender people) into a narrow and less potent piece of legislation that prohibits discrimination in (some) workplaces—ENDA. It was argued then, as it is today, that compromise in the present is necessary in order to make incremental advances in the future. Religious institutions (to which the state grants tax-free status), small businesses, and the military were among the workplaces kept out of the 1994 version that went down to defeat two years later.[24] There have been several versions since then, including one that contains gender-identity language, but none has ever passed both houses of Congress. As it stands today, twenty states and Washington, D.C., along with many cities and towns, bar discrimination based on sexual orientation; laws in each locality have exceptions depending on size and type of employer.[25]

Openly gay Congressman Barney Frank and Senator Ted Kennedy, both liberal Democrats, joined with HRC in defending the 2007 version of ENDA that passed the House (not the Senate) that year, which does not include transgender people, arguing that this is the most realistic deal on offer. To their credit, groups such as the National Gay and Lesbian Task Force (NGLTF) and the major LGBT labor advocacy group, Pride at Work, have joined with transgender groups and others to oppose any compromise legislation that excludes transgender people. The issue here is not whether it is ever acceptable to make political compromises, but rather what terms are nonnegotiable and principally unconscionable. A 2006 study by the *San Francisco Guardian* and the Transgender Law Center found that 60 percent of transgender people in San Francisco earn less than $15,300 per year, only 25 percent have a full-time job, and nearly 9 percent have no source of income.[26] Three hundred national and statewide LGBT groups joined together to form United ENDA to push for transgender inclusion, arguing that "most discrimination against gay, lesbian, and bisexual people who were not transgendered was rooted in prejudices about gender-normative appearances and behaviors—that is, it was the too-effeminate gay man, or the too-masculine woman, who was more vulnerable to employment discrimination."[27] Typical of the kinds of letters compromisers received was the one from a transgender person, using a pseudonym, who wrote to Congressman Frank before the vote asking for an all-inclusive ENDA, "Why don't we deserve your support to protect our right to make a living?.... Someday I hope to be able to leave the closet and be able to share who I am with the world, but without basic protections such as ENDA provides that day will be further off."[28]

Transgender activists are right to argue that after more than thirty years of attempting to gain civil rights for sexual minorities, they shouldn't have to sit at the back of the bus and accept the latest gender-identity "compromise" as just another "gap," in Congressman Frank's words.[29] Instead of representing demands of the LGBT community to those in power, these "leaders" perceive their role as quelling demands from activists and selling deals forged in backrooms to those whose lives are directly affected by this legislation.

This is nothing new. When the Hawaii Supreme Court ruled in 1993 that the denial of marriage licenses to same-sex couples was a violation of that state's laws protecting people from discrimination on the basis of gender, instead of providing momentum for movement activists to win marriage rights the case became a political football. Predictably, Republicans chose the pre-election period in 1996 to push for the Defense of Marriage Act (DOMA), a bill that allows states as well as the federal government not to recognize same-sex marriages consecrated in other states and that defines marriage as a union between a man and a woman. Rather than standing up to the bigots, Clinton caved along with the majority of Democrats in both houses of Congress. As one historian reported the event: "In the dead of night, without cameras or microphones to record his shame, President Clinton signed DOMA into law."[30] Seven years later,

Vermont's governor Howard Dean signed legislation granting same-sex couples civil unions, rather than marriage, also in the dead of night. As with the 1972 gay convention speaker who addressed the crowd at 2 a.m., the Democrats appear committed to a strategy of dealing with gay civil rights out of public sight— "in the closet" is perhaps a more apt metaphor.

The national LGBT leadership scrambled in the weeks leading up to the 1996 election to sell the "*Denial* of Marriage Act" to their constituency, even forking over thousands of dollars in hush money to local groups.[31] Despite the rhetoric of die-hard Clinton supporters at the time who alluded to his reversing the legislation once back in office for a second term, Clinton himself went on record denouncing gay marriage: "I remain opposed to same-sex marriage. I believe marriage is an institution for the union of a man and a woman. This has been my long-standing position, and it is not being reviewed or reconsidered."[32] Vaid drew a parallel between the Carter and Clinton administrations: "The major difference in sixteen years seems to be that we have graduated from meeting with senior staffers to meeting directly with the President. But measured in action, the difference is negligible."[33]

By the 2004 election when the battle over full marriage rights resumed in Massachusetts and California, it was the liberals of the Democratic Party who reined in the movement and then later blamed their electoral loss on activists who, they claimed, gave the right wing "a position to rally around."[34] Once again, it was gay Congressman Barney Frank who tore into those seeking reform, such as San Francisco mayor Gavin Newsom, for performing "spectacle weddings" ahead of the presidential election.[35] Aside from the obvious opportunism behind the attacks, Democrats presume that

LGBT people must wait for conservative Americans to catch up with their desire for civil rights. Yet rights cannot wait for the approval of reactionaries. According to that logic, Blacks too should have waited for public opinion to catch up with their demands. But in 1968, one year *after* the Supreme Court struck down bans on interracial marriage as unconstitutional, Gallup polls showed that only 20 percent of Americans approved of marriages between Blacks and whites.[36]

In 2008, there was something profoundly disturbing about Barack Obama, the son of a Black man and a white woman, calling for "states' rights" when it comes to same-sex marriage. This is especially so since the California court cited as precedent in its 2008 decision overturning the gay marriage ban the sixty-year-old decision that opened the door for biracial couples like Obama's own parents to legally marry. Ironically, opinion polls taken on the eve of the 2008 election showed overwhelming opposition to any constitutional ban on same-sex marriage as well as support for marriage rights equal to opposition, with the trajectory on all relevant questions clearly heading toward approval of same-sex marriage.[37] Activists can only contemplate where opinions would lie if there were actually vocal support coming from political leaders like Obama.

No leading Democrat has ever gone before the public on prime-time television or in the front pages of the nation's newspapers to discuss the ongoing injustices, violence, discrimination, and daily humiliations that LGBT people face in order to advocate the abolition of institutionalized discrimination. In other words, these leaders do not lead; instead they echo the aspirations of elites and use their prestige, money, and sexual orientation to fob off political palliatives as victories. So long as high-powered attorneys and Democratic

WHATEVER HAPPENED TO GAY LIBERATION?   151

Party officials—regardless of their sexual orientation—are permitted to dominate the debate, full rights will never be achieved for the vast majority of the oppressed. The legacy of corporate-driven strategies and reliance on the Democrats for delivering civil rights for sexual minorities is a poor one. A successful movement strategy, therefore, must begin with independence from the Democratic Party.

From movement to market

Millions of LGBT people and their allies commemorate the Stonewall Riots each year in gay pride marches that draw enormously diverse crowds in major cities around the world. Whether the majority of participants are aware of the origins of these colossal celebrations is a mystery. These events have been largely stripped of historical or political content and given over to major banks, beverage manufacturers, and other businesses as means to sell their commodities to the ever-widening LGBT market. There is something both heartening and deflating about these events. Heartening because for many they present opportunities to come out and be part of a community and celebrate in unity, even meet new friends or potential lovers in a society in which it remains difficult to do so. Deflating because enormous corporate entities like Miller Brewing Company and Citibank are provided venues to shroud their exploitative enterprises in feel-good rainbow colors.

In most big cities with gay enclaves, like New York and Chicago, these marches that once started in the neighborhoods where LGBT people congregate and flowed outward to spread the message of gay liberation begin today in nearby areas and flow into the neighborhoods, often called "gay ghettos" or "gayborhoods," where participants are encouraged to disperse into bars and clubs. Whatever one thinks of this rerouting, it is not accidental. In fact, it was the manager of the Stonewall Inn, Ed Murphy, who first noted the marketing potential of these marches-cum-parades and, in an ironic twist of history, formed the Christopher Street Festival Committee in 1972, successfully reversing the march route two years later to provide gay ghetto business owners with both cash and caché.[38]

That a once universally despised minority was partially transformed in the public eye into a chic market niche is testament to the ability of capitalism to commodify sex and repackage a layer of its own social dissidents into madcap consumers and purveyors of style. While one wing of the American ruling class continues to press for socially reactionary policies and ideas, another profits from creating a picture of LGBT folks as fun-loving, free-spending, upwardly mobile, campy, mostly white, sexy (but often sexless) sidekicks to their straight counterparts. But just as television and film distort the reality of most straight lives and living conditions to conform to a middle-class or even wealthy lifestyle and worldview, so too does the mainstream media project an utterly false picture of who is gay and how most gays live. This marketing offensive reached new heights in the early 1990s in response to the greater visibility of LGBT people who went on the attack to demand AIDS drugs and treatment, opening the door ever wider for millions who had previously remained closeted. This schizophrenic approach, pillorying gays one moment and pitching to them the next, has since remained a feature of advanced capitalism in many Western countries.

As *Homo Economics* points out "In a stark illustration of the discrepancy between image and reality, in 1993, at the height of the 'gay moment,' nineteen initiatives around the nation to repeal pro-gay legislation or to institute antigay policies passed, while not one local or statewide legislative effort on behalf of gays prevailed."[39] This was the same year that "lesbian chic" became all the rage in popular media. The glossy culture and high-society magazine *Vanity Fair* ran a cover in August that year with lesbian singer k.d. lang wearing a suit and getting a mock shave while lying back in a barber chair enjoying the attentions of supermodel Cindy Crawford. Meanwhile *Newsweek* proclaimed lesbians had finally arrived—at least white, affluent, and conventionally attractive ones—in their cover article posing the question, "Lesbians Coming Out Strong: What Are the Limits of Tolerance?"[40] Absolut vodka, Benetton clothing, Miller beer, and dozens of other products began appearing in gay magazines with ads targeting the new audience, while advertising executives proclaimed: "The Gay Market: Nothing to Fear But Fear Itself."[41] The gay advertising drought of the eighties, resulting from the explosion of AIDS and a spate of gay militancy that advertisers shunned, gave way in the nineties to a dramatic rise in national brands targeting the market. One spokeswoman for Miller beer explained her company's ubiquitous ad campaigns in gay neighborhoods and bars matter-of-factly, "We market to gays and lesbians for business reasons because we want to sell our product to consumers. It doesn't get more complicated than that."[42]

Dollars and Sense magazine ran a fascinating story on this paradox entitled "The Gay Marketing Moment."[43] In it, they exposed how gay marketing services peddled unrepresentative statistics about LGBT wealth and lifestyles to business executives in order to create the myth of the rich gay that persists in many circles to this day. Strub Media Group, led by gays, surveyed readers of certain lesbian and gay magazines to arrive at the much-touted income for the average gay household that year, a remarkable $63,100, compared to $36,500 in the wider population.[44] To this figure was added the insight that, as most LGBT households had no children (more so then than today), marketers could enjoy a bonanza of opportunities targeting these newly baptized DINKS (double income, no kids). The *Wall Street Journal* declared gay households "A Dream Market," with educational and lifestyle "characteristics sought by many advertisers."[45]

Beginning in 1988, the National Gay Newspaper Guild conducted studies of LGBT newspaper readers, which determined that 59.6 percent had graduated college, compared with 18 percent in the overall population. In addition, this guild—representing gay businesspeople who owned magazines and papers and therefore had a stake in publicizing these results to woo advertisers—also concluded that 49 percent of LGBT readers were professionals, as opposed to only 15.9 percent overall.[46]

But the statistics gathered by groups like Overlooked Opinions on consumer preferences, education, and income turned out not to be at all reliable for the wider LGBT population beyond those who read glossy style magazines or attended certain types of gay events from which these studies were drawn. Like Black readers of *Ebony, Essence*, and *Jet* magazines, who earn between 41 and 82 percent more than the average African American, LGBT magazine readers do not represent a monolithic community whose income levels can be generalized to the wider population.[47] In fact, when scientific surveys were conducted in 1994, rather than being upwardly mobile "guppies" (gay urban professionals), most individual gay men were found to earn incomes slightly below straight men ($21,000 vs. $22,500) and individual lesbians were discovered to have slightly higher incomes than straight women ($13,300 vs. $13,200).[48] In addition to the growing data that show that LGBT people have similar or lower incomes than heterosexuals, it stands to reason that a population long targeted for discrimination and attacks is not likely to be uniformly open to marketers about their sexuality. Also, those who are most likely to have the financial and support networks that allow them to more easily come out—that is, the middle and upper classes—may continue to skew even the more reliable statistics.

Katherine Sender, a researcher in this field, extrapolated from the ongoing pay differential between men and women and its relationship to LGBT household income. "The 'Double Income, No Kids' stereotype of gay male affluence reflects gender inequities in household income, not higher-than-average incomes of single gay men." She continues, "Gender differences in earnings, where women earn on average only 74 percent of male incomes, are compounded in household incomes: gay male and heterosexual couples earn about the same, whereas lesbian couples earn 18 to 20 percent less."[49] Though years of studies have attempted to correct these phony statistics, even today a simple Google search on gay incomes quickly nets Community Marketing's 2008 figures showing the median household income for both gay men and lesbians is "approximately $80,000," far in excess of straight households.[50] As in the past, these figures represent a small slice of lesbians and gays of the upper-middle class whose purchasing habits put them in contact with market researchers. Not surprisingly, this study was cosponsored by Absolut vodka. In reality, according to the Urban Institute's latest figures, for 1999, median earnings for households with gay men in their peak income years (twenty-five to fifty-four) are $3,000 *less* than households with a man and a woman, regardless of their marital status.[51]

Despite the facts, any casual TV viewer or magazine reader is treated to a steady diet of distorted images of LGBT people who are almost always white, male, and rich—except for the *L Word*, where the women are mostly white and wealthy, with an extraordinary amount of leisure time for partying and dining out. Shows like *Will and Grace* (rich gay attorney and campy sidekick), *Queer Eye for the Straight Guy* (vacuous, product-driven, fashion savants), and *Queer as Folk* (white gay male professionals doing the club scene) drive home the fantasy life that is sold as the norm. Notable exceptions include HBO's breakthrough series *The Wire*, which portrayed the first openly gay Black gangster living in a ghetto as a featured character on a series. However, this special cable channel show drew less than one percent of the American TV viewing audience.[52] HBO's successful *True Blood* series featured a muscled, unabashedly queeny, Black, gay line cook with a sassy mouth, who stole the show—and in one episode had sex with a middle-aged white male politician, a TVland, Southern gay first, no doubt.

While attempts by the right to attack corporations like Miller and Levi's that openly market to gays or provide equal benefits to their LGBT employees have failed,[53] the right wing has successfully latched onto the skewed statistics about lesbian and gay incomes and lifestyles in its battles to reverse civil rights gains. The first major success of this strategy was scored in 1993 with the creation of a slickly produced antigay video challenging the very notion that LGBT people are oppressed, *Gay Rights/Special Rights: Inside the Gay Agenda*. Splicing together footage of the 1987 and 1993 marches on Washington, groups like the Christian Coalition and Traditional Values Coalition (TVC) took aim at the very idea that gays should receive civil rights protection as a "special minority class." Comparing the false data on gay and lesbian household incomes to the U.S. Census data on median African-American household incomes in 1990 ($12,166), they make a case for denying this "privileged" group "special rights." The video was sent free to all members of Congress, Black and white churches, and many community groups. Senator Trent Lott (R-MS), ever the bigot, drew the desired conclusion: "It makes a mockery of other legitimate civil rights that people have worked for for years…. To give this kind of recognition is going to undermine all kinds of laws that are already on the books and is going to hurt a lot of people that deserve these kinds of protections."[54]

Colorado for Family Values used the video and statistics to successfully push antigay ballot initiative Amendment 2, arguing, "not only are gays not economically disadvantaged, they're actually one of the most affluent groups in America!"[55] And just as LGBT activists have argued for years, these ideological attacks can have deadly consequences. A rash of gay murders in Texas that year led *Vanity Fair* to interview one convicted murderer, Donald Aldrich, to understand what was behind these killings. Aldrich explained his reasoning this way:

> About the best job I can get is working in a restaurant makin' minimum wage or just barely over it, and it's like, I get no breaks…. Yet here they are, they're doing something that God totally condemns in the Bible. But look at

everything they've got, they've got all this nice stuff. They've got all these good jobs, sit back at a desk, or sit back in an air-conditioned building, not having to sweat, not having to bust their ass, and they've got money…. So, yeah, I resented that.[56]

Part of the LGBT marketing craze that took off in the 1990s alluded to the presumption that gays' marginalization from mainstream society could be alleviated through becoming a desirable market. Like abandoned waifs awaiting corporate rescue, gays and lesbians are portrayed as socially vulnerable and therefore not only a marketer's dream but also desperate for means of taking the sting out of repressive laws and inferior social status. *American Demographics* wrote, "because these consumers are disenfranchised from mainstream society, they are open to overtures from marketers."[57] In the absence of any organized means to achieve genuine political and social power, LGBT folks are offered capitalist society's substitute, niche consumer "power," that is, the option to spend one's money on products whose advertisers pander to some notion of gay middle-class desire. As one analyst explains, "The gay business class…uses an open rhetoric of liberation and self-expression through commercial strength and consumer power. It offers a version of gay freedom which is based on the visibility and power of gay markets."[58]

This is hardly unique in the world of capitalist marketing techniques. Like "You've come a long way, baby," the ingenious 1968 tagline for Virginia Slims' cigarette ads, which introduced a new generation of young women to smoking (and lung cancer), the tactic is effective at winning market share. It is also an expression of how gay and straight business owners were able to manipulate the politics of identity that implicitly accepts a cross-class alliance of LGBT people into a conception of group success. Gay businesspeople and gay-identity marketers work to convince working-class LGBT people that their own advancement is tied to purchasing certain consumer goods, travelling to certain gay destinations, and shopping at targeted gay locales. This rainbow-festooned market not only papers over real class divisions among LGBT people, but, as with consumer society generally, also equates success and achievement with ownership, fashion, and, in this case, the attainment of gay cultural bling.

The proliferation of a gay male physical aesthetic over the last two decades is an extension of this as well. With the health of gay men in particular under scrutiny and their masculinity as always challenged, increasing numbers of American gay men seek to defy stereotypes and sickness by cultivating a male aesthetic of chiseled abs and muscular bodies that is supposed to be the aspiration of every man, regardless of sexuality. Leaf through any gay men's magazine—or just glance at its cover—and this becomes patently obvious. One painful irony of the modern era is how the obsessive objectification of women's bodies that has endured for ages has now become a cross-gender phenomenon. The marketing of gym bodies (and unnaturally hairless ones at that) has brought gay and straight men down to the same appearance-obsessed level as women. Whether this is social retrogression for men or perverse progress for women as we meet each other in the appearance-anxiety middle, it is surely to the benefit of gym owners and marketers of diet aids across the nation. This dynamic encapsulates the transformation from the struggle for liberation into "the business of liberation."[59]

The rise of the "homocons"

Perhaps the nation's most famous gay conservative of the twentieth century was McCarthy-era attorney Roy Cohn, a politically repugnant and closeted self-hating Jewish gay man. His treachery in pursuing Ethel and Julius Rosenberg to the electric chair in the early 1950s through his battle to conceal the AIDS virus that killed him in 1986 was captured in brilliant cinematic style in Tony Kushner's *Angels in America*. Today's gay conservatives, or "homocons," are out of the closet, are published in major newspapers, and appear on TV chat shows as representatives of the LGBT community. As with the legions of highly paid female executives with expensively coiffed hair and power suits, the ranks of the upper class are now peppered with gay men and lesbians who wield considerable clout as a result of struggles waged by LGBT people whom most homocons of today shun. In a bizarre expression of the law of unintended consequences, these homocons too are products of struggles past, though few would admit this historic irony.

The most prominent right-wing gay organization is the Log Cabin Republicans, whose Web site proudly explains, "We believe in limited government, strong national defense, free markets, low taxes, personal responsibility, and individual liberty."[60] In other words, they are unabashed pro-imperial free-marketeers who happen to be attracted to folks of the same sex. What is most notable about this troupe, aside from perhaps a generous dose of self-loathing, is how they have plugged away inside the Republican Party for thirty years yet still cannot garner respect from the leadership and most members of a party they continue to campaign for and endorse. Although presidential candidates refuse to meet with them, party conferences ban them from the premises, and Bob Dole once famously returned their financial contribution, the Log Cabinites refuse to take "no" for an answer. If nothing else, they are persistent.

Exit polls in 2000 and 2004 showed that 25 percent of gay voters went for George W. Bush.[61] Whatever one thinks of the reliability of such polls it is worth noting that there has been a considerable easing of "culture war" rhetoric from the Republican right since its heyday in the early nineties, when gays were aggressively attacked in speeches by Pat Buchanan and other paleoconservatives at their 1992 convention. Today, Buchanan himself sits beside the first openly lesbian and self-described "butch dyke" news anchorwoman, Rachel Maddow, debating global events on prime-time television.[62] The evangelical Christian running mate of John McCain, Governor Sarah Palin, who was chosen to shore up the far right Republican base in 2008, felt compelled to call for "tolerance" for gays and lesbians in her vice presidential debate. Setting aside the fact that most people would prefer to think of toothaches, not people, as things to be tolerated, this too represents a sort of milestone. This transformation is due primarily to two factors. One, there are today a greater number of wealthy gays who are out and among the ranks of the powerful than ever before. Republicans may not care for what gays do in bed, but business is business. And two, public opinion has shifted considerably as LGBT people come out, making zealots' attacks unseemly, even at gatherings of reactionaries, some of whom, like Dick Cheney and Newt Gingrich, have lesbian and gay family members.[63]

This is *not* to say that homophobia is about to disappear anytime soon. So long as the dominant political class has a need to both shore up the nuclear family and forge divisions among ordinary people, homophobic ideas along with reactionary gender norms will persist. And in times of economic downturn, when social tensions run highest, the class in power has an even greater stake in pushing their repressive sexual and gender order. Nothing terrifies the rich and powerful quite as much as solidarity among ordinary people across racial, gender, and sexual orientation lines to focus their ire at the top. What stands out about the current crop of lesbian, gay, and bisexual conservatives (transgender people do not yet appear represented among them)—aside from the overwhelming dominance of men in their ranks—is how many project themselves as social rebels of a sort, some even hailing from activist backgrounds.

Referred to as "Rush Limbaugh with monster pecs,"[64] Andrew Sullivan is the most prominent U.S.-based homocon of the last twenty years. Once the editor of the *New Republic*, Sullivan's writings have frequently appeared in the *New York Times* and *Time* magazine, and his blog, The Daily Dish, is a widely read online commentary. His regular appearance on prime-time news shows and the publication of several books have helped promote him as an official voice of American gaydom. The *Village Voice*'s Richard Goldstein characterizes Sullivan's ubiquitous appearance in the liberal media this way: "Imagine Ward Connerly, the black opponent of affirmative action—or a scathing antifeminist like Katie Roiphe—getting a column on race or women's issues in the [*New York*] *Times*. Yet when it comes to gays, the more 'politically incorrect' you are—and the more cutting toward queer culture—the farther you get in the liberal media."[65]

Like Bruce Bawer and others of the genre, Sullivan derides the left-wing association of the historical LGBT movement, slams queeny men and butch women for giving gays bad press, promotes sexual prudery against the "libidinal pathology"[66] of gay promiscuity, and argues for gay marriage as the final frontier for gays, a right that would render any further movement moot in his mind. His libertarian conservative leanings, witty and passionate defense of same-sex marriage, and current opposition to the Iraq War often place him in the company of progressive LGBT people, despite his generally reactionary politics. Sullivan's biological determinism, however, exposes the conservative logic at the heart of his worldview. Differences between the sexes are "based on deep biological realities that are reflected across all cultures and all times,"[67] he explains. This essentialist notion that our sexuality and gender behavior are natural and inborn lies at the heart of the homocon project of "policing the sexual order."[68]

Homocon sexual moralism is most dangerous when applied to the HIV/AIDS epidemic. Gabriel Rotello's *Sexual Ecology: AIDS and the Destiny of Gay Men* has played a role in arming the law-and-order bigots who police gay sex in the name of health care. Rotello is not just any conservative commentator—as he puts it himself, he "not only followed the party line" of gay AIDS activism, he "helped write it."[69] Rotello was an active member of AIDS Coalition to Unleash Power (ACT UP) and was a founding editor of *Outweek* magazine. Like gay writers Larry Kramer, founding member of Gay Men's Health Crisis, and Michelangelo Signorile, best known for outing billionaire Malcolm Forbes, Rotello blames gay male promiscuity for the devastation of AIDS among gay men. He writes that the virus that causes AIDS, HIV (human immunodeficiency virus) "did not have the means to become an epidemic in most of the world until the vast liberalization of human behavior combined with the vast increase in technology in the mid to late twentieth century."[70] He thus argues "the gay sexual revolution of the seventies was profoundly anti-ecological."[71]

Not only are these conclusions politically reactionary, they are scientifically false. Over 90 percent of the world's nearly thirty-three million people who have AIDS or the virus that causes it live in the developing world, and only 5 to 10 percent of them are men who have sex with other men, according to United Nations AIDS statistics.[72] In other words, AIDS is largely a disease of poverty, uneven economic development, and worldwide government neglect. Its spread has coincided with huge rises in the occurence of tuberculosis, another disease of poverty, and rampant industrial development without regard to environmental or human needs.

In the United States, where nearly six hundred thousand people have died of AIDS since its detection in 1981,[73] AIDS is not the tragic outcome of sexual promiscuity among gays—assuming one could even define the number of partners that would qualify someone as promiscuous. Today, Blacks and Latinos make up 64 percent of those with AIDS in the United States, and a decreasing number of those cases each year since the 1990s are men who have sex with other men (regardless of how they classify their sexual orientation). [74] AIDS has spread to such alarming numbers of people in the United States because the government and pharmaceutical CEOs are antigay, racist, and greedy. By naming the newly diagnosed virus Gay Related Infectious Disease (GRID) in 1981, the Reagan administration and Democratic-led Congress could easily rationalize doing nothing about a disease that was killing off what they viewed, along with intravenous drug users, as a disposable population. Their refusal until 1986 to spend millions to screen the nation's blood supply condemned fifteen thousand hemophiliacs and thousands more transfusion recipients to painful, unnecessary deaths. Rotello's meager nod to corporate greed in his writings doesn't even hint at the fact that no other disease in history has made pharmaceutical company shareholders salivate so much. AZT, the first failed miracle drug, cost more than $8,000 per year and shot Burroughs Wellcome's profits sky high. One crucial component of today's "drug cocktail" treatments, Norvir, quintupled its price to $7,800 in 2004, which brought a flurry of lawsuits. AIDS drugs still provide some of the most lucrative profits in pharmaceutical history.[75]

Rotello's attack on gay men for being promiscuous, and therefore "unnatural," is typical right-wing, blame-the-victim politics. His dismissal of the "condom code" as a "mere technological fix," is perhaps his most specious and anti-intellectual argument. The condom code, better known as safer sex, is the prescription of doctors and AIDS activists that states that latex condoms must be used for anal, vaginal, or even oral sex whenever bodily fluids are being exchanged. Rotello argues that the 8 to 10 percent failure rate of condoms leaves an unacceptably high risk for contracting a deadly disease. True. But the problem is not the condom code; it is poorly manufactured condoms and little to no education on exactly how to use them in this era of abstinence-only education in most public schools.

Why, for instance, in a system that has managed to create the notion that men and women sweat differently and require different deodorants, are there no anal sex condoms? Anal sex, the way most gay men contract AIDS, requires a stronger and more durable condom, which companies have refused to manufacture and explicitly market because they might be perceived as "promoting" gay sex. Though Rotello attempts to retain his progressive credentials by cautioning readers against homophobia, the implications of his writing are startlingly clear. He diverts blame away from the politicians and corporations and focuses attention on the sexual multipartnerism of many gay men. His book, packaged as an argument about the causes of the AIDS crisis, actually contributes to its continuation.

Not all homocons are rich, of course, but the worldview they promote certainly works to reinforce reactionary and repressive sexual laws and ideology that most benefit those in power. They also remind us that the notion that all those who share a common oppression must have a common interest in fighting side by side is flawed.[76] In fact, one's perspective and interests appear quite different from behind the wheel of a Mercedes than from the driver's seat of a Chevy. Most LGBT people, as the statistics above show, are working class and have no stake in uniting with and perpetuating the backward myths promoted by the elite—regardless of the sexual preference of the person palming off personal biases as "the gay perspective."

In Defense of Materialism: Postmodernism, ID Politics, and Queer Theory in Perspective

For Marxists, theory is a guide to action, not an end in itself. "The philosophers have only *interpreted* the world in various ways; the point, however, is to *change* it,"[1] as Marx and Engels famously put it. Their aim was not to denigrate theory or philosophers but to challenge them to take on real-life struggles to end the exploitative and oppressive state of affairs that all working-class people face under capitalism.

This is not, unfortunately, the thinking that has dominated the political and theoretical discussions around LGBT liberation over the past few decades in the United States. LGBT politics have been centered inside the academy since the decline of social struggles in the Western industrialized nations in the 1970s. Some of the participants of the late 1960s movements who went on to academic careers perceived the failures of those struggles and of pseudo-socialist states to achieve liberation as indicators that Marxist politics and the strategy of collective struggle were, at best, anachronisms or, at worst, fatally flawed. In an era of rampant consumerism and neoliberalism that marked the 1980s and beyond, many of these academics sought alternative theories to Marxism for understanding the world, including LGBT oppression. They discovered postmodernism.

Despite the radical intentions and proclivities of many exponents and adherents of postmodernism and its political offshoots—identity politics and queer theory—these ideas do not arm people with a worldview that can overthrow the oppression that LGBT people face. In fact, they are a retreat from not just class politics, but from a materialist analysis of how the world works and how to change it. While postmodern ideas appear to be on the wane in this newly developing political era, they have dominated LGBT scholarly and movement thinking for a long time and will not simply disappear without activists and theoreticians rising to the challenge of replacing them. What follows is a brief exposition of postmodernism, identity politics, and queer theory and a polemic against them, because our understanding of these often abstract concepts has an impact on the strategies activists develop to challenge the status quo. After all, "Without revolutionary theory there can be no revolutionary movement," as V. I. Lenin argued in *What Is to Be Done?*[2]

Postmodernism and the politics of identity

Marxist literary critic Terry Eagleton defines postmodernism as:

> [T]he contemporary movement of thought which rejects totalities, universal values, grand historical narratives, solid foundations to human existence and the possibility of objective knowledge. Postmodernism is skeptical of truth, unity and progress, opposes what it sees as elitism in culture, tends toward cultural relativism, and celebrates pluralism, discontinuity and heterogeneity.[3]

This sophisticated-sounding set of ideas—often written in highly complex, unintelligible prose—masks a profoundly anti-materialist and pessimistic outlook on the possibility for change. Whereas modernism was an intellectual trend marked by adherence to rational thought and scientific inquiry, *post*-modernism is a philosophical critique of objective knowledge. Postmodernists argue that objective knowledge is an illusion because what we call "truth" or "knowledge" is only particular to our culture and the language or "discourse" that comes down to us from those in positions of power. Whether it is critiquing political systems, literature, or fine arts, postmodernism places all theoretical assumptions into question and regards all assertions as contingent and culturally relative.

Many progressives and radicals, including some socialists, came to embrace postmodernism and poststructuralism[4]—a variant of postmodernism—in the 1970s after the apparent failures of Stalinist and Maoist parties and states to deliver the social transformations they claimed to herald. Several of the originators, Jean Baudrillard, Jacques Derrida, and Michel Foucault among them, were French intellectuals born in the early twentieth century who were profoundly influenced by both the horrors of fascism and the treachery of the massively influential French Communist Party (CP).

One event that shaped their thinking about the world was the betrayal by the French CP in the midst of the largest general strike ever, in 1968, when ten milllion workers linked with mass student struggles to raise radical demands. What began as a student revolt against the Vietnam War at Nanterre, a university in the western suburbs of Paris, became a mass economic and social upheaval that expressed the French working class's discontent with police repression and the mirage of postwar consumer gratification for some in the face of poverty for many.[5] A mix of antiauthoritarian outrage and socialist visions for total economic and social transformation were expressed through ubiquitous graffiti and banners with slogans such as "Be Realistic, Ask for the Impossible,"[6] and "The Boss Needs You, You Don't Need Him."[7] Yet the top-down, Moscow-led French CP betrayed the aspirations of millions of workers and students when it cut a deal with Charles de Gaulle's regime, thus short-circuiting the massive economic and social rebellion, channelling broader demands into bread-and-butter reforms and ending the weeks-long strikes and factory occupations that threatened General de Gaulle's government. As socialist historian Daniel Singer summarized: "The Communist leadership opted for the safety of 'parliamentary battles between frogs and mice.' It chose the road of electoral defeat."[8]

While early postmodernists engaged with Marxist principles to seek a way out of the crisis, initially without a wholesale rejection of class struggle, jettisoning class politics was precisely the final outcome as followers of Foucault and others abandoned any belief in the possibility for a new social order. Foucault himself, once a member of the French CP, remained a lifelong opponent of both Western bourgeois ideology and the Moscow-dominated communist parties that he identified with Marxism. As a gay man who died in 1984 of AIDS, Foucault has a nearly iconic status among many LGBT intellectuals for his theoretical contributions to an understanding of sexuality. Marxists agree with his constructionist viewpoint of sexual identities, as discussed in the first chapter. However, his conflation of Stalinism with socialism as well as his theoretical excursions away from the material and social roots of power and oppression, discussed below, render his legacy a contradictory one for the left. "Foucault professed no ability to explain historical causation," writes William B. Turner. "All of Foucault's major works contain numerous causal statements. They do not, however, contain attempts to explain causally the major shifts from one period or episteme to another,"[9] Turner explains. Hence, without a materialist understanding of where sexual oppression came from, Foucault could offer few ideas for combating it. According to the author of *Saint Foucault*, "Foucault evaded occasional efforts by left-wing gay intellectuals to credit his writings with contributing to the gay liberation movement: 'My work has had nothing to do with gay liberation,' he reportedly told one admirer in 1975."[10]

Postmodernists' rejection of class struggle as a means for liberating the oppressed lies not just in their disillusionment with the 1960s, but also in their assessment of the shifts taking place in world capitalism. Advances in the globalization of mass production and rise of the information age led some to argue that the United States and Western Europe had become "postindustrial" societies. As the British journal *Marxism Today* argued:

> Our world is being remade. Mass production, the mass consumer, the big city, big-brother state, the sprawling housing estate, and the nation-state are in decline; flexibility, diversity, differentiation, mobility, communication, decentralization and internationalism are in the ascendant. In the process our own identities, our sense of self, our own subjectivities are being transformed. We are in transition to a new era.[11]

While capitalism has undoubtedly undergone massive changes in the modern era, including shifts in how and where production takes place, the production of goods has never ceased to be a central feature of capitalism, even in the West. During the very period when postmodern ideas triumphed, the eighties and nineties, the size of the U.S. manufacturing workforce alone actually increased by five million, despite American industrial workers' decrease relative to the overall workforce.[12] What's more, these postindustrial thinkers imply that the vastly expanding service sector inside Western economies is made up of workers whose power is somehow diminished by the non-industrial character of their labor. In fact, the teachers, nurses, baristas, data processors, fast-food servers, and cashiers are indeed exploited workers in the classic Marxist sense of the term—they sell their labor power to capitalists who profit from the difference between the value of the service or product and the wage paid to the employee. Despite structural changes in the workforce, blue- and white-collar workers from industry to services still possess the central power Marx and Engels attributed to them in *The Communist Manifesto*. Simply put, as the class that produces wealth in capitalist society, workers hold the potential for transforming it.

The middle-class origins of many of the ex-radicals who developed and promoted postmodern ideas shaped their outlook. Raised during the biggest economic boom in capitalism's history, in particular in the United States, where higher education was more accessible than ever and the level of class struggle was low, these thinkers often saw workers as backward. The fact that the Vietnam War, which radicalized the sixties generation, was supported for many years by most white workers only stoked the notion that workers were "bought off."[13] As radical philosopher Herbert Marcuse once put it, "Why should the overthrow of the existing order be of vital necessity for people who own, or can hope to own, good clothes, a well-stocked larder, a TV set, a car, a house and so on, all within the existing order?"[14] However, the declining living standards of the U.S. working class over the last thirty years reveals the limitations of taking a snapshot of the conditions and consciousness of some workers at one point in history. A decades-long employers' offensive that has left tens of millions without health care and in precarious jobs or unemployed exposes how workers, even in the wealthiest nation, remain an exploited and oppressed class.

Having theorized out of existence the human force Marxists place at the center of struggles—i.e., workers—postmodernists sought alternative agents for changing the world, and some questioned whether fundamental change is even possible or desirable. Two leading postmodernists, Ernesto Laclau and Chantal Mouffe, in their work *Hegemony and Socialist Strategy*, proposed that "new social movements" could replace the "disappearing" working class.[15] Each oppressed group, according to this notion, could form its own separate or "autonomous" movement, which came to be known in the 1980s as identity politics, also known as ID politics. Identity politics activists and scholars raise autonomy, that is, separation from others as opposed to unity, as their key organizing principle. "The politics of identity must also be a politics of difference,"[16] argues proponent Jeffrey Escoffier. In lieu of the working class, advocates of ID politics argue that women, Blacks, LGBT people, and other oppressed minorities are uniquely capable of both defining and fighting against their own oppression. Lesbian scholar Dana Cloud explains, "The key to identity politics is the idea that one can somehow explain oppression simply by referring to one's own *experience* of it. In identity politics, there is no attempt to *ex-*

plain the origins of and strategies against racism and sexism, as these phenomena are theorized as psychological, experiential events rather than as ideological systems with a basis in material reality."[17]

It should go without saying that those who experience racism, sexism, and/or homophobia have an interest in ending it—and should and usually do play key roles in organizing any movement against it. But identity politics goes much further. It exalts the "personal is political" framework that contends that one's lifestyle, personal relationships, and consumer choices are central forms of political resistance, often leading to moralistic and individualistic notions of challenging the system. "The identity politics of minority groups is an attempt to gain access to power outside the public arena (i.e., in private, in *culture*),"[18] explains AIDS historian Cindy Patton. It does so "not only by articulating the 'authentic' subjective experience of oppression—by 'speaking out,' 'coming out,' 'telling it like it is'—but also by using the community constructed on that identity as a base of block power."[19] The aim, according to Patton and her co-thinkers, is not human liberation or even an end to oppression, but the creation of cultural spaces where oppressed groups can express themselves freely.

Identity politics activists and scholars' adherence to identity-based power blocs is tantamount to a rejection of the notion that class is a fundamental divide in society, thus they sever the link between exploitation and oppression. Escoffier is blunt about how his pessimism for working-class opposition led him to embrace identity as the alternative: "We are now in a period of decline and discouragement.... The recent history of the American working class clearly shows that it lacks the organizational and political capacity to struggle effectively for the fundamental transformation of society."[20] To the degree that class is acknowledged in this schema at all, it is "classism" or snobbery that is condemned, rather than the actual division of society into classes. When academics uprooted the cause of LGBT oppression from class society—if they sought the source of oppression at all—it was found in the realm of ideas, not the material world. The problem, for these academics, is reactionary ideas held by straight people, popularized by a straight-run media, and enforced by a state dominated by straight people. Patton, like many others, argues that homophobia is the result of a "bad attitude" or "state of mind" of some individuals, not the result of any structural inequality produced by capitalism.[21] This commonsense notion is given credence through LGBT peoples' real lived experience with homophobia from personal interactions with some straight people who have been theorized as being part of the problem and in some way even as being beneficiaries of the oppression of others.

The theory of sexual oppression as ideologically based, drawn from such writers as Foucault, shares many of the same conclusions as patriarchy theory. Patriarchy theory came to be nearly hegemonic in the feminist movement and radical exponents of it, such as Heidi Hartmann, argue that male domination is not a product of class society, but is a universal feature of human society. Sex, not class, is the key division in society, according to patriarchy theory, and all men benefit from the oppression of all women. Hartmann defines patriarchy as "a set of social relations between men, which have a material base, and which, though hierarchical, establish or create interdependence or solidarity among men that enable them to dominate women." In addition, "the material base upon which patriarchy rests lies most fundamentally in men's control over women's labor power…. Control is maintained by denying women access to necessary economically productive resources and by restricting women's sexuality."[22] The main problem with this theory is that it defies historical proof that male dominance is not a universal feature of all human societies, but arose alongside class divisions, as anthropological evidence in *Myths of Male Dominance* by Leacock shows.[23] Another problem is that patriarchy theory attempts to lump all men, including poor and working-class men, into the same category, concluding essentially that homeless men oppress the likes of Hillary Clinton, for example. Despite Hartmann's nod to a material base, as a theory it replaces the materialist analysis of women's oppression rooted in the nuclear family with the notion that ideology is the basis of oppression and exploitation.

Patriarchy theory found a parallel in ID politics' conceptions of gay liberation in the idea that straight people benefit from the oppression of gays. This idea that straight people are the problem is aggressively argued in the "I Hate Straights" manifesto, first distributed by anonymous members of Queer Nation at New York's Gay Pride celebration in June 1990. It reads in part:

> Straight people have a privilege that allows them to do whatever they please and fuck without fear…. I want there to be a moratorium on straight marriage, on babies, on public displays of affection among the opposite sex and media images that promote heterosexuality. Until I can enjoy the same freedom of movement and sexuality, as straights, [*sic*] their privilege must stop and it must be given over to me and my queer sisters and brothers. Straight people will not do this voluntarily and so they must be forced into it. Straights must be frightened into it. Terrorized into it….
>
> It is easier to fight when you know who your enemy is. Straight people are your enemy.[24]

This hostile sectarianism against the majority of the population could hardly be a model for collective struggle in a society in which LGBT people are likely to be a minority. Its rejection of straight people, posing as rebellion against the status quo, reads like a primal scream, not the political strategy of an organization aiming to challenge homophobia. One veteran Black lesbian activist of the 1970s movements, Barbara Smith, responded to this manifesto in a letter to *Outweek* "suggesting that if queers of color followed its political lead, we would soon be issuing a statement titled, 'I Hate Whitey,' including white queers of European origin."[25] For Marxists, consciousness under capitalism is mixed, sometimes contradictory, and capable of being shifted by experience, argument, and struggle. The positive change in attitudes toward LGBT people in the media and reflected in opinions polls since the 1980s shows that hostility to people due to their sexual orientation—or race and gender, for that matter—is not static.[26]

What's more, as D'Emilio infers, "movements based on identity probably act as a barrier to solving class-based injustices because they place a premium on group loyalty across class lines."[27] As in any cross-class alliance, those with the most confidence, time, and connections—usually those who are middle or upper class—drive the agenda and outlook of new social movements to suit their own aspirations and not those of the working class and poor. "In every case, the primary beneficiaries have been members of the middle class, those with access to education and training and privilege that have allowed them to take the most advantage of equal rights and equality of opportunity," D'Emilio explains.[28] His critique here is not of individual middle-class activists or academics, but an accurate assessment of the middle class as a social force. The proliferation of queer and gender studies departments at major universities and LGBT-focused media and other cultural outlets are some of the outcomes from these identity politics movements, and they are welcome advances. However, they do not actually meet the material needs of most sexual minorities nor do they confront the fundamental problems facing most LGBT people who are working class.

Discourse—fighting phrases with phrases

One of the basic precepts of postmodernism, from which identity politics and queer theory draw inspiration, is that there are no objective truths, at least none that we can know for certain. Truth or reality for postmodernists is a question of perception, since we cannot really know reality because it is mediated through language. This is a remarkably oxymoronic concept, for if ever there were a claim to truth posing as an anti-truth, it is that there is no objective truth at all—or if it exists, we cannot really know it.

Postmodernists challenge the validity of any and all universalizing worldviews, which they often refer to as "metanarratives." As Jean François Lyotard explains, "I define postmodern as incredulity toward metanarratives,"[29] that is, skepticism toward "the existence of any general pattern on which to base our conception of a true theory or a just society."[30] With Marxism perceived as "the god that failed," not only did academics reject existing models of "socialism," but they rendered moot class interests, class struggle, and, along with the working class, all material agents of change. Some of these postmodern thinkers, such as Ernesto Laclau and Chantal Mouffe, refer to themselves as "post-Marxist," which while true chronologically, would be best described as *anti*-Marxist. Ellen Meiksins Wood explains in her appropriately titled *Retreat from Class*, that Laclau and Mouffe:

> set out to undermine the very foundations of the Marxist view that the working class will be the agent of socialist transformation, and to replace it with a political project whose object is "radical democracy" and whose subject is a popular alliance constituted not by relations of class, nor indeed by any determinate social relations, but rather by discourse.[31]

Why "discourse"? After the defeat of the French general strike in 1968, some went casting about for alternative theories to explain their disappointments. Foucault posed discourse as the means through which human interaction is regulated and thought is derived. For Foucault and others discourse was "a group of statements which provide a language for talking about...a particular topic at a particular historical moment." "Nothing," he argued, "has any meaning outside of discourse."[32] Foucault wasn't denying material reality so much as positing the notion that objects only have meaning through discourse, which governs the way reality can, and cannot, be discussed. "Through the various discourses," he wrote, "legal sanctions against minor perversions were multiplied; sexual irregularity was annexed to mental illness; from childhood to old age, a norm of sexual development was defined and all the deviations were carefully described."[33] Rather than being part of society, Foucault believed language constructs society, thus giving "language reality-creating powers quite as formidable as those to be found in claims that language is society-free.... For him, discourse itself constituted and reproduced power relations in society."[34]

This form of linguistic idealism in which language shapes reality rather than being a means of social intercourse that both reflects and is a product of reality was further refined by the philosopher Jacques Derrida. He wrote, "There is no out-side-text,"[35] meaning that we cannot really know objects out-side of what can be spoken of or written about, not that there is no reality exactly. This is an awful lot of power with which to imbue concepts and words; in fact, it amounts to flipping reality on its head. Postmodernism's worldview—all protestations against metanarratives aside—is that our consciousness ex-pressed through discourse determines our material world. However, our language describes the outside world more or less accurately, and our ideas and the language we use to ex-press them are shaped by and in turn help shape that outside world—the process is dynamic. As Marx and Engels wrote:

> In direct contrast to German philosophy which descends from heaven to earth, here we ascend from earth to heaven. That is to say, we do not set out from what men say, imagine, conceive, nor from men as narrated, thought of, imagined, conceived, in order to arrive at men in the flesh. We set out from real, active men, and on the basis of their real life-process we demonstrate the development of the ideological reflexes and echoes of this life-process.... Morality, religion, metaphysics, all the rest of ideology and their corresponding forms of consciousness, thus no longer retain the semblance of independence. They have no history, no development; but men, developing their material production and their material intercourse, alter, along with this their real existence, their thinking and the products of their thinking. Life is not deter-mined by consciousness, but consciousness by life.[36]

Postmodern logic has led some to draw reactionary con-clusions. Images, for Baudrillard and his co-thinkers, don't represent the world; instead "we have a world *of* images, of hallucinatory evocations of a nonexistent real."[37] This postmodern dystopia leads to a sense of fatalism and passivity in the face of a world in which we cannot assume reality beneath the surface appearance of things. If truth is simply perception, even the oppression of LGBT people must be called into question as merely the bugaboo of a sexual minority and not a systematic, institutional, and cultural force that can crush peoples' lives. Eagleton perceptively locates the class character of this theoretical posturing in the academy: "Those who are privileged enough not to need to know, for whom there is nothing politically at stake in reasonably accurate cognition, have little to lose by proclaiming the virtues of undecidability."[38]

For Marxists, commonsense ideas are shaped in part by the "ruling ideas" in society. As Marx and Engels put it, "The ideas of the ruling class are in every epoch the ruling ideas, i.e., the class which is the ruling material force of society, is at the same time its ruling intellectual force."[39] For example, the late nineteenth-century shift from certain sex practices evolving into the concept of fixed sexualities grew out of the material needs of industrial capitalism. The capitalists' need for workers and attaining their reproduction and upkeep on the cheap developed into the ruling class's ideological defense of the nuclear family, and with it "natural" gender roles and sexual dos and don'ts. Changes in the material world shape the ideological needs of the class in power to alter and confine our sexual lives.

Among the most disorienting concepts of postmodernism is the understanding of what power is and how to challenge it. Marxists locate structural relations of power between the vast class of workers who sell their labor power and the small class of employers who exploit them and in whose interests the state and its police, courts, military, etc., serve. In contrast, post-modernists locate power all around them. Foucault explained, "Power is everywhere; not because it embraces everything, but because it comes from everywhere...power is not an insti-tution, not a structure."[40] He went on to argue, "The individual which power has constituted is at the same time its vehicle."[41] Despite providing elaborate examples of how the penal system and medical establishment are used as tools of social control, there is no accounting for how and why these systems came to be and in whose service they function. For Foucault

> power is not a substance, but a relation. Power is therefore not *possessed*, but *exercised*. That means that power should not be conceptualized as the property of someone who can be identified and confronted, nor should it be thought of (at least in the first instance) as embedded in particular agents or institutions. Power is not a possession of the Monarch or the Father or the State, and people cannot be divided into those who "have" it and those who don't. Instead, power is what characterizes the complex relations among the parts of a society—and the interactions among individuals in that society—as relations of ongoing power.... Power, then, is not to be understood according to the model of a unidirec-tional vector from oppressor to oppressed. Rather, it's a fluid, all-encompassing medium, immanent in every sort of social relation....[42]

Disengaged from its class basis, power becomes a rootless, ubiquitous, and vague notion. If power is everywhere (and nowhere), then fundamental social change is an illusion. Using similar concepts, John Holloway's popular 2002 book rallied the global justice movement to *Change the World Without Taking*

Power by dissolving power and creating "anti-power" within ourselves. Revolution for the postmodernists has ceased to mean transforming the world; instead the world must be metaphysically tweaked. Or as is explained in *Saint Foucault*, "The aim of an oppositional politics is therefore not liberation but resistance."[43] The goal of resistance becomes survival, "finding the best way to cope...within existing social arrangements,"[44] not victory over oppressive powers.

With this notion, language itself becomes the site of struggle, not just one tool that people can use to challenge their oppression. The words "queer," "dyke," and "fag"—slurs that generations of effeminate men and masculine women have found scrawled on their high school lockers—become weapons to contest power. In 1990, a new LGBT group calling itself Queer Nation was founded to fight homophobia, often through small direct actions, called "zaps," aimed at shocking straight people, such as dressing in stereotypical butch or femme garb and staging kiss-ins at suburban malls. Queer Nation's founding members explained the group's name this way: "It's the idea of reappropriating the words of our oppressors and actually re-contextualizing the term 'queer' and using it in a positive way to empower ourselves.... Now we can really rally around the word, and that confuses our oppressors. It makes us feel stronger." The other activist added, "We have disempowered them by using this term."[45] As Sharon Smith argues, "This reflects the belief that using certain 'politically correct' language can affect the conditions facing the mass of gays and lesbians in society. It does not. Whether or not Queer Nation activists feel personally 'empowered' by using the term 'queer,' the vast majority of people will continue to regard it as a term of abuse."[46]

At the group's launch meeting in New York City, a dispute about the name revealed the mindset of many who championed "queer" as a celebration of marginalization and expressed a desire to wear the outcast status as a badge of honor. As one defender explained his use of queer, it means "We're not pathological, but don't think for that reason we want to be normal."[47] While the word queer has morphed in recent years into a broader term for gender and sexuality rebel, it reflected for many at that time a rejection of power and an embrace of social exile. Preeminent queer theorist Eve Sedgwick appears to actually hold up the unreformability of "queer" as a good thing: "If queer is a politically potent term, which it is, that's because, far from being detached from the childhood source of shame, it cleaves to that scene as a near inexhaustible source of transformational energy."[48] Queer Nation's birthmark then was one of militant defeatism—rhetorical militancy replaced collective struggle. The goal of these new postmodern social movements, as one advocate explains, was "less 'the end of domination' or 'human liberation' than the creation of social spaces that encourage the proliferation of pleasures, desires, voices, interests, modes of individuation and democratization."[49]

The postmodernists' fascination with discourse as determinant recalls an earlier generation of philosophers from whom Marx and Engels broke away, the Young Hegelians, who similarly believed that "human progress is held back primarily by illusions, mistaken ideas, and false consciousness."[50] In a critique that could be applied more than 150 years later, Marx and Engels argued:

> This demand to change consciousness amounts to a demand to interpret the existing world in a different way, i.e.,

IN DEFENSE OF MATERIALISM 185

to recognize it by means of a different interpretation. The Young-Hegelian ideologists, in spite of their allegedly "world-shattering" phrases, are the staunchest conservatives. The most recent of them have found the correct expression for their activity when they declare they are only fighting against "*phrases*." They forget, however, that they themselves are opposing nothing but phrases to these phrases, and that they are in no way combating the real existing world when they are combating solely the phrases of this world.[51]

Transgender activist and author Riki Wilchins captures this dilemma with a more contemporary twist: "if discourse is so all-powerful, then freedom is impossible. We can no more escape discursive power than we can our own subjectivity…. Discourse becomes like the Borg on *Star Trek*: 'Resistance is futile.'"[52]

Discourse as determinant stands in sharp contrast with the earlier movements for Black Power and women's and gay liberation, where terms like "colored," "Negro," "girl," and "queer" were rejected through mass fightbacks to claim monikers demanding power, which fit the combative era. It is telling that these earlier struggles looking to broaden and expand their influence never named themselves using racial or sexual epithets. But whereas Marx and Engels chastised the Young Hegelians for the inapplicability of their ideas to the outside world, a perfect storm of circumstances in the late twentieth century thrust into action many who looked to the concepts of these neo-idealists for guidance. The marriage of antimaterialism and activism was not always a happy one.

Identity politics in action

"Silence=Death" was not only a poignant rallying cry for the new AIDS movement; it was perfectly suited to the political age that spawned it. This slogan, in white print on black posters with an inverted pink triangle reminiscent of the Nazi-era badges for homosexuals, first appeared on the lampposts and walls of lower Manhattan in 1986.[53] Not until the final days of Ronald Reagan's second term in 1987 did the president even bother to utter the word "AIDS," a disease that had by that time killed more than 20,000 Americans and infected more than 50,000 people in 113 countries in the six years since it was diagnosed.[54] That year, three out of four AIDS cases in New York City were diagnosed in gay men, according to playwright Larry Kramer, who helped initiate both the service-oriented group Gay Men's Health Crisis (GMHC) and the direct-action group ACT UP.[55] Kramer's urgent demand for action first appeared in the New York *Native* in the 1983 piece, "1,112 and Counting," which began, "If this article doesn't scare the shit out of you we're in real trouble. If this article doesn't rouse you to anger, fury, rage, and action, gay men may have no future on this earth. Our continued existence depends on just how angry you can get."[56]

As much as the disease itself, it was the nasty political climate that fueled the escalation of the crisis that drove Kramer to sound the alarm. Reagan's communications director, Pat Buchanan, said that AIDS was "nature's revenge on gay men," while Christian right-wing bigot Jerry Falwell said, "AIDS is the wrath of God upon homosexuals."[57] Moral Majority, one of the most prominent right-wing groups of the era, did a mass mailing for funds that read, "Why should the taxpayers have to spend money to cure diseases that don't have to start in the first place?.... But let's let the homosexual community do its own research. Why should the American taxpayer have to bail out these perverted people?"[58] Anti-sodomy laws in Texas and Georgia in 1983 were justified on the basis that homosexuality "caused" disease.[59] And the *New Republic*'s Charles Krauthammer argued that year, "Just as society was ready to grant that homosexuality is not an illness, it is seized with the idea that homosexuality causes illness."[60] All of them, through indifference and/or invective, expressed the callous homophobia that dominated U.S. media in the 1980s.

Any critique here of the movements that arose to challenge this state of affairs takes solidarity with their aims as its starting point. Groups like ACT UP won some significant victories, including unprecedented early drug trials, escalation of experimental treatments, and widespread attention to, sympathy for, and acceptance of people with AIDS. Nevertheless, the political perspectives that guided many of these activists often led to bitter and unnecessary splits and also often rejected straight allies of every race while creating an inhospitable climate for committed activists on the organized left, including those who were LGBT and themselves had HIV/AIDS.

Groups such as ACT UP, which burst onto the scene in March 1987, and Queer Nation, which branched out from ACT UP in 1990 to take on homophobia, adhered to the concept of identity politics that regarded only those who share a common identity and directly experience a form of oppression as capable of fighting against that oppression. Many of ACT UP's founders who themselves were HIV-positive were successful advertising executives, filmmakers, TV producers, playwrights, and other professionals who had the financial means, education, and confidence to build a splashy network of activists across the country in the era before the Internet.[61] One thirty-five-year-old Manhattan business consultant who joined ACT UP after his lover died of AIDS explained his life before activism: "I was on kind of a typical yuppie materialistic trip."[62] Meetings began each week with the commemoration of a member, friend, or lover who had died that week, adding a sense of urgency and sobriety to the often chaotic proceedings where multiple actions were debated and planned. But the surface militancy driven by the lethality of the disease masked a political perspective that was extremely narrow and middle-class in its orientation. As one journalist with AIDS described it, "ACT UP was always part theater, part group therapy."[63]

In keeping with postmodernist suspicions of unity and collective struggle, zap actions—small, targeted events organized by affinity groups often made up of friendship cliques—won out over proposals for broader rallies and marches that could draw in allies and mobilize others. One of the leading members of ACT UP New York's Treatment and Data Committee describes how some zap actions, despite good intentions, could be counterproductive:

> Some ACT UP factions wanted to disengage from research meetings and didn't want to work with other community groups and activists. They interrupted conferences to protest two studies, ACTG 076 and ACTG 175. Rather than propose improvements to those trials, they wanted to "Stop 076!" and "Stop 175!" If they'd been successful, two of the most dramatic discoveries of the 1990s would never have occurred. Activists can impede research as well as improve it.[64]

One GMHC staffer suggests that some ACT UP actions were counterproductive because "The goal became more about personal expression and less about change."[65] For example, a small group of Washington, D.C., ACT UP members handcuffed themselves to AIDS lobbyists in 1992 due to a disagreement about the lobbyists meeting with the Centers for Disease Control (CDC). Lesbian attorney and activist Urvashi Vaid argues, "The decline of ACT UP and direct action began, in my view, the instant media coverage of actions displaced the political calculus of right and wrong."[66]

While government officials snidely created a hierarchy of patients and pitted "worthy" breast cancer victims against "unworthy" AIDS sufferers, in its early years ACT UP refused to take up the call for universal health care, despite growing numbers of Americans facing a lack of health care.[67] (At their twentieth-anniversary march in lower Manhattan in 2007, however, ACT UP announced its launch of a two-year campaign to fight alongside allies for single-payer universal health care.[68]) As Bob Nowlan rightly surmises, when the gay movement accepted the medical establishment's treatment of AIDS as a separate health issue that only affected certain marginal populations of society, it played into the hands of those in power who were all too content not to have to put resources into a disease that initially affected mostly gay men and intravenous drug users.[69] Strategies for the movement were determined on the basis of personal experience, as opposed to lessons from history or through collaboration with those not afflicted with AIDS. Activists with a broader political strategy, such as Marxists, were viewed with suspicion by AIDS writers like Cindy Patton and Simon Watney. For example, in *Policing Desire: Pornography, AIDS and the Media,* Watney denounces Marxists as "puritanical separatists" and rejects any unified theory of how to approach the AIDS crisis, opting instead for "pragmatic" strategies like lobbying and looking to Princess Diana, who occasionally interrupted her monarchal duties to hold AIDS babies or attend a benefit concert.[70]

In keeping with its ID politics framework, ACT UP always embraced the active participation of lesbians through the insistence that women who have sex with other women were as likely as men to contract HIV/AIDS and thus had a direct stake in the struggle.[71] Yet, while many prominent AIDS activists then and today are lesbians, studies do not bear out the claim that women who have sex exclusively with women are very likely to contract HIV/AIDS. Anyone who is sexually active *can* get AIDS, and there are risk factors for sex workers—many if not a majority of whom are women. But according to the CDC's latest figures on those who tested positive for HIV/AIDS, "Of the 534 (of 7,381) women who were reported to have had sex only with women, 91 percent also had another risk factor—typically, injection drug use."[72] The point here is not to peddle a falsehood about lesbian immunity to AIDS but rather to challenge the narrowness of a political outlook that starts with the assumption that people must be rattled into believing they are likely to get AIDS in order to become involved in a movement to fight for a cure and against institutional indifference.

The prevalence of postmodern concepts in Queer Nation and other LGBT movements of the late twentieth century corresponded not only with the educational and class background of many leading activists, but also with a common notion that in a postindustrial society the working class could not be looked to as an agent of change. And even if it could, the resurgence of hostility to LGBT people early in the American AIDS epidemic surely translated in the minds of many activists that working-class straight people were not allies. Health-care and pharmaceutical workers (and their unions) employed by the giant corporations that were often targeted in actions were not perceived as potential supporters to be won over to the struggle for research and development funding. This us/them mindset dictated the groups' actions. One of Queer Nation's frequent activities was to gather members and head out to suburban shopping malls, where the Queer Shopping Network would dress and act in ways meant to jolt people and stage kiss-ins in order to "shock" straight customers at the mall. The dominant chant at protests was "We're here, we're queer, get used to it!"—a defiant assertion of identity that can also repel all those who do not identify as queer.

Splits in local chapters were endemic in this divisive atmosphere. ACT UP chapters often divided into mini-groups over differences of focus or over whether to allow Republicans, cops, or socialists to join. In 1990, for example, the ACT UP San Francisco chapter split into two groups, one devoted to AIDS treatment.[73] Four years later, one of the San Francisco chapters broke away from the rest of the group when some members disagreed with the strategy of fighting for more and cheaper antiretroviral drugs, which they claimed were lethal. The breakaway group opted to run a marijuana dispensary instead.[74] Some engaged in "bigot busting," a campaign of spitting at Mormons for their antigay religious teachings.[75] According to the *Village Voice*, by 1992, internal arguments in the New York chapter about the effectiveness of direct action, which had been raging for a couple of years, led some to split off into the Treatment Action Group (TAG). TAG then accepted $1 million from the pharmaceutical giant Burroughs Wellcome, the profiteering drug company that had been the target of ACT UP's ire since its founding.[76]

Queer Nation began as a splinter from ACT UP to fight homophobia; some lesbians left gay males to form Lesbian Avengers; debates about whether to extend membership to bisexuals and transgender people led to their own splits; and Women's Health Action Mobilization (WHAM!) formed to take up abortion rights, and on and on. Women's Action Coalition (WAC), a women-only group calling for "patriarchal demolition," drew hundreds to weekly meetings in the early 1990s but its New York chapter soon imploded in a brittle battle over whether a butch lesbian could appropriately represent the group on CNN.[77] Similar shrinkage occurred in other groups as weekly meetings originally numbering in the hundreds dwindled to dozens and then handfuls of participants. Ironically, perhaps, most of these groups' members were enthusiastic supporters of Bill Clinton's 1992 campaign, even if some groups withheld formal endorsement. ACT UP did not officially endorse candidates, and millions watched when a New York chapter member, Bob Rafsky, aggressively confronted candidate Bill Clinton in April 1992. In a clip aired on *Nightline*, Rafsky argued, "We're not dying of AIDS as much as we are dying of eleven years of government neglect," to which Clinton famously replied, "I feel your pain."[78] However, as the ACT UP Capsule History Web site for 1992 displays, their ubiquitous poster for that year read, "Campaign 1992: Vote as if your life depended on it!"[79] The clear signal was that a vote for Bill Clinton (against George H. W. Bush) was a life-sustaining choice.

Despite the theoretical limitations of ID politics that informed movement leaders' strategies, many actions were enormously successful at drawing in allies who were not directly affected by individual struggles.

Some of the most successful and prominent actions defied separatist identity principles. Thousands of LGBT and straight people turned out to protest the anti–safe sex message of the Catholic Church at St. Patrick's Cathedral in December 1989. Similar numbers turned out to well-publicized actions starting in March 1987 and repeated each March for many years to protest pharmaceutical companies' and Wall Street's outrageous profiteering on AIDS drugs.[80] Mass actions to defend abortion clinics from right-wing bigots were frequently led by young lesbians in WHAM! and a campy and politically savvy offshoot of gay drag queens known as the Church Ladies for Choice, who would show up wearing old-lady dresses, wigs, and practical shoes, singing "This Womb Is My Womb" (to the tune of "This Land Is Your Land") and other send-ups of American classics.[81]

But most often the strategies were zap actions driven by an in-your-face irreverence for authority that ignored the real fulcrums of power and failed to embrace the Black, Brown, and white working-class people of all sexual orientations who would soon become the rising face of AIDS in America and around the world. Rather than building alliances with labor and Black and Latino community leaders, as well as challenging the Democrats who controlled Congress until 1994, zaps expressed defiance without offering a way forward in the struggle. Today, AIDS in the United States is increasingly infecting African Americans. The latest figures from the CDC on HIV/AIDS in the United States show that despite Blacks' making up less than 13 percent of the U.S. population, since 2005 they account for 49 percent of all those diagnosed with HIV/AIDS.[82] This is why future AIDS organizing must orient on all working-class people—LGBT, straight, Black, and of every race.

Queering identity

Where identity politics argues for the autonomy of separate oppressed groups and struggles, queer theory challenges identity categories altogether. Ostensibly, it is an open rejection of identity politics, though queer theorist David Halperin concedes that it is still a "brand of identity politics."[83] Queer theory makes the claim of being able to include people who aren't just gay, lesbian, bisexual, or transgender, but could embrace straight people who behave or think "queerly," while excluding some gays, especially those white gay males who aspire toward ideals like monogamy or marriage. As Lisa Duggan puts it, "We might begin to think about sexual difference not in terms of naturalized identities, but as a form of *dissent*, understood not simply as speech, but as a constellation of nonconforming practices, expressions and beliefs."[84] Queer theory is often invoked to provide a space for women and people of color who have been excluded from mainstream LGBT politics. It is seen as a challenge to both gender and sexual binaries, which are conceived as constructed and changing over time and geography.

In the 1990s, queer theory arose out of some left-wing academics' discontent with the assimilation of middle-class gays and lesbians into the mainstream of American society. Many of queer theory's leading theoreticians and activist followers are left-wingers who reject identity politics and the conservative direction in which many of its leaders took the LGBT movement, primarily into the halls of corporate and political power. Yet they do so on terms that do not challenge the basis of ID politics' conservatism—its cross-class character. One of queer theory's most prominent theorists, Judith Butler, is undeniably a leftist who adamantly opposes the Iraq war and is a self-described internationalist.[85] Yet queer theory puts forward a profoundly pessimistic, even paralyzing, worldview in which people are all just atomized beings for whom common group identity acts as a sort of social kryptonite or Achilles' heel that somehow weakens or lessens us each. Hence, following from identity politics, and taken to postmodernism's logical extreme, it is based on the middle-class idea that we are all oppressed primarily as individuals by other individuals and therefore any resistance to oppression must be individual. Queer theory contends, "resistance is through the refusal to identify with the other."[86] In effect, queer is a/n (non)identity that is supposedly unique to every individual. The *Genealogy of Queer Theory* explains, "The work of queer theorists...tends toward the following suspicion: If our rights depend on our common identity as humans, then we all have to look alike, act alike, be alike in order to have rights. Of course, this is not how the system is supposed to work, but the experiences of women and minorities in the United States indicate that it does, in fact, work this way."[87]

While identity politics tends to strengthen the divisions between oppressed groups, queer theory unwittingly lends itself to disavowing the validity of oppression entirely by denying the common points of identity between members of subjugated groups. For example, Halperin argues that "The most radical reversal of homophobic discourses consists not in asserting, with the Gay Liberation Front of 1968, that 'gay is good' (on the analogy 'black is beautiful') but in assuming and empowering a marginal positionality.... Those who knowingly occupy such a marginal location, who assume a de-essentialized identity that is purely positional in character, are properly speaking not gay, but *queer*."[88] Therefore, "queering" something, including queering identity politics, is tantamount to subverting it as the theory suggests. In other words, "Queer theory is oppositional."[89]

In defining queer theory one runs immediately into a theoretical conundrum. Its major thinkers caution against precision: Judith Butler writes, "normalizing the queer would be, after all, its sad finish," Lauren Berlant and Michael Warner insist, "because almost everything that can be called queer theory has been radically anticipatory, trying to bring a world into being, any attempt to summarize it now will be violently partial."[90] It is the theory that dare not define itself.

Judith Butler explains queer theory's aversion to identity this way:

> [T]he prospect of *being* anything, even for pay, has always produced in me a certain anxiety, for "to be" gay, "to be" lesbian seems to be more than a simple injunction to become who or what I already am.

She is, therefore,

> not at ease with lesbian theories, gay theories, for as I've argued elsewhere, identity categories tend to be instruments of regulatory regimes, whether as normalizing categories of oppressive structures or as the rallying points for a liberatory contestation of that very oppression.[91]

What does it mean to argue that "identity categories tend to be instruments of regulatory regimes?" Simply because sexual identity is constructed by capitalism does not mean that the category of lesbianism, for example, is a tool of oppression or inequality any more than is classifying people who live in a certain region of South America as Venezuelans (an identity that is also a historical creation). Defining or labeling someone doesn't create the oppression; likewise, changing what we call someone, such as queer, does not challenge the oppression in the least. Again, Marx's and Engels' words to the Young Hegelians seem apropos: "On the basis of the philosophical belief in the power of concepts to make or destroy the world, they can likewise imagine that some individual 'abolished the cleavage of life' by 'abolishing' concepts in some way or other."[92] Even Wilchins, a founder of both Hermaphrodites with Attitude and Transsexual Menace—perhaps the quintessence of non-normalized categories—argues, "social groups cannot exist without shared norms of structure and meaning.... Thus, [postmodernism] is unable to propose any notion of group action that is positive and rewarding."[93]

One of the objections to identity by queer theorists is that its emphasis serves to exclude others, which is true. If one is a lesbian, then by definition one cannot also be a man. But historically, classifying people by identity—and, in the case of LGBT people, coming out of the closet to embrace one's identity—has also enabled similarly oppressed people to find each other, organize, and agitate for civil rights. In their opposition to civil rights struggles to "normalize" and "assimilate" LGBT people into wider society by fighting for reforms such as same-sex marriage or equal employment rights, queer theorists' fundamental conservatism is exposed.

Beneath a veneer of radicalism lies a profoundly anti-working-class agenda. Butler, while opposing homophobic attacks on gay marriage, makes an argument against activists' focus on this issue because it supposedly takes away from the fight against AIDS, somehow diminishes the alternative lifestyles of LGBT people with no partner or with multiple partners, and attempts to promote an image of gays as "a religious or state-sanctioned set of upstanding couples."[94] In other words, queer theorists oppose reforms such as gay marriage that would provide material benefits to LGBT couples on the basis that it would corral sexual minorities into "heteronormative" lifestyles, essentially meaning assimilation into "straight society." The notion that there is such a thing as "straight society" is a confused concept. It means that all straight people regardless of class, race, nationality, etc., share common perspectives and lifestyles; this is patently untrue. If what is meant by "heteronormative" is the middle-class lifestyle portrayed in the media, then Butler and others are conflating the family values claptrap promoted by powerful institutions and right-wing ideologues who defend them with the outlook of working-class straight people. For example, Martin Manalansan IV invokes Lisa Duggan's criticism of "homonormativity" and struggles for gay marriage this way:

> Homonormativity is a chameleon-like ideology that purports to push for progressive causes such as rights to gay marriage and other "activisms" but at the same time it creates a depoliticizing effect on queer communities as it rhetorically re-maps and re-codes freedom and liberation in terms of privacy, domesticity and consumption. In other words, homonormativity anesthetizes queer communities into passively accepting alternative forms of inequality in return for domestic privacy and the freedom to consume.[95]

Aside from the incorrect and moralistic caricature of heterosexuals, this conception of LGBT folks smacks of Hollywood fantasy gays and lesbians, not the working-class majority. Any truly oppositional politics must stand unapologetically in defense of the right to same-sex marriage—as leftists did sixty years ago with mixed-race marriage—despite critiques of the state, religion, and monogamy. Counterposing the radical re-structuring of society, in which benefits are not tied to relation-ships—straight or gay—to reforms in the here and now is a recipe for passivity.

First, gay marriage is a reform. Like *all* reforms under capitalism, it leaves the structure of the system intact while al-leviating a grievance—in this case, the denial of both material benefits and the desire to have LGBT relationships acknowl-edged as equal to those of heterosexuals. Like the demand for unionization, under which the terms of workers' exploita-tion are renegotiated—with workers gaining higher wages and benefits but not eliminating the power of bosses—equal marriage would end some discrimination without eliminating oppression altogether.

Second, to challenge the demand for same-sex marriage for not delivering sexual liberation is a bit like disparaging the civil rights sit-ins to desegregate lunch counters in the early 1960s for not eliminating racism. It sets up a false expectation for a reformist demand and then assails it for not delivering revolutionary transformation.

Some queer theorists have managed to drown even the Stonewall rebellion in the murky waters of historical rela-tivism, in which we supposedly cannot even be certain of the significance of a central event in modern gay history. In *Queering Gay and Lesbian Studies* Thomas Piontek decon-structs the 1969 Greenwich Village riots that gave birth to the modern gay movement, concluding that Stonewall was "a messy and ambiguous historical event."[96] In his chapter "For-get Stonewall," Piontek can only see a seamless narrative be-tween the early conservative homophile movement of the McCarthy era and the mass upheaval that gave rise to the

Gay Liberation Front. Aside from some indisputable remarks presented as visionary insights about historical continuity, this argument serves only to belittle protest, struggle, and political organization. The reader is left questioning if his point is that nothing we do really matters or if anything we do, no matter what, matters equally.

Resistance to convention and hostility to assimilation are two of queer theory's hallmarks. Michael Warner explains that the trouble with normal, in his book of that name, is that it is "a kind of social suicide."[97] Going to work, paying the rent, raising children, etc., are not simply inglorious acts of normalcy, but what kind of sex and how much of it one has are judged the arbiter of resistance and radicalism. Queer theorists place an exhaustive focus on "nonnormative" sexual practices, such as sadomasochism and fist-fucking, because they are conceived as ways of overcoming the "traditional construction of pleasure."[98] While transgender queer theorist Patrick Califia, formerly a lesbian S/M activist and now living as a man,[99] does "not believe that we can fuck our way to freedom,"[100] the condescension he and other queer theory writers express against "vanilla" sex and those who are monogamous creates a hierarchy of sex acts and privileges polyamory, that is, multiple sex partners. Aside from its moralism, the larger problem of setting up a hierarchy of sexual tastes in which the more outré the better is that it poses no challenge to oppression and simply mirrors bourgeois sexual norms. The promoters of bourgeois sexual propriety promote the missionary position while queer theorists "oppose" it with fisting—yet both attempt to place moral standards on intimate activities; they just disagree on which ones are better. Califia explains that he'd rather be shipwrecked with a "male masochist" than a "vanilla lesbian."[101]

Califia's boredom with lesbians who prefer conventional sex (presuming there is such a thing as conventional lesbian sex) is posed as a challenge to the dominant order, whereas it's merely a personal preference. A casual stroll through any of the nation's red light districts or a perusal of the Internet's mind-boggling display of sexual variety proves that capitalism is perfectly capable of accommodating unconventional sex tastes, and entrepreneurs are all too happy to make billions off any kind of sexual appetite and fetish. Attempts by queer theorists to pose sex as a front for opposition represents what Cloud rightly calls "an anti-politics of intimate life."[102]

Not surprisingly, queer theorists attack Marxism for refusing to place sex acts on equal par with class in the struggle against oppression. Patton argues that Marxists have "erotophobia,"[103] meaning presumably that Marxists are antisex. Aside from there being no proof of this offered, the fact remains that sex is a need recognized by Marxists, but not in the same way as food, health care, or housing are needs. It is the real world that imposes on society the centrality of these economic needs as opposed to those of one's intimate life, not Marxists. This is not due to prudery; after all, there is nothing implicitly radical about what kind of sex one has or how much of it. Bolshevik leader Alexandra Kollontai summed up the issue rather well:

> The conservatively inclined part of mankind argue that we should return to the happy times of the past, we should reestablish the old foundations of the family and strengthen the well-tried norms of sexual morality. The champions of bourgeois individualism say that we ought to destroy all the hypocritical restrictions of the obsolete code of sexual behavior.... Socialists, on the other hand assure us that sexual problems will only be settled when the basic

reorganization of the social and economic structure of society has been tackled.[104]

Kollontai's point is simply that true freedom in the realm of
sexual morality can only be achieved through a larger struggle against all forms of oppression and exploitation. The sex
politics of queer theory are essentially the politics of bourgeois individualism. As Califia admits, we really cannot "fuck
our way to freedom."

Opposition to all convention presents some other obvious
problems. First of all, there are all sorts of social conventions
we adhere to not because we are compelled by force or tradition, but because they enable us to live harmoniously with
other human beings. Waiting one's turn in line and opening
the door for the next person are social conventions most people readily adopt because they make sense and allow us to
live in a world cooperatively with others. There is nothing inherently bad about conventions. In fact, few of us would desire or be able to live in society without many of them. Sorting
out those that serve to extend oppression from those that enable us to live as collaborative social beings may give rise to
useful debates, but these are resolvable in practice, not in the
realm of abstraction. Most rhetorical snipes at all convention
have little to offer in the sphere of the practical.

The trouble with "gender trouble"

Queer theorists' project of deconstructing given truths to reveal how they have been created by society also translates
into denying gender and sexual categories. They argue that
gender is "discursively constructed," and therefore can be
"discursively" deconstructed—to define is to "reify" or make

something concrete, and therefore part of our struggle, they argue, is to reject definitions. Marxists, in contrast, see gender and sexual categories as socially constructed, and therefore they can only be socially deconstructed, with language following behind. Most famously among the queer theorists, Butler writes that gender is a sort of "cultural fiction, a performative effect of reiterative acts": "Gender is the repeated stylization of the body, a set of repeated acts within a highly rigid regulatory frame that congeal over time to produce the appearance of substance, of a natural sort of being."[105] In her book *Gender Trouble*, Butler argues that "there is no gender identity behind the expressions of gender,"[106] and so feminists as well as LGBT liberationists who take these "cultural fictions" as givens are trapped. However, it appears that is it Butler and company who have trapped themselves in a discursive enigma of their own creation.

It is one thing to argue that the way we physically comport ourselves, dress, style our hair, etc., is at least partly an involuntary performance shaped by the culture in which we are raised. No doubt that is true and Simone de Beauvoir's 1949 book *The Second Sex* makes this case eloquently, as Butler acknowledges. It is quite another to conclude from this that all gender is a hoax that can be contested through parody, as Butler suggests. She writes: "Practices of parody can serve to reengage and reconsolidate the very distinction between a privileged and naturalized gender configuration and one that appears as derived, phantasmatic, and mimetic—a failed copy, as it were."[107] She argues that positive political change can arise from destabilizing society's construction and assumptions of gender through drag and other forms of parody. Cloud takes on Butler's utopianism for substituting struggle with a "theater of the self in which intimacy is staged and words are detached from their material referents. The theory of performativity locates agency in the 'consciousness'...of individuals and not in posing a collective challenge to capitalism."[108] Yes, gender and its norms are both socially constructed and constricting, and some people, such as those who are transgender, find these norms asphyxiating. But the problem is that we live in a sexist society in which the way one is treated, how much one is paid, one's physical vulnerability, and a zillion other considerations are shaped by one's gender—not that we each have a gender. As the introduction to Butler's piece in the *Transgender Studies Reader* asks, "if gender is not real, how real can its oppression be?"[109] Naturally, any liberatory politics must embrace the multiplicity of sexual behaviors and mannerisms, styles of dress, and physical demeanors that human beings desire to express. It must reject the legal norms that demand a person's physical sex must conform to their gender identity. But arguing that gender is a meaningless category, rather than a more ambiguous one than some social scientists believe, raises interesting philosophical questions yet drives us into a theoretical and organizational cul-de-sac.

If woman is a fiction, it raises an obvious difficulty in fighting for her rights. Butler argues, "the premature insistence on a stable subject of feminism, understood as a seamless category of women, inevitably generates multiple refusals to accept the category."[110] She then draws the conclusion that feminism itself, in fighting for this fictional category, is "coercive and regulatory."[111] Here, stable concepts and clarity of meaning are construed as "regulatory." Rather, it is the coercive powers of the law that impose the notion that a person's genitalia must necessarily conform to their gender identity.

Butler and Sedgwick rightly take on feminists who raise essentialist arguments—that women are nurturing and more passive as a result of their biology, for example—but don't get at the real-world issues that confine most women, and men for that matter, such as their income, access to education, health care, and so on. In fact, one glaring deficiency of queer theory is how little it even attempts to engage with the realities of most peoples' lives. While "bodies" are analyzed ad nauseam by these theorists, their writings assume that peoples' gender and sexuality are the most defining aspects of their lives. Surely peoples' bodies are partially constructed by society, more specifically by what class someone is born into. One is more likely to be obese, smoke, die young, and have greater stress if one must work long hours, sit in horrendous traffic jams, have little leisure time, and all the other class-influenced aspects of our lives. Historian Harriet Malinowitz's quip about queer theorists rings true here: "The queer theorist network often resembles a social club open to residents of a neighborhood most of us can't afford to live in."[112]

Many who have theorized about gender and sex have conceived of a distinction between the two in a way that Butler describes as, "Sex is to nature or 'the raw' as gender is to culture or 'the cooked.'"[113] While some may agree that femininity and masculinity are social creations, biological sex, it is usually argued, is not—you are either born with one set of bits or the other. On the contrary, Butler and others rightly challenge the limited notion of a sexual binary of male/female given the evidence of millions of intersex people with ambiguous genitalia who do not fit neatly into either category. The scientific fact of anatomical variation that runs the spectrum of possibilities, however, is not a clarion call to erase male and female from our vocabularies—these words signify real live beings in the world, several billion in fact. Instead, it raises the concept of ambiguity in the realm of sex for a minority of people who are traumatized not by the terms "male" and "female," but by a society that will not allow for sexual fluidity, uncertainty, and difference.

The Intersex Society of North America explains, "we've learned that many intersex people are perfectly comfortable adopting either a male or female gender identity and are not seeking a genderless society or to label themselves as a member of a third gender class."[114] In the real-life experiences of those whose interests queer theorists tell us their ideas serve, it is not the labels that transgender and intersex people abhor, rather it is the medical establishment and other institutions that create their dilemma. The labels merely serve to describe what has been codified by law and social practice. It is interesting to note that even those drawn to these ideas and who sometimes use the contorted vocabulary of queer theory must abandon them when the rubber hits the road, so to speak, as transgender activist and writer Riki Wilchins does in her movement organizing. Tragically, because of the distorted tradition of socialism and a weakened left, ID politics and queer theory play off each other in some academic quarters as if in a hermetically sealed bubble. Yet neither is capable of delivering sexual liberation, and their shared suspicions of objective truth and skepticism about the possibilities for common mobilization lead both to an interminable standoff.

Postmodern ideas developed and flourished in the post-1960s period, when a generation of Americans grew up without participating in or even witnessing class struggles on a mass scale. Tens of millions have now come of age in a society where these politics of difference and individualism appear as common sense, which perhaps accounts for the continued widespread acceptance of the language of these theories even as their social relevance recedes. As anthropologist Max Kirsch astutely points out,

> Queer theory's highlighting of the impossibility of identity and the relativity of experience closely follows the development of current capitalist relations of production, where the self-contained individual is central to the economic goal of creating profit through production and its by-product, consuming.... It is thus my view that the tenets of Queer theory closely pattern the characteristics of social relations that it claims to reject. Rather than building resistance to the capitalist production of inequality, it has, paradoxically, mirrored it.[115]

As Kirsch puts it, "we are not alone."[116] Human beings are social animals who cannot exist or thrive without each other. We are weakest as individuals. While ruling-class ideology promotes rugged individualism and the development of personal attributes as means toward success, it is as a collective class that ordinary people have power to make change. Not because we are all the same—obviously not—but because we all have a common enemy in the system and the tiny class of parasites who run it. Regardless of our differences and how experiences of oppression manifest themselves, workers have more in common than not. What class society has constructed, organized forces in opposition to it can tear down. However, the philosophical poststructuralism of queer theory is a fetter on the physical deconstruction of this oppressive system.

Queer theory takes some of the problems created by identity politics activists, who often draw barriers between oppressed groups, and attempts to resolve them by theorizing out of existence both groups and barriers. What neither seems to accept is that simply because someone cannot identify *as* a lesbian does not mean that she cannot identify *with* lesbians. Nobody can refute, of course, that only a gay man with AIDS, for example, can know what it is like to go through this world as a sexual minority often blamed by right-wingers for having brought onto himself a potentially fatal ailment. Similarly, only a Black woman can know what life is like in her skin. However, queer theorists elevate the realities of differences into insurmountable obstacles to common identity, and by extension, common action is called into question as well.

The ideas that gave theoretical expression to an era of low struggle, a tiny organized left, and neoliberal economic policies that ran roughshod over ordinary peoples' lives no longer appear to have the same currency in social movements. As we enter an era in which demands are being made on a new administration and the first shoots of struggle are surfacing in labor and among LGBT people, activists drawn from the ranks of the downwardly mobile middle and working classes are seeking practical strategies and politics to achieve real change. Great possibilities lie in the leftward shifting consciousness regarding homosexuality in U.S. society and the growing sense that in unity there is strength.

CHAPTER SEVEN

Biology, Environment, Gender, and Sexual Orientation

Since the early 1990s, there has been considerable research and an enormous amount of media coverage speculating about the existence of a "gay gene." From magazine cover stories like *Newsweek*'s "Is This Child Gay? Born or Bred: The Origins of Homosexuality"[1] to television exposés like *ABC News*'s "Are You Born Gay?"[2] the idea of a biological origin for homosexuality is now widely accepted. Whereas twenty years ago, most lesbians, gays, and bisexuals would have referred to their sexuality as a "preference," it has become increasingly common for people to regard their own and others' sexuality as innate. D'Emilio sums up the social utility of this viewpoint:

> The idea that people are born gay—or lesbian or bisexual—is appealing for lots of reasons. Many of us experience the direction of our sexual desires as something that we have no control over. We just are that way, it seems, so therefore we must be born gay. The people who are most overt in their hatred of queer folks, the religious conservatives, insist that being gay is something we choose, and we know we can't agree with them. Hence, again, born gay. Liberal heterosexual allies love the idea. If gays are born that way, then of course they shouldn't be punished for it. "Born gay" is also a relief to any of us who have some doubts about our

sexuality or who feel ourselves sinking under the weight of the oppression. If we're born gay, then it's not our fault, and we're certainly not choosing to be oppressed: we just can't help it, so leave us alone. It also answers those who worry about the effect of too many out-of-the-closet gay men and lesbians: if people are born this way, then young people won't be influenced by us.[3]

Is Anyone Born Gay?

Despite its current popularity, the scientific evidence for biological causes of sexuality and other complex human behaviors is inadequate, while the political and social implications are often downright reactionary. Whatever the intentions of the scientists who study the biological causes of sexuality and the activists who promote their findings, the quest for a strictly biological explanation for our behavior is misguided.

The main studies that have been performed are the neuroanatomical research of Simon LeVay, the studies of sexual inheritance by Michael Bailey and Richard Pillard, and genetic linkage research by Dean Hamer and Peter Copeland.[4] In 1991, researcher Simon LeVay's study was widely interpreted as strong evidence that biological factors directly wire the brain for sexual orientation.[5] But several considerations militate against that conclusion. First, LeVay's work has never been replicated in any other study, which surely should be required before any theory is to be considered potentially valid. Furthermore, in his published study, all the brains of gay men came from deceased AIDS patients. His inclusion of a few brains from presumed heterosexual men with AIDS did not adequately address the fact that at the time of death virtually all men with AIDS have decreased testosterone levels as a result of the disease itself or the side effects of particular treatments.

LeVay studied forty-one brains, nineteen of them from men who died of AIDS, itself a quite small and unrepresentative sample. He concluded that since the hypothalamus, a part of the brain slightly smaller than a golf ball, was smaller in the brains of gay men that he studied and similar in size to that of women, the sexual behavior of a gay man is similar to that of women.[6] LeVay, a gay man whose lover died of AIDS, undoubtedly had the best of intentions, but he also had to rely on the medical information available to him about the brains of deceased subjects he studied—and may have assumed sexual histories that are unfounded and not confirmable. He also took for granted the binary view of sexuality—that one is either gay or straight—ignoring the possibility that any of his subjects might have been bisexual. Finally, LeVay disregarded the possibility of the alternative conclusion that brain structure might be the effect rather than the cause of homosexuality. LeVay remains convinced of his research and argues, "Hirschfeld was right. I support the idea that we're a third sex—or a third sex and a fourth sex, gay men and lesbians. Today, there's scientific documentation behind this."[7]

Studies hypothesizing that sexual orientation runs in families by Bailey, Pillard, and others demonstrate that same-sex siblings of openly avowed gay men are more likely to be gay than others, but this research raises more questions than it answers. Siblings raised in the same household not only share genes but a common social environment, raising the prospect of social influences on the siblings' sexual preferences. In addition, gay men were recruited for these studies through gay publications and men with gay brothers were more likely to respond than those with straight brothers, thus skewing the sample.[8]

Some studies on twins separated early in life rely on samples far too small for clear conclusions.[9] One Minnesota twin registry has "only six recorded cases of identical twins separated at birth in which at least one of the siblings is reported to be homosexual."[10] Four pairs of twins were women; the others were men. In one of the two male identical twin pairs both were gay; one of the four female pairs included a lesbian and a bisexual. Due to the tiny sampling from which drawing generalizations would be scientifically unsound, this research shows no direct correlation between genes and sexuality. Yet this study has been widely reported as showing a 25 percent and 50 percent sexual orientation match, respectively, despite the fact that the researchers themselves raise the problem of generalizing from this study and leave the door open for other explanations. "That the twins are highly selected cannot be doubted; they are not representative of twins or homosexuals.... Our evidence, though based on a small sample, implicates environmental factors as the major determinant of female homosexuality,"[11]

Dean Hamer argues that male homosexuality is inherited from the mother's X chromosomes (females have one X chromosome from each parent, while males have an X chromosome from their mother and a Y chromosome from their father). He studied 114 families and recruited subjects that openly identified as gay, thus skewing the research results against findings of bisexuality, for example. In fact, Hamer deliberately eliminated bisexuality from his study, concluding that it was not significant enough to be included.[12]

Hamer's 1994 study with Peter Copeland found a pattern of higher rates of homosexuality among male relatives of gay men on their mother's side and thus concluded that, similar to color blindness, also passed on via the X chromosome, the maternal genetic line is where gayness can be located, though they never claimed to have identified any specific genetic sequence. Other studies since then that attempted to replicate Hamer and Copeland's findings were unable to correlate gay sexuality with the X chromosome. Edward Stein challenges the findings of the Hamer and Copeland study, arguing, "Taken as a whole, Hamer's study faces various methodological problems, its results are open to various interpretations (several of which are more plausible than the existence of a gay gene), and it has not been replicated."[13]

Arguments against a genetic origin for homosexuality do not necessarily assume that one's sexual orientation is a choice in the sense that, for example, one's political affiliation is. After all, in a society where LGBT people are oppressed, why would people choose to be discriminated against? For that matter, nobody wakes up one morning and suddenly decides to be attracted to one sex or another. Yet there is an act of will involved in deciding to acknowledge and pursue the desire to engage in a same-sex relationship or to eschew the possibility altogether. Socialist Phil Gasper argues against the false dichotomy of genes versus choice.

> Even identical twins exhibit differences at birth because of tiny differences in their prenatal environments. Tiny environmental differences after birth can equally produce noticeable differences in behavior and psychology. It's also worth noting that the fact that something feels natural to an individual is no evidence that it is innate. Speaking English feels perfectly natural to me, while speaking Chinese seems strange and exotic, but obviously languages are learned (even though no conscious choice is involved with

respect to our first language or languages). I think many gay people make the mistake of thinking that because they were attracted to members of the same sex from a very early age, and because their desires weren't the result of a conscious choice, that the desires must be innate. But even when that is true, the conclusion doesn't follow.[14]

Neither biological nor environmental determinism

Scientific writings by many researchers, including the prominent feminist, biologist, and historian of science, Anne Fausto-Sterling—whose works are blessedly accessible to the non-scientist—make a compelling case for rejecting *both* biological determinism and environmental determinism in attempts to understand anything as complex as human behavior. She explains, "If the first take-home lesson in thinking about complex human traits is that linear chainlike causal explanations...are simply wrong, then the second is that the alternative idea of 'environmental determinism' is also an oversimplification."[15] In discussing the interplay between environment and biology, Fausto-Sterling provides a useful example. Studies of pregnant Dutch women and their offspring during a famine of 1945 showed that those children born to women who were starving during the first six months of pregnancy tended to have a higher incidence of obesity later in life, largely due to the way a part of their brains involved in appetite developed. Those children born to women who suffered starvation in the final trimester, however, tended to develop into thin adults due to the inhibited growth of fat cells in gestation. The ostensibly genetic causes of these children's rates of obesity were also environmental, resulting from a famine at the end of the Second World War. What's more, environmental factors are both "multitiered" and "without time limits."[16] Although children born with severe malnutrition in the United States have been found to be at higher risk for mental retardation, when those same children are placed in an environment where there is good nutrition, health care, and other economic and social benefits, their mental development can be perfectly normal. [17]

This interplay between environment and biology and the complexities involved in discussing both features has profound implications on the debate surrounding the formation of sexuality and gender. Some LGBT organizations, most notably Human Rights Campaign—which released a press packet on the research[18]—sincerely believe that advancing a gay gene theory will help win civil rights and defeat discrimination. Their approach is similar, in fact, to the one taken by an early advocate for eliminating sodomy laws, Karl Heinrich Ulrichs, who published a series of pamphlets in the 1860s that essentially argued for the innate character of what he referred to as the "third sex," a concept later taken up by German sexologist Magnus Hirschfeld (discussed in chapter 1). Like Hirschfeld and pro-gay advocates of the past, many today who believe homosexuality is biologically determined are attracted to an explanation that could potentially counter oppressive legislation against LGBT people. The thinking goes, if LGBT people's sexual orientations are simply hard-wired, denying them rights in the modern era would be widely seen as cruel, arbitrary, and bigoted. *Newsweek* posed the argument for a gay gene this way: "Theoretically, it could gain them [LGBT people] civil rights protections accorded any 'natural' minority, in which the legal linchpin is the question of an 'immutable' characteristic."[19]

But this theory does not challenge the idea that hetero-sexual behavior is "normal" while homosexuality is "abnor-mal." Tying civil rights to biology avoids the central argument that human beings deserve humane and equitable treatment regardless of what others think of their sexual preferences. Moreover, the right has been able to co-opt the biological argument, advancing ideas about physically "curing" homosexuality. These conservatives conclude that if homosexuality is a genetic disorder, like sickle cell anemia, then a medical solution to the "problem" can be found. The president of the Southern Baptist Theological Seminary, Dr. Albert Mohler, Jr., argues, for example, that a biological basis for homosexuality would "not alter God's moral verdict on homosexual sin." Christians, he argues, ought to consider the possibility of a genetic or hormonal "treatment" administered to a mother to alter her child's sexual orientation.[20]

Aside from the politically backward notion that homosexuality ought to be "cured," there is also an implicit misconception about what genes are and how they operate. As the example of the pregnant Dutch women above indicates, genes function differently from the way they are popularly discussed. Fausto-Sterling explains how they operate:

> [A]n individual's developmental and environmental history, in combination with his or her total genetic endowment (all the genetic information encoded in the DNA), as well as chance, contribute to the final phenotype [external presentation]. By the same token, genes alone do not determine human behavior. They work in the presence and under the influence of a set of environments.[21]

Even if there were scientific proof of a genetic cause for sexual behavior, it would not prevent the oppression of LGBT people. After all, there is a biological explanation for the color of people's skin, yet widespread discrimination against those with darker skin persists.

Of the many scientific and political problems with the search for a gay gene, one seems primary. What does it even mean to say someone is gay? We cannot identify LGBT people across time and place, which would have to be the case if sexuality were biologically determined. It is neither historically nor culturally accurate to argue that sexual activity between older men (who also had sex with women) and younger boys in ancient Greece, same-sex activity inside prisons (where options are by definition limited), and consensual sex between two men in twenty-first-century Brooklyn amount to behavior displayed by the same sexual human type. Even men in some Latin cultures today who are married to women but periodically have penetrative sex with other men would never consider themselves to be gay or even bisexual. To these men (*machos* or *activos*), only those in the receptive sexual role (*jotos*) are homosexual.[22] Some Americans might insist that they are simply in denial and must own up to our society's definition of gay and straight. In fact that's precisely how one scientist described his approach: "there are societies in which people don't call themselves gay…but they certainly do stuff we would call gay."[23] However, this approach amounts to viewing others through a biased cultural lens. And what about bisexuality? Or how transsexuals did not emerge as a separate type of person until the twentieth century? Viewed in this way, the search for a genetic origin of human sexual behavior is a quixotic endeavor at best.

The prevalence of a sexual binary in most gay gene studies flies in the face of both long-standing empirical research and at least some LGBT peoples' lived experience: much of sexual identity is fluid and not fixed. Alfred Kinsey's team questioned thousands of individuals in detail for their ground-breaking 1948 book, *Sexual Behavior in the Human Male*, using a scale from zero to six to reflect the sexual desires, fantasies, and activities of men. They accorded zero to those who were exclusively heterosexual and six to those who were exclusively homosexual, while those in between reflected varying degrees of bisexuality. In addition, Kinsey's team took on the still dominant idea about the link between effeminacy and homosexual men. As he wrote:

> It should be pointed out that scientific judgments on this point [effeminacy] have been based on little more than the same sort of impression which the general public has had concerning homosexual persons.... Males do not represent two discrete populations, heterosexual and homosexual. The world is not to be divided into sheep and goats. Not all things are black nor all things white. It is a fundamental of taxonomy that nature rarely deals with discrete categories. Only the human mind invents categories and tries to force facts into separated pigeon-holes. The living world is a continuum in each and every one of its aspects. The sooner we learn this concerning human sexual behavior, the sooner we shall reach a sound understanding of the realities of sex. [24]

Much recent biological research into human sexual behavior has ignored insights Kinsey offered six decades ago. As author Robert Alan Brookey concludes, "the gay gene discourse imagines male homosexuality as a biological state of effeminate pathology; accordingly, it reintroduces the dualistic notions of sex and sexual orientation that informed psychoanalytic theory...prior to Kinsey." [25] Given the mixed historical record of gays and the field of psychiatry, which until 1973 categorized homosexuality in the United States as a mental illness, it is best to view ideas that pathologize human sexual behavior with suspicion. The ubiquitous assumption of "Sissy Boy Syndrome" (that's what perceived effeminate behavior in men is often called)[26] among researchers of gay men sounds more like locker room chatter than scientific inquiry. And the almost universal presumption that tomboyish behavior and a "masculine" appearance in women are signs of lesbianism provides a window into the internalized belief system some researchers employ. The near-absence of inquiry into female sexuality in most of these studies is startling. Much as Sigmund Freud conceived of female sexuality as "a dark continent,"[27] these biological studies seem to perceive lesbianism as a kind of enigma.

What we can say for certain is that modern class society has created the material conditions for a multiplicity of desires to be realized—or frustrated. Although we are physiologically suited to a wide range of sexual options, what individuals decide to act upon depends on a vast web of environmental and social conditions. So long as we live in a society where social norms limit and proscribe our sexual behavior, we cannot really know how humans would behave sexually if unhampered freedom of choice existed.

Sissies, Tomboys, and Trannies

From popular books like *Men Are from Mars, Women Are from Venus* to TV sitcoms and comic book caricatures of heterosexual relationships, we are blitzed with social "truisms" about the supposedly fixed natures of men and women. Men and women are intrinsically different, we are told over and over again. One hardly needs to venture farther than the nearest Baby Gap store with its vast displays of blue and pink to encounter images, clothing, and infant doodads that promote popular notions of nurturing, passive, soft femininity and aggressive, confident, strong masculinity. These distinct gender roles, cultivated from birth, foster the belief that men and women are by nature significantly different—even polar opposites. But despite its commonsense appeal, this idea does not stand up to scientific inquiry. Rigid gender roles and behavior aren't essential to our biological nature. Rather, they are essential to the nature of our society.

The global variety of gender expressions is proof that, if nothing else, our natures are "incredibly malleable," as pioneering anthropologist Margaret Mead put it.[28] In New Guinea, Mead found cultures with no concept of distinct sexual natures between men and women, both of whom expressed maternal behavior well into the mid-twentieth century when she studied them. In the Arapesh culture, Mead found that both men and women were expected to share child-rearing responsibilities and to raise male and female children to be full equals. In another tribe, the Mudugmor, she found extreme aggression in both sexes and in a third, the Tchambuli, Mead discovered gender roles completely reversed from our own traditions. The women there were dominant and the men were emotionally submissive.[29]

The great diversity of gender expressions throughout a variety of cultures and time periods challenges the modern Western conception of biologically fixed gender roles. Native American berdaches, also known as two-spirited individuals, are usually anatomical males who may marry other men and perform functions we would associate with traditional women's roles, though they are considered in their societies to be male.[30] The *hijras* of India, with a reputed four-thousand-year-old history, could be classified as eunuchs, effeminate men, or transsexuals in U.S. society.[31]

The Marxist understanding of gender roles under capitalism, as explained in chapter 1, is that they are shaped by the system's need for women's unpaid reproductive labor in the home. Homosexual behavior is a challenge to this function, even when lesbian or gay men choose to lead lives similar to those of heterosexuals and raise children as millions today often do. The behavior of LGBT people weakens and even defies traditional sex roles, thus undermining the attitudes most desirable to the smooth functioning of capitalist society. As historian Jeffrey Weeks summarizes, "If social roles are so flexible, if there is no necessary connection between reproduction, gender and sexual attributes, it is not clear why sharp sexual dichotomies should be so crucially necessary—unless we make a prior assumption about their inevitability."[32]

Yet walk into any day care center, and it's hard to ignore what many parents of very young children see—small boys running about shooting things and little girls playing more quietly. There are always exceptional cases, but they only appear to confirm the observation of gender differences appearing so early in life that they must be inborn. But humans are social animals—who require the longest time of any primate to mature into adulthood. Quite literally, from our earliest moments, we learn gender. And even if there were some biological basis for psychological and behavioral differences between males and females, there is no reason to assume these are unchangeable, given the complexity of both human psychology and behavior and the multitude of factors that shape these features.

Developmental psychologists have performed studies since the eighties on very young children to discover how and when they begin to discern and understand gender. At two years old, children could not identify boys from girls or women from men, yet just six months later they were able to correctly identify all of them. The slightly older children who could pick out boys from girls also showed gender-typical behavior in ways that their younger peers did not—they preferred same-sex play groups, boys were more aggressive, and girls were more passive. When studied in the children's homes, toddlers as young as twenty months could not identify boys from girls; the 50 percent of children at twenty-seven months who could also had parents who gave them either positive or negative feedback for "sex-type toy play," that is, boys playing with trucks and girls with dolls. These "early labelers" displayed greater awareness of traditional gender roles as they got older as well. When children younger than three were shown pictures of naked girls and boys, they could not identify them until those same images were shown clothed. Even 60 percent of four- and five-year-olds could not consistently identify the sex of these images naked, but required hairstyle and clothing cues to do so correctly. In fact, even once they learned what the different genitalia look like, these slightly older children sometimes got the sex identity wrong if the clothing and hairstyle signals were switched. For them, gender was still not fixed to sex.[33] These behavioral psychologists concluded, "the child's construction of a gender schema reflects back the behavioral, cognitive, and affective dimensions of the familial environment.[34] Unfortunately for those parents seeking an upbringing free of gender bias for their kids, families are not the only institutions that acculturate young children. As every parent eventually discovers, to one degree or another, the world will eventually have its way with their kids.

Even widespread notions of psychological differences between boys and girls ignore considerable research that points to the dominance of similarities between them. A 1974 book that reviewed two thousand studies on personality, social behavior, and memory "dismissed as unfounded many popular beliefs...including beliefs that girls are more 'social' than boys; that girls are more suggestible; that girls have lower self-esteem...whereas boys are better at higher level cognitive processing; and that girls lack achievement motivation."[35] What researchers then and since have discovered is that by the onset of puberty children of both sexes have been socialized sufficiently to express differences that are widely claimed to be inherent in our biological makeup. These myths have serious consequences for everything from lower expectations for girls in math class and pressure for boys and men to repress their emotions to women being passed over for jobs requiring high technical skills.

Those who do not conform to these assigned roles are often victims of prejudice, humiliation, and even violence. Perhaps none more so than "effeminate" males. In a society where maleness reigns supreme, male gender benders are perceived as weak and vulnerable, yet also as threatening to the social order. As anyone who has ever played in, worked at, or walked past a schoolyard and heard the timeless epithet "faggot" hurled at the kid who missed the ball (or anyone who was that kid), it is apparent that nothing is meant to sting quite so badly as this slur against a boy's masculinity.

In their report on anti-LGBT violence in 2007, the National Coalition of Anti-Violence Programs recorded twice as many violent incidents against men who display gender-atypical behavior than against women; the greatest increase in violent attacks were against transmen, those who were physically female at birth and identify as male.[36] The most famous case in recent years was that of Brandon Teena, a female-to-male transgender person, who was raped and murdered and then memorialized by Hollywood in the award-winning movie *Boys Don't Cry*. Certainly, girls and women who flout the gender order are also taunted and victimized. In the most recent studies on harassment and violent attacks in middle and high schools, female and male teens who exhibit atypical gender behavior were more than three times as likely to experience a physical assault than teens who are victimized due to race, and only slightly less likely to be victimized than those who were perceived to be LGBT.[37]

The link between gender-atypical behavior and male gayness goes back to the nineteenth century and prevails to this day. Dubbed "Sissy Boy Syndrome" by sexologist Richard Green in 1987, but formally referred to in both sexes as Gender Identity Disorder (GID), gender-atypical behavior is considered by many psychologists to be a condition requiring psychological treatment, though Green himself argued that therapy would do more damage than good. Green's research on the sissy-gay link concluded, "Barbie dolls at five, sex with men at twenty-five."[38] Like other behavioral scientists, Green found that "feminine" boys were closer to their mothers than fathers, which he believed accounted for their gender-discordant behavior. Whether this is an outcome or cause or entirely unconnected to the boys' sexuality, however, is not scientifically proven. In fact, if it is true that gender-atypical boys are closer to mom than dad, it could be the result of the father's homophobic treatment of his "sissy" son, in which case the father's behavior pushed the son closer to his mother, not the son's gayness or any perceived atypical behavior. GID was first named and listed in 1980 in the American Psychiatric Association's *Diagnostic and Statistical Manual of Mental Disorders*.[39] The findings of Green's study are also undermined by the fact that there are also males who, though closer to their mothers than to their fathers, do not grow up to be gay. Transgender persons seeking sex reassignment surgery must go through a costly and lengthy process to get diagnosed and treated for this "psychopathology," though most insurance companies consider transsexual health care treatments to be "experimental" or "elective" and therefore not worthy of coverage.[40]

That many adult gays and lesbians can recall childhood gender-atypical behavior has been extensively studied. A review of forty-eight such studies concluded that 50 percent of boys who acted like "sissies" turned out to be gay adults, while only 6 percent of girls who recounted tomboyish behavior in childhood grew up to be lesbians.[41] One factor that must be taken into account is that gender-typical behavior itself has morphed over time, advancing the argument that it is socially constructed. Infinitely more fathers today change diapers, stay at home with their kids, and share child-rearing with their partners than at any point in modern history. The appearance of diaper-changing stations in men's restrooms is but one indication of this. And everything from men's and women's hairstyles to body shapes and clothing allow today for a more androgynous appearance, reflecting shifting material conditions and social mores. D'Emilio even suggests that the emergence of a transgender identity at the end of the twentieth century is connected to the "increasingly porous boundaries that have come to characterize gender roles" in late capitalism, making it comparatively easier than in previous eras to cross over to another gender.[42]

In addition, gender-atypical behavior might be a way for young children to relate to peers whose company and activities they prefer, rather than being an expression of some inner sexual yearnings. For adults living in a society in which it is difficult to meet potential sexual partners, especially for LGBT people who are today a small minority, behavior, clothing, and mannerisms are means of identifying one another. The modern women's liberation movement may have more to do with the gap between tomboys becoming lesbians and "sissies" maturing into gay men than anything else. Since the 1970s, girls who display a talent and desire for sports and rough-and-tumble play are far less likely to be perceived as sick than boys who dress up in mommy's clothes or play with dolls. It is a reflection of the sexism of our society that women's traditional gender roles are devalued while men's are lauded, regardless of the sex of the person displaying the behavior. In essence, "effeminate" men are derided for dragging men down to the unenviable position of women. "Masculinity" in women, on the other hand, evinces disapproving looks from some, but is often perceived as self-reliance, confidence, and strength—characteristics our society extols. Those men most threatened by and hostile to "masculine" women seem to take umbrage at the notion that such subordinate creatures dare stand toe to toe with them.

But it's not just bigots who hold onto gender stereotypes. Many progressives, including some feminists, adhere to notions of behavioral norms that are intrinsically conservative, even if the aims of the advocates are not. Two feminist scientists, Susan Pinker and Louann Brizendine, have presented themselves as "reluctant truth-tellers" in their books, which argue there are innate psychological differences between men and women.[43] In *The Female Brain*, Brizendine not only asserts that women have "a nearly psychic capacity to read faces and tone of voice for emotions and states of mind,"[44] but also that women are real chatterboxes compared to their fellows—with women using twenty thousand words per day compared with men's mere seven thousand. It turns out that when researchers actually wired men and women with recording devices to test out her theory, both uttered around the same number of words, approximately sixteen thousand each day.[45] While Brizendine acknowledged that study, which appeared in *Science*, her reissue of the book in the subsequent paperback repeated her original claim. In a video interview, Slate.com's Amanda Schaffer goes through some of the various claims made by both Pinker and Brinzendine, one of which relies on a study sample of only nine people, and concludes that they are basing their arguments on "unsettled science."[46]

Some feminists hew to the notion that domestic violence is a predominantly male trait, but scientific inquiry reveals otherwise. Janice Ristock opens her book on violence in lesbian relationships by taking on feminist myths about women's and men's supposed natures and challenging the notion that by exposing lesbian domestic violence she is either minimizing heterosexual violence or aiding the right.[47] Ristock's work es-

timates the rate of lesbian domestic abuse at anywhere between 17 and 52 percent, and her book recounts harrowing
stories of domestic violence between women.[48] Clearly,
women display a similar capacity to men for aggression and
violence in their relationships.

Intersex people and the male/female binary

Five times a day in American hospitals doctors surgically alter
a newborn infant's genitalia for cosmetic purposes often
amounting to mutilation that prevents the grown child from
ever experiencing an orgasm.[49] Ever since the 1950s doctors
have considered it a "medical emergency" to assign a fixed sex
to a baby born with elements of both male and female genitalia.[50] Sometimes a baby is born with internal organs of a male
but external genitalia of a female or vice versa; other times
there are outward genitalia of both sexes; and in still other
cases the baby isn't really intersex at all, but was born with a
clitoris the doctor perceived as "too big" or a penis that was
seen as "too small" (newborns' penises are evidently never
"too big"). These intersex children are not as rare as one might
assume. There are about as many intersex people in the United
States alone as there are Jews, more than five million today—
many more than albinos, for comparison, suggesting that most
of us have encountered, and perhaps some of us are ourselves,
intersex individuals.[51] There exists intense secrecy and shame
surrounding this issue. Some people don't even know they are
intersex, as parents are directed not to tell their children and
doctors are sometimes evasive about the nature of the surgery
even with the parents, leaving them in the dark as well. Spain's
top hurdler in the 1988 Olympics, Maria Patino, discovered her

intersexuality during gender testing at that year's Olympics and she was initially disqualified.[52]

Scientists believe that intersex people have been around for as long as males and females, evidenced by ancient depictions and tales of hermaphrodites, the common name for intersex people until recent years. The Roman sculpture Sleeping Hermaphrodite from the second century AD depicts what appears to be a reclining woman from behind, but when one views the front, an erect penis and breasts are revealed. Foucault wrote an introduction to the memoirs of Herculine Barbin, a nineteenth-century intersex person who lived as a woman but was forced to have surgery to become a man.[53] The incidence of intersex births appears to be on the rise in the last decades; some scientists suggest the possibility of environmental and other factors.[54]

LGBT struggles of the recent past have opened the way for those who are intersex to speak out about what has been done to them by the medical establishment. Groups such as Intersex Society of North America (ISNA) and activists in Hermaphrodites with Attitude expose the intense psychological and physical damage caused by these medically unnecessary surgeries. Cheryl Chase, who founded ISNA, was born as "Charlie," but doctors decided when "he" was one-and-a-half that "his" small penis was actually a clitoris ("he" was also born with ovaries). Rather than acknowledge Charlie's intersexuality, which doctors assumed would be traumatizing, they decided to cut off his penis, thus rendering the adult Cheryl incapable of ever having erotic sensation to the point of orgasm.[55] ISNA demands an end to these surgeries until and unless the mature child decides for him or herself and, crucially, it argues that intersex children should be raised as either male or female. ISNA also provides useful information about how to discern which gender identity a child is likely to adopt later in life according to their own experiences and scientific studies.

> At ISNA, we've learned that many intersex people are perfectly comfortable adopting either a male or female gender identity and are not seeking a genderless society or to label themselves as a member of a third gender class. Although it's true that the urge to perform surgeries on intersex children's sex anatomies is sometimes born out of the belief that children must have sex anatomies that are clearly male or female in order to be comfortable in either a male or female gender (and this is clearly a harmful belief born out of antiquated notions about gender identity corresponding directly to genital anatomy), the idea of raising a child as a boy or girl isn't what most adults with intersex conditions point to as their main problem.
>
> In fact, many of the people with intersex we know—both those subjected to early surgeries and those who escaped surgery—very happily accepted a gender assignment of male or female (either the one given them at birth or one they chose later for themselves later in life). Instead, adults with intersex conditions who underwent genital surgeries at early ages most often cite those early genital surgeries and the lies and shame surrounding those procedures as their source of pain. Later in life, like many people with typical anatomies, intersex people take pleasure in what some gender scholars (like Judith Butler) might call *doing* their gender. Thus, intersex people don't tell us that the very concept of gender is oppressive to them. Instead, it's the childhood surgeries performed on them and the accompanying lies and shame that are problematic.[56]

The heretical bodies of intersex people call into question the male/female sexual binary and advocate for a more fluid understanding of physical sex. While we are never encouraged to conceive of bodies this way, both primary and secondary sexual characteristics are awfully similar in function and occasionally even in appearance. The clitoris is stimulated like a penis and comes in various sizes as does the penis, and breasts come in a wide range of sizes on both men and women. The rest of our bodies are more similar than they are distinguishable from each other. For example, it is increasingly difficult to tell the difference between some of the best-trained male and female Olympic swimmers when they are wearing state-of-the-art one-piece speed suits. The impact of Title IX, the 1972 law mandating equal funding for girls' and boys' sports in schools that was one outcome of the women's liberation movement, has helped to radically alter not only women's fitness and emotional well-being, but their bodies as well.

Obviously, there are some physical differences between men and women, but it is our culture and not biology that gives them their meaning. Even the notion that only women can give birth is challenged by the reality of Thomas Beatie, popularly known as the "pregnant man," a female-to-male transgender man who gave birth in 2008 to a baby girl. The media's snide references to his being a "man" as opposed to a "real" man because he retained the physiological ability to have a child exposes our society's discomfort with his unconventional body and gender choices.

It is society, not biology, that imposes the capacity for nurturing uniquely on women as a result of child-bearing, however. Even differences in female and male muscularity and size have been shaped over thousands of years by our gender roles, diet, and shifting cultural preferences. Anthropologist

Eleanor Burke Leaçock notes that male and female Neanderthals had the same muscularity, and that with the rise of a social division of labor in early modern humans thousands of years ago, women and men's muscularity developed differently.[57] This continues to evolve as our work lives and lengthy commutes tend to dictate a more sedentary lifestyle for many people. Contemporary American men and women are more likely to be muscular if they have either manual labor jobs or leisure time to enjoy physical activity, both of which are shaped by class, not biology.

The discovery in the early twentieth century in India of two female "wild children," raised by a pack of wolves, challenges our conventional notions of human physical capacities. These two children could outpace other humans easily by running on all fours, rather than on just their two legs. Like wolves, they were nocturnal and ate and digested raw meat easily, and communicated through barks at feeding time to establish a pecking order at the same food bowls.[58] This is a rather dramatic example of the plasticity of even our skeletal and nervous systems.

Even when it comes to hormones we have been misled. Scientific investigation into the hormonal secretions of testes and ovaries, beginning in the nineteenth century, presumed inherent differences and female inferiority. The mischaracterization of the "sex hormones," testosterone and estrogen, dates back to the Victorian era when these two hormones, found in all humans, were first studied and took on antagonistic characteristics that mapped political notions onto human physiology. As Fausto-Sterling explains, "Physiological functions became political allegory—which, ironically, made them more or less credible, because they seemed so compatible with what people already 'knew' about the nature of sex difference."[59] Despite the fact that these hormones affect bones, blood, liver, kidneys, and heart, testosterone and estrogen took on properties that were entirely social, not biological. Even the naming of these hormones reflected cultural biases: *estrus*, derived from Latin, means "crazy" or "insane" and came to be the root of the name for the female hormone estrogen in the late 1930s.[60] There is a correlation between amounts of testosterone and estrogen and one's physical sex; these hormones are often prescribed for those transgender people who are transitioning from one sex to another. But the popular concept that they are exclusively sex hormones does not correspond to science.

Biological determinism also appears to run into difficulties with evolving consciousness and science. Though a minority of men and women have "passed" as the other gender for centuries, it is only with the rise of medical technology and the social consciousness that arose from the LGBT struggles in the late twentieth century that transsexuality became possible and more widely desirable. Transsexuals are a relatively new category, despite evidence cited earlier regarding the sex reassignment surgeries in Russia after the 1917 revolution. The existence today of tens of thousands of people who have used surgery and hormones to alter their birth genitals—though not all transgender people alter their bodies—raises the prospect of other sexual types developing in the future as well.

Transgender people, those whose gender identity does not jibe with the gender assigned them at birth, do not necessarily seek any alteration of their genitalia. They do, however, seek equitable treatment and respect, starting with full legal rights as included in an International Bill of Gender Rights.[61]

Among the many ways that transgender peoples' lives are deprecated and invalidated is through the ubiquitous, and unnecessary, requirement to specify gender on legal forms from passports to drivers' licenses. They are caught in a legal and social quandary. If transgender people check the "wrong" box they can be subject to harassment or arrest if discovered to be biologically at odds with the box that was ticked. Like forms requiring us to announce our relationship status as married, single, or divorced, these gender boxes provide more information about the society we live in than the individuals we are. After all, why would any divorcée choose to identify herself for all time by a failed relationship that has ended? For that matter, why in a society in which millions of women go years or even decades without wearing a dress is the universal sign for the women's room a stick figure in a dress? It is the most perverse and pervasive enforcement of gender norms we all encounter on a daily basis. Of course, even the fact that we have separate restrooms for men and women is an outgrowth of social norms, not a biological necessity. Being accosted or derided for going to the "wrong" bathroom is one of the most noted daily humiliations of transgender people, thus their demand for gender-neutral bathrooms.

The fact that conventional gender roles today prevail throughout much of the world is not proof of their biological link but a testament to the globalization of capitalism and its social prerogatives. Class society's need for the nuclear family and its attendant gender roles have allowed gender to acquire the status of human nature—as have greed, competition, and militarism. Biology does impose certain limits on our behavior, but not nearly to the degree many scientists would have us believe. Evolutionary biologist Stephen Jay Gould explains,

"Violence, sexism, and general nastiness are biological since they represent one subset of a possible range of behaviors. But peacefulness, equality, and kindness are just as biological—and we may see their influence increase if we can create social structures that permit them to flourish."[62] Or as one theorist puts it, "biology is politics by other means."[63] Socialist Phil Gasper sums up the pursuit of genetic origins to our behavior effectively:

> The attempt to explain important features of society in evolutionary or genetic terms—biological determinism—has two goals. First, it tries to convince us that the social order is a consequence of unchanging human biology, so that inequality and injustice cannot be eliminated. Second, in the case of problems that are impossible to ignore, it tells us to look for the solution at the level of the individual and not at the level of social institutions. The problems lie not in the structure of society, but in some of the individuals who make up society. The solution is thus to change—or even eliminate—the individuals, not to challenge existing social structures.[64]

In sum, sexuality and gender are socially constructed and in order for human beings to achieve self-determination, we must transform the social order that narrows and pathologizes some kinds of human behavior.

CHAPTER EIGHT

An Injury to One
Is an Injury to All

The prospect for building solidarity among LGBT people and other oppressed and exploited people exists today to a degree unthinkable in previous generations. As a result of past struggles and the resulting shifts in consciousness, increasing numbers of sexual minorities no longer feel the need to remain closeted. According to the most recent Harris Poll, nearly three-quarters of the American population personally knows or works with someone who is gay, lesbian, bisexual, or transgender.[1] This has had a demonstrable impact on heterosexuals' consciousness. Nearly 80 percent of U.S. adults say their attitudes toward LGBT people are more favorable today than in the past.[2]

Census figures show that LGBT people live in every city, suburb, and many small towns throughout the United States, despite the fact that San Francisco, New York, and Los Angeles remain urban meccas for LGBT people. Wilton Manors, Florida, is probably unknown to most readers of these pages, yet it has the third largest concentration of gay men in the country.[3] The Dakotas, Montana, Wyoming, and West Virginia have the largest numbers of senior same-sex couples; while small towns like Sumter, South Carolina, and Pine Bluff,

Arkansas, are among the Southern communities that large numbers of African-American gay and lesbian couples call home.[4] Though the Census Bureau does not ask about sexual identity directly, and does not track transgender or bisexual people, the most recent survey, taken in 2000, asked about the sex of each person in the household and respondents could check either "husband/wife" or "unmarried partner." Extrapolating from those figures and a smaller 2005 sampling, experts at the Williams Institute, affiliated with the UCLA School of Law, suggest that there were approximately 8.8 million gay, lesbian, and bisexual adults in the country in 2007.[5] Given that some remain closeted or would not feel comfortable responding truthfully to official surveys, and transgender people are not officially counted, it's clear that the population of sexual minorities in the United States must be even greater. The fact that people no longer must move to major urban centers in order to live openly gay lives is a reflection of progress from previous struggles and drives the advance of civil rights battles beyond the traditional LGBT-friendly urban enclaves.

Alongside these advances, bigotry, institutional discrimination, and violence persist. However, unity among ordinary people who share common experiences of exploitation and oppression—regardless of sexual or gender identity—is possible. Straight working-class people do not benefit from the continued oppression of LGBT people, even if some believe otherwise. Under capitalism, the ongoing oppression of sexual minorities serves the interests of the ruling class—those who own and control production, the dissemination of ideas through media and education, and other resources. The ruling class needs the nuclear family and divisions among workers to continue making profits and to maintain its control over the majority. The nuclear family's role in privatizing child-rearing, housework, and cooking, etc., lets bosses off the hook from paying for these services. LGBT people flout the gender norms that families are supposed to embody through their mere existence. If any and every sexual and gender arrangement were permissible, the wage gap between men and women and the privatized burdens of family life would be placed into question.

Though some working-class straights buy into the notion that they benefit from gender stereotypes, sexual repression, and homophobia, they are in fact hurt as well. While some individual working-class straights do use nasty slurs or commit acts of violence against LGBT people, it is not in their interest to do so. Screaming "faggot" at a coworker is not only insulting, it also corrodes the potential for solidarity against the boss who denies them both decent benefits and wages. Battering a neighbor because he wears a dress is not only potentially lethal, but also prevents both batterer and victim from waging a common fight against a landlord for heat or services. A minority of heterosexuals carry out acts of bigotry against LGBT people because, in addition to the competition under capitalism that exists between bosses for profits, there is competition among workers as well, for jobs, housing, education, etc. Set against each other in this way, atomized and isolated, workers at times express their rage by turning against one another rather than the system and the class that exploits and oppresses them. After all, it is always easier to kick down than to kick up. Viewed in this way, instead of gay and trans bashings expressing the power of straight people over others, these are acts of powerlessness. This is not to excuse or in any way justify discrimination or violence—far from

it. Rather, if activists are to pose a serious challenge to the status quo, they must be able to explain why working-class
straight people sometimes lash out at LGBT people.

Marxists argue that workers can only fundamentally alter
their oppressive and exploitative conditions by organizing as a
class to transform the material conditions that stoke bigotry
among ordinary people. This is why Marx argued that capitalism creates its own "gravedigger" in the working class. Sharon
Smith explains:

> [W]hen Marx defined the working class as the agent for
> revolutionary change, he was describing its historical poten-
> tial, rather than a foregone conclusion. While capitalism pro-
> pels workers toward collective forms of struggle, it also
> forces them into competition. The unremitting pressure
> from a layer of unemployed workers, which exists in most
> economies even in times of "full employment," is a deterrent
> to struggle—a constant reminder that workers compete for
> limited jobs which afford a decent standard of living.[6]

Solidarity between LGBT and straight workers is impeded
so long as some workers cling to backward ideas—whether
they're homophobic, sexist, or racist. Italian socialist Antonio
Gramsci explained how most people walk around with "contradictory consciousness":

> The active man-in-the-mass has a practical activity, but has
> no clear theoretical consciousness of his practical activity,
> which nonetheless involves understanding the world in so
> far as it transforms it. His theoretical consciousness can in-
> deed be historically in opposition to his activity. One might
> almost say that he has two theoretical consciousnesses (or
> one contradictory consciousness): one which is implicit in
> his activity and which in reality unites him with all his fel-
> low workers in the practical transformation of the real

world; and one, superficially explicit or verbal, which he
has inherited from the past and uncritically absorbed.[7]

In other words, people simultaneously hold onto ideas that
both reflect their lived experiences, which are popularly interpreted for us by those who own and control power, while also
having commonsense ideas that are inherited from the past.
Straight workers who express homophobic and transphobic
ideas do so because they live in a society devoted to profit,
which requires the bombardment of ideologies to help shore
it up through educational, religious, and popular means. One
inbuilt contradiction of capitalism is that the same forces that
aim to crush working-class people also create conditions for
unity. Material conditions exist to allow most people who are
exploited and oppressed to shed reactionary ideas and to em-
pathize and organize with others. However people may identify their sexual preferences and desires, all workers must
work and struggle to pay the bills. And since straight working-class people are neither the oppressors of LGBT people
nor beneficiaries of that oppression, the conditions exist for
them to break with homophobic and other reactionary ideas.
Just because someone cannot identify *as* gay or transsexual
does not mean that they cannot identify *with* gays or transsexuals. Workers who reject these discriminatory ideas that
serve as obstacles to unified action must challenge their
coworkers, friends, classmates, and family members who
hold them.

What's class got to do with it?

Rather than one community with a common experience and
perspective, LGBT people—like straights—are significantly

shaped by their economic class. Though sexual minorities can be found in every occupation and class, it is logical to assume that because the overwhelming majority of the population is working class, so too are most LGBT people. That is, whether they are white-collar professionals or blue-collar workers, most LGBT people must sell their labor to an employer in order to live, thus creating a common class interest with others who may not share their sexual identity. This creates the potential for solidarity along class lines.

The most authoritative demographic studies of the LGBT population in the United States come out of the Williams Institute. Their latest figures have been compiled from the data of same-sex couples in 2005, numbering 776,943—up 20 percent from 2000, a drastic increase that is likely a reflection, in part, of the easing social stigma many LGBT people feel regarding their sexuality.[8] Despite the popular culture's stereotypes about gay men, men in same-sex couples in the United States earn significantly less on average than their straight counterparts, $43,117 compared to $49,777, while the median income of men in same-sex couples is 15 percent less than straight married men, $32,500 compared with $38,000.[9] While women in same-sex couples earn less than men, their incomes are actually higher than that of married women, $34,979 on average (with a median income of $28,600) compared with heterosexual married women's average income of $26,265 (and their median income of $21,000).[10] This discrepancy is likely due to the fact that only 20 percent of all same-sex couples have children under eighteen in the home, thus far fewer lesbians than straight women are likely to have taken years off work or delayed paid employment to have children, which suppresses earnings.

One ethnographic study of gay and bisexual blue-collar men in the United States found that most of these men at the turn of the twenty-first century were out to their families, friends, and coworkers.[11] Greater class pressure to be macho means working-class gay men often defy gay stereotypes in their dress and mannerisms and are assumed to be straight by casual acquaintances. Though many reported antigay discrimination at certain points in their lives and some offensive slurs on the job, most felt they were looked down on by middle-class gays and said their greatest challenges were economic. Comments like these about bourgeois gay men are peppered throughout their interviews:

> Middle-class men are clones who like to mess with us but won't give us the time of day when it's over. They are focused on identity and determined to overcome it. They try too hard to be accepted.

> They are less inclined to develop political alliances but cling to right-wing models of individuality.

> Every middle-class fag wants to snag a doctor. Working-class men are more apt to experience discrimination from the middle-class queers than from the straights.[12]

These comments echo similar ones from working-class lesbians interviewed in another study.[13] One lesbian complains about the political coalitions most LGBT groups seek out. "I'm disturbed by the push for alliance with the corporate boardroom and not the union hall," Joanna Kadi says.[14] Others are irritated by middle-class assumptions about higher rates of homophobia among workers, who have less free time for movement involvement and so are not as well represented in groups like Parents and Friends of Lesbians and Gays (P-FLAG), although working-class family members are as likely as middle-class ones to be supportive. These studies are by necessity anecdotal given the difficulty of gaining accurate statistics on sexuality, yet point to a crucial truth. Middle-class presumptions about "the LGBT community" that in the past have driven movement organizing are not only offensive to many working-class gays but are also often inaccurate.

The interaction between workplace organizing and the fight for LGBT rights has a long history. Some of the research that historian Allan Bérubé did on the Marine Cooks and Stewards Union (MCS) in the 1930s and 1940s shows how, prior to the emergence of gay rights organizations in the United States, a largely gay and multiracial group of workers led by communists on passenger ships transformed a reactionary union into one that defended gay rights, challenged racism, and won material gains for all of them until McCarthyite tactics tore them apart in the 1950s.

> Bérubé explored the connections of class, race and sexuality in the life of this union. Former members of MCS told him that gay men made up the majority of the stewards on many passenger lines. Decades before the first U.S. gay rights organizations, the MCS won the first on the job protection for gay workers. There were so many gay men in the union that straight stewards were often also queer-baited and understood how such baiting was a tactic used to divide workers. Gay men were accepted because they were workers just like any other.[15]

There was nothing automatic about the overt pro-gay and antiracist positions of MCS, which had initially been formed in 1901 by white workers attempting to keep Chinese immigrant workers from gaining jobs on the passenger lines.[16] It was the militant San Francisco general strike in 1934 and active participation from organized communists on the passenger ships in the 1930s that sparked the fight to racially integrate the union and take on homophobia at a time when there was no organized force doing so. Workers learned from their own experiences that if they didn't welcome Blacks, gays, and other oppressed groups into their ranks, the bosses would use racism and homophobia to divide them and bust their union. Revels Cayton, a Black, gay MCS leader, posed the argument this way, "If you let them red bait, they'll race bait. If you let them race bait, they'll queen bait. These are connected—that's why we have to stick together."[17] MSC grew in strength, numbering twenty thousand workers at its height, and was legendary for its Black, gay, militant leadership and the sign that hung in their union hall that read: "Race-baiting, Red-baiting, and Queer-baiting is Anti-Union."[18] In the anti-communist hysteria of the 1950s, the union was smashed with help from the FBI.

Harry Hay, the founder of the first U.S. gay organization, the Mattachine Society, got his start as a union organizer in the 1930s and 1940s in New York's Department Store Workers Union with the International Workers of the World (IWW). Hay drew on the invaluable experience he and the other four Mattachine Society founders got in their clandestine union activities.[19] Because their union drives needed to stay underground early on in order to prevent the bosses from learning about their doings until they had developed a critical mass of supporters, Hay and the others learned certain skills that informed their later practice. He explains, "The first five members of the Mattachine Society were all union members experienced in working in underground unions. We took an oath that we would plead the Fifth Amendment before we divulged information of any sort about the group."[20] Obviously, after Stonewall this kind of cloak-and-dagger approach was no longer necessary.

Harvey Milk and labor versus the bigots

By 1977, more than thirty American cities or counties had legislation barring discrimination against lesbians and gays. Thirty years later, twenty states, Washington, D.C., and 140 counties and cities have sexual identity non-discrimination laws, while California also bars discrimination based on "gender identity, appearance and behavior."[21] These civil rights protections have not come easily.

The rise of the religious right in the late seventies took gay activists by surprise when pop singer and orange juice spokeswoman Anita Bryant threw down the gauntlet launching the culture war. Her Save Our Children campaign in Dade County, Florida—a response to antidiscrimination legislation—set a combative tone with Bryant's verbal salvo: "What these people really want, hidden behind obscure legal phrases, is the legal right to propose to our children that theirs is an acceptable alternate way of life.... I will lead such a crusade to stop it as this country has not seen before."[22] Save Our Children was not only successful at winning over a majority of voters to repeal the Dade County pro-gay legislation, but went on to wage successful repeal campaigns in St. Paul, Minnesota, Wichita, Kansas, and Eugene, Oregon.[23] This flurry of setbacks was stemmed by the organizing efforts of newly formed LGBT groups organizing alongside labor unions in California, with the creative spokesmanship of the nation's first openly gay elected official, San Francisco supervisor Harvey Milk.

Milk was a former marine and ex-stockbroker from New York, whose irreverent and charismatic flair and humor are captured in Randy Shilts's *The Mayor of Castro Street* and brilliantly portrayed by Sean Penn in the movie *Milk*. He was hardly a born radical, having campaigned for segregationist Republican Barry Goldwater, and he was a supporter of the war in Vietnam early on.[24] But Milk left New York and his conservative politics behind and embraced populist and often radical politics as a small businessman operating in the nation's swiftly evolving gay ghetto, Castro Street, San Francisco. There, the local movie marquee announced: "Give me your weak, your huddled, your oppressed and your horny looking for a little action."[25] The Castro district's working-class neighborhood was rapidly transforming in the 1970s into a vibrant and popular LGBT quarter.

In 1974, Teamster representative Allan Baird took the unprecedented step of approaching gay labor activist Howard Wallace and Milk, considered an unofficial local gay leader before his 1978 election, to help truckers win a boycott against Coors beer for refusing to sign a union contract. Not only did Milk and Wallace win over gay and lesbian bars and clientele to join the boycott, but they also won Teamster jobs for gays in exchange, including a truck-driving job for Wallace.[26] Their organizing efforts were so successful that they eventually slashed Coors's sales in California from 43 percent to 14 percent, spread the boycott to thirteen other states, and established links with Latino workers and organizations like Crusade for Justice that endured for future battles.[27] In response to Coors's policy of denying employment to gays and lesbians, labor leaders argued, "Anyone who pays dues to the union should not have their private life the subject of anything of an employer on the job. It's only elementary human rights to defend the rights of lesbian and gay workers."[28] Born and raised in the Castro district, Teamster organizer Allen Baird, who was married and straight, had to endure verbal harassment and aspersions cast his way for organizing with gays, yet he argued with union brothers and sisters about the need for unity. Milk's ongoing collaboration with labor unions led to official political endorsements from the city's truckers, firefighters, and construction workers, who filled his Castro Street camera shop to stamp campaign flyers, along with the unlikely promotion from firemen whose rubber coats bore the message: "Make Mine Milk."[29]

In 1978, an Orange County conservative state legislator, John Briggs, placed Proposition 6 on the ballot calling for the firing of any California teacher caught "advocating, imposing, encouraging or promoting" homosexuality.[30] Initially, Briggs' attempts to stoke bigotry were successful, with more than 60 percent of those polled supporting the measure.[31] However, the earlier Coors boycott had set the stage for organizing against the Briggs Initiative.

Howard Wallace's Bay Area Gay Liberation (BAGL) committee, which formed in 1975 out of the Coors boycott, joined twenty-one local unions in pledging support for gay rights and opposition to the Briggs Initiative.[32] Statewide rallies, speakouts, popular concerts, and aggressive campaigning against this anti-union and homophobic legislation won over the majority of Californians, who voted down the ballot measure, which lost by more than a million votes.[33] Thousands of previously in-

active and apolitical gays and lesbians as well as straight unionists mobilized together in an effort that opened the door to a
partnership that introduced some workers to new allies and allowed some LGBT workers to come out at work and begin
fighting for civil rights within their unions. In some workplaces
homophobic language and behavior on the job was openly
challenged and derided as anti-union. The hospital workers'
union leader announced, "There will be no more derogatory
language or references to lesbian and gay people in the staff of
the union."[34] BAGL's mass organizing tactics, which con-
sciously mirrored militant trade unionism's pickets, demon-
strations, and mass leafleting campaigns, signaled a sharp
departure from the traditional backroom power-brokering, according to the *San Francisco Bay Guardian*.[35] Their aggressive
organizing tactics led the California Teachers Association to
mail out 2.3 million "No on 6" voter cards throughout the
state.[36] In an interview with gay labor activist Susan Moir, she
points to the Briggs battle as a touchstone for future fights and
explains how many straight unionists have come to view LGBT
rights. "A lot of union people don't understand it [gay rights]
intellectually and are not going around talking about it, but
they recognize that in society there are winners and losers and
that the losers don't stand a chance if they're not united against
the winners.... An attack on queer teachers was an attack on
teachers, and teachers are workers."[37]

Just weeks after the Briggs Initiative went down to defeat,
a conservative ex-policeman, former fireman, and city official
named Dan White slipped into City Hall and assassinated the
liberal mayor George Moscone and newly elected supervisor
Harvey Milk. Having anticipated his own killing a year earlier,
Milk had made a tape that friends played upon hearing the

news of his death. In an act of political chutzpah, Milk's recording declared himself a committed gay movement activist to the end, named and derided moderate political gays who equivocated and quelled struggles rather than leading them, and then named who he believed his successors should and should not be in the event of assassination. Finally, he repeated a sentiment he had expressed many times on the campaign trail, "Let the bullet that rips my brain open every closet door in America."[38] As if heeding his call, at least forty thousand gays and straights marched in a funeral procession through the streets of San Francisco.[39] Milk's killer, White, was treated as a hero by the local police, who had abused the gay community for years. White received seven years' prison for manslaughter (he served five) instead of premeditated murder, and the jury's light punishment sparked fury throughout the city. Thousands of people took to the streets upon hearing the verdict, chanting "We want justice" and "Remember Harvey Milk." They overturned and set fire to police cars and smashed through the ornate glass doors of City Hall.[40] Police responded violently, raided the gay Elephant Walk bar, and beat patrons bloody. One hundred gays and lesbians and sixty cops were hospitalized in what has come to be known as the White Night Riots.[41] Twenty-year-old Nina D'Amato wrote the following account of her participation in that riot in a letter to her twin brother, Paul:

> I participated in a riot of about 10,000 people (*10* thousand people, that is humanoids of almost every age, race and sexual preference, not *5* thousand *gays* only) that began at the Civic Center. You probably read that it began as a result of the Dan White verdict, which is true, but it became more than that…. [W]e were like AMAZED and HORROR

SHOCKED to find ourselves in the midst of what looked like the DESTRUCTION of the AMERICAN DEMOCRATIC CONSTITUTIONALLY SANCTIFIED CAPITALIST WAY...or something...The windows of city hall had been broken (that's lots of windows) so the riot squad was surrounding the building. They were being kept occupied by lots of verbal threats and broken glass being thrown at them, so...everyone else started trashing everything in sight and lighting every police car within a mile on fire. It was great. It was amazing how well everybody worked together—most of the buildings in the civic center were trashed (mainly windows broken) but everyone agreed not to touch the library, and it wasn't. When the police started chasing sections of the crowd people were warning and helping each other right away (consequently, very few people got hurt). It was so strange, people would scream, "Kill the Pigs," etc., as they ran from them, but would all be laughing when we got to a safe spot.... I think just about anybody who was angry about anything showed up... (Did you know that asshole was an advocate of the death penalty??).... My bank branch had all its windows broken.[42]

One fascinating aspect of Nina's colorful account of the riot is how seamlessly an explosion ostensibly in response to an antigay verdict became a broader struggle against the economic and political forces that confine all working-class people's lives. The police, the seat of municipal power, and the banks were targeted, while the library was not; and the people in the crowd identified with and helped each other. In other words, the explosion of rage that night was not only against a system that let off with minimal punishment a killer of a popular gay leader but also an assault on the symbols of power and wealth.

Organizing in the downturn

The long-term impact of the Coors boycott, Briggs battle, and response to the assassination of Harvey Milk continued to shape LGBT activists' consciousness even during the 1980s and 1990s' downturn in protest activity. After the White Night Riots, there was an uptick in gay-labor organizing that at times reflected the class divisions within the LGBT community. A Castro district gay and lesbian caucus of the Hotel Restaurant and Bar Employees union Local 2 put out a newsletter called *Dishrag* to express their displeasure with both the continued low wages paid by gay bar owners and the antigay harassment Local 2 employees experienced. In it, workers declared:

> We are NOT gay mascots of the present union administration, easing the way for a union drive that builds the union treasury while disrespecting individuals and institutions within the gay community. NEITHER are we in cahoots with bar owners represented by the Tavern Guild who promote a false 'Gay Unity' that secures profits but not wages, benefits or decent working conditions for gay employees.... We won't choose any longer between job security and simple respect and support around being gay—we want it all.[43]

Their union drive at a gay-owned Castro Street café brought out class tensions between LGBT workers and bosses who fought their six-month picket line. As one striker put it, "It was the first strike in the gay Castro. It didn't go down easily. It left a kind of bitterness in a lot of people's craw for a while."[44] It was the first time class lines in the heart of the gay ghetto were so starkly drawn and many of the most class-conscious LGBT workers began to throw in their lot with labor.

The AFL-CIO's Industrial Unions Department, which oversees the organizing of "hard hat" workers, came out against antigay discrimination in 1982, long before most cities and states. One year later, the AFL-CIO's national convention unanimously voted to support gay rights, which it has since reaffirmed.[45] Wallace and other vets from those earlier fights went on to found the labor movement's official LGBT caucus, Pride at Work.

The 1987 March on Washington presented an opportunity for left-wing LGBT labor activists, some of whom were organized socialists, to meet and begin coordinating activities inside the union movement to expand nondiscrimination efforts in more workplaces and unions. These groups were often small initially and received little or no union funding. For example, only ten activists from New York's 135,000-member District Council 37 representing city and state employees met to start a local caucus there in 1989.[46] Their perspective of linking labor and gay rights led them to close collaboration with other minority caucuses like the Coalition of Labor Union Women and Coalition of Black Trade Unionists to fight in local struggles to win concrete gains. Howard Wallace was appointed by the largely Latino United Farm Workers (UFW) president Cesar Chavez to be a full-time liaison to LGBT people to spread a grape boycott that was under way, while the UFW pledged support for gay and lesbian issues.[47] Lavender Caucuses began springing up in different workplaces to demand domestic partnership benefits, which in a society lacking universal health care in the midst of the AIDS crisis took on new urgency for gay men in particular. The case of one Black gay New York City librarian, Nat Keitt, who fought for health benefits for his AIDS-afflicted lover, is featured in the 1996 documentary *Out at Work*. Keitt and other LGBT workers, including previously closeted Chrysler electrician Ron Woods, used their struggles against workplace discrimination to promote the national launch of Pride at Work in 1994, which was recognized as an AFL-CIO constituency group in August 1997.[48]

Pride at Work's consistent commitment to fighting for LGBT rights inside American workplaces has coincided with the steady decline of unionization, an employers' offensive to increase profits at any human cost, and the stranglehold of the Democratic Party over the trade union leadership and progressive movement activists. As discussed earlier, the strategy of looking to the Democrats without mobilizing mass pressure has not been an effective one. Unionization, while up slightly in 2008 to include 12.6 percent of the American labor force (more than sixteen million workers), has been in steady decline since 1979.[49] This leaves the overwhelming majority of all workers outside the protection of organized labor, inside which wages and benefits tend to be better. The willingness of union and movement leaders to view the Democrats as the main vehicle for change has meant there has been no activist strategy to win the federal workplace antidiscrimination legislation, ENDA, which continues to languish in Congress after more than three decades. As socialist Lance Selfa writes,

> Historically, the two-party system has played the role of shock absorber, trying to head off or co-opt restive segments of the electorate. It aims to manage political change so that change occurs at a pace that big business can accept. For most of the last century the Democratic Party has been the most successful at playing this shock-absorber role.[50]

Perhaps the biggest bright spot for LGBT workers has been the steady growth in the number of corporations offering domestic partner benefits. New York City's independent, unionized weekly paper, the *Village Voice*, in 1982 became the first company to secure equitable benefits for non-married partners of employees regardless of sexual orientation.[51] Today, thousands of non-union and union corporations offer domestic partner benefits, but they are often misconceived as a special accommodation to same-sex couples when in fact most beneficiaries are straight. In most workplaces that offer them, from 1 to 5 percent of the workforce apply for them and typically 50 to 70 percent of those who take advantage of the benefits are non-married heterosexual couples.[52] Health insurance companies' homophobic and unscientific claims that gays are more costly to insure due to AIDS has often led them to add a surcharge to companies and municipalities offering such benefits. However, that surcharge is often returned at the end of the fiscal year as such fears prove unfounded. In fact, the City of West Hollywood actually saved $65,000 in the first six months of offering these benefits.[53]

The low cost of domestic partner benefits to employers is one significant reason why thousands of companies, universities, and cities offer them today. Another is the goodwill factor. As greater numbers of LGBT people come out of the closet, and younger straight couples forgo or delay marriage, Corporate America has hit upon these benefits as a way of presenting themselves as open-minded, socially conscious conservators of the bottom line. Nearly 90 percent of the five hundred largest publicly traded companies, the Fortune 500, prohibit discrimination against gays and lesbians on the job, while more than 50 percent provide domestic partner health insurance benefits.[54] The more profitable a firm is, the more likely it is to provide them. The fact that CEOs of some of these conglomerates have signed on to local pro-gay legislation, however, is most often an expression of crass business logic. In a society in which gays and lesbians are in the boardroom as well as on the shop floor, corporations are in competition with each other for talent—regardless of sexual identity. In the face of proposed legislation against LGBT people in Indiana, for example, pharmaceutical giant Eli Lilly weighed in this way: "Given the great lengths Lilly takes to attract and retain top talent from around the world, we oppose any legislation that might impair our ability to offer competitive employee benefits or negatively impact our recruitment and retention."[55]

However, Exxon Mobil and Wal-Mart, which have traded number one and two slots on the Fortune 500 list for years, continue to discriminate against LGBT people on the job, exposing the fact that even these rights have not come easily. Workplace LGBT caucuses inside white-collar and often non-union companies have been instrumental in pushing for reforms. It is no coincidence that some of the most rapid growth in workplace nondiscrimination codes and benefits came about along with the last high point for LGBT struggles, during the early 1990s AIDS movement when employee networks sprouted to organize and advocate for them.[56] But with the demobilization of movement activists, who relied on the Clinton administration to deliver reform without struggle, many worker activists adhered to a course of "unobtrusive mobilization" and "professionalism"—in other words, backroom meetings in lieu of protests.[57]

By the time ABC aired the historic TV episode in which Ellen Degeneres came out as a lesbian on her sitcom *Ellen* in 1997, 42 percent of Americans believed that equal workplace rights for LGBT people already existed.[58] In response to this misperception, HRC tried to broadcast an ad explaining that forty-one states still discriminated against sexual minorities at work, yet ABC refused to allow them to buy air time nationally, limiting the ad's visibility to select markets. The cultural right protested the show and the ad for their advocacy of "special rights" for gays and continues to promote this fiction.

Myths about Black homophobia

One section of the U.S. population has been singled out in the media as being particularly homophobic—Blacks. If accurate, this would pose a significant obstacle to class unity in a society where nearly 13 percent are African American. However, polls show a marginal difference in attitudes between the races and indicate that people of all races between eighteen and thirty-four have more favorable opinions on issues directly affecting LGBT people than those over the age of sixty-five.[59] In fact, regarding the question of expanding hate-crimes legislation to include LGBT people, 71 percent of African Americans approve, far more than other polled racial groups (61 percent of whites and Latinos approve, by comparison).[60] On other issues, such as adoption rights and allowing gays and lesbians to serve openly in the military, Blacks and whites differ by only two or three percentage points.[61]

In the wake of Barack Obama's historic 2008 presidential victory, a false and reactionary narrative emerged that blamed Black voters for the gay marriage ban, Proposition 8, that passed by a 52 to 48 percent margin in California. While Florida and Arizona also passed same-sex marriage bans, the vote for Prop 8 in the politically progressive state of California was widely attributed to the enormous surge of Black voters, 70 percent of whom approved the ban, according to exit polls, reversing the state's May 2008 Supreme Court decision allowing lesbians and gays to marry. The widely publicized exit poll numbers are challenged by a January 2009 study commissioned by the National Gay and Lesbian Task Force (NGLTF), which conducted an in-depth analysis of election returns in several California counties. Researchers found that between 57 and 59 percent of African Americans voted in favor of Prop 8, not 70 percent. In addition, four pre-election polls among Blacks on Prop 8 showed support for the antigay marriage initiative between 41 and 58 percent.[62] The exit polls showed that 53 percent of Latinos voted for the ban, as well as around 49 percent of white voters.[63] The state's Black population is 6.2 percent, and it accounted for 10 percent of the overall vote. In other words, blaming African Americans for the referendum's passage ignores 90 percent of the vote.

It also ignores recent history. To judge from social research, had there been an unapologetically pro-civil rights campaign, there would have been the prospect of a different outcome. The most recent comprehensive study of Black attitudes toward homosexuality, which combines thirty-one national surveys from 1973 to 2000, came to a fascinating conclusion. The Georgia State study found that "blacks appear to be more likely than whites *both* to see homosexuality as wrong *and* to favor gay-rights laws,"[64] indicating that African Americans' religiosity has many believing homosexuality is a sin, while their own experience of oppression leads them to oppose discrimination. This was borne out in the 2004 elections, where in the six states with substantial Black populations that had same-sex marriage bans on their ballots, Blacks were slightly *less* likely than whites to vote for them.[65]

Nationally, 55 percent of all Americans approve of "legally sanctioned gay and lesbian unions or partnerships,"[66] a dramatic shift from just a few years ago. If an explicit case in favor of gay marriage were made by activists, a multiracial majority could be won over in coming years. The exit poll statistics from California don't explain the more important story of why so many of California's Black, Brown, and white citizens—who voted overwhelmingly for the first African-American president by a 56 to 37 percent margin—also supported striking down civil rights for lesbians and gays. The most critical reason was the ineffective strategy used by pro–gay marriage forces that adhered closely to the Democratic Party's—and Barack Obama's—equivocal position on the issue. While formally opposing Prop 8, both Obama and his running mate Joe Biden were vocal throughout the campaign about their personal discomfort with and opposition to same-sex marriage. It seems reasonable to assume that the outcome of the Prop 8 vote could have been quite different if Obama had come out against it, given his massive popular appeal.

Despite the unprecedented and astonishing sums of money raised to fight the referendum—the pro-equality side took in $43.6 million, compared with $29.8 million for the anti–gay marriage forces—the No on 8 side lost. The statewide No on 8 Coalition didn't use the money for a grassroots organizing campaign. It didn't put out a call for activists to hit the phones, knock on doors, and hold rallies and actions to publicly denounce the bigotry of the measure—though in a few cases, most notably the California Teachers Association, activists took the initiative to do so on their own.

Prominent African Americans such as Martin Luther King's widow, Coretta Scott King, and civil rights activist Al Sharpton have frequently spoken out for gay civil rights, including marriage, and repeatedly warned against the divisive tactics used by the right. Sharpton was a frequent participant in ACT UP rallies and marches for AIDS funding in the late 1980s and early 1990s. Reverend Jesse Jackson, long a vocal supporter of LGBT rights, has taken an equivocal position on gay marriage, yet opposes any bans. In a prominent Harvard Law School speech, Jackson made a point of distancing the civil rights struggles of Blacks and that of gays by arguing that as gays have never been enslaved or denied their voting rights they should not agitate for reforms in the terms of the civil rights movement. Yet, as members of the National Black Justice Coalition have asserted, one doesn't have to experience the same history of oppression to "share a common denominator" and demand civil rights.[67]

The legacy of identity politics organizing in the United States often lends itself to an unproductive "oppression Olympics" in which different groups compete, in a sense, for which one is lowest on the totem pole. It seems a politically useless endeavor, as it only mirrors the ideological framework of the dominant class in whose interest these divisions persist. The unique history of African-American enslavement and the persistence of systematic dehumanization on the basis of skin color are undeniably woven throughout the fabric of many aspects of American society. Arguing for civil rights for LGBT people doesn't diminish the oppression and struggle of Blacks; rather, it draws lessons from them and expands society's concept of justice. What is key to liberation is not the ranking of oppressions but devising strategies for uniting the oppressed.

When the AIDS crisis first surfaced in the early 1980s in the United States, it was largely white gay men and intravenous drug users who were its initial victims. Today, the face of AIDS in the United States is increasingly Black. The latest figures on

HIV/AIDS in the United States from the Centers for Disease Control show that 49 percent of those newly infected with HIV are Black, and more than half of them are gay or bisexual men; the infection rate among Black women is fifteen times that of white women.[68] African-American civil rights leader Julian Bond argues, "Our inability to talk about sex, and more specifically homosexuality, is the single greatest barrier to the prevention of HIV transmission in our community. Intolerance has driven our gay friends and neighbors into the shadows. Men leading double lives—on the 'down low'—put our women at extreme risk."[69] Bond is correct, though there has been some progress and new initiatives have been undertaken in the Black community to educate people and fight for AIDS funding, with little federal support. The high cost of AIDS treatment drugs and the disproportionate numbers of Blacks who do not have access to health care creates a deadly combination.

It is a feature of continued racism in America that the Black church is often held uniquely accountable for its homophobia and inactivity in the face of AIDS. The mostly white Catholic Church, like the Black churches, also turned its back on HIV/AIDS sufferers and demonized the lifestyles of all those who were dying horrific deaths in isolation from any societal support, which is why its leading clergy and institutions were targets of some of the most heated protests of the late 1980s and early 1990s. However, the enormous wealth of the Catholic Church, in stark contrast to most Black churches, renders its culpability that much worse.

The Christian right has not been alone in using divide-and-conquer tactics. The self-styled bête noir of the gay right and former editor of the *New Republic*, Andrew Sullivan, has stoked this notion of exceptional Black homophobia. "Why would we want to be involved with the Black community? After all, they're so much more homophobic than whites," he insisted in an interview with Charlie Rose.[70] Barbara Smith, a Black lesbian feminist historian, took on his challenge brilliantly:

> I think that racist white lesbians and gay men like to pretend that people of color are more homophobic than white people as an excuse for not working with people of color or working on issues of concern to people of color. The fact that the right wing is more than 99 percent white doesn't seem to make any difference in their assessments. Institutionalized homophobia in this society is definitely a white monopoly. And when we do see examples of homophobia in people-of-color contexts, what that should motivate people to do is to increase the level of solidarity with gay men and lesbians of color so that we can challenge homophobia wherever it appears.[71]

Here Smith is not just taking on the implicit racism of the notion that Blacks are somehow more homophobic than whites; she raises a key point for white gay progressives to consider and act upon. Unless LGBT struggles solidarize with the struggles of people of color, gay struggles will not only be less diverse, they are less likely to succeed, especially as U.S. society becomes increasingly multiracial.

The fight for reforms

One question raised by the struggles of the recent past is whether activists should fight for reforms *or* revolution. As stated earlier, incremental change and total transformation can be reciprocal, that is, winning gains in the here and now can often lead to the kinds of organizational methods and confidence to fight for even more. Winning an end to the pathologization of homosexuality in 1973 opened the doors for further gains and the battle continues to this day.

If President Obama follows through on his promise to repeal the "Don't Ask, Don't Tell" ban on LGBT people serving openly in the military, it would be a victory despite the reactionary role of the U.S. armed forces. Lifting the ban would be a reform LGBT activists could leverage to wage a broader argument about civil rights for sexual minorities. The hypocritical logic of allowing LGBT people the right to kill or die for the American Empire, while denying them basic workplace and marriage rights, would be exposed. One need not support the actions of the military or encourage anyone to serve in its forces in order to use the federal government's acknowledgement of LGBT rights in one instance to demand equal rights across the board. That two-thirds of the U.S. population already supports a repeal of "Don't Ask, Don't Tell" reflects a higher level of respect for LGBT people among ordinary Americans than exists at the highest levels of power.[72]

A victory such as this would also push the envelope on questions of gender norms. While the issue of gays in the military may not ordinarily be posed as an issue that takes on traditional gender roles, it is implicit. Stereotypical notions of what women and men are supposed be like are subverted by acknowledging the ability of sexual and gender rebels to serve alongside everyone else. This seemingly ambiguous reform calls into question widespread social beliefs inside one of the most backward institutions in the United States, the military.

In the face of mass protests to roll back the recent antigay marriage ballot measures, especially California's Proposition 8, some leftists are a bit queasy. *Nation* columnist Alexander Cockburn has called it a "sidestep on freedom's path" and queer theorist Judith Butler has expressed discomfort that the "sense of an alternative movement is dying."[73] Why, they ask, should radicals be so adamant about defending the right of gays and lesbians to enter into an institution that is decidedly mainstream and tied to the state and religion?

The conclusion by some to stand aside or even oppose the nascent explosion of outrage demanding gay marriage is misguided. Same sex marriage is a civil right that must be unapologetically defended by socialists and other leftists—not only for its own sake as a material and social benefit under capitalism, especially to working-class and poor LGBT people, but because the reform is not a barrier to further struggles—it can be a gateway to them instead.

A few facts are needed to clear away some of the misconceptions. Because of the Clinton-era Defense of Marriage Act (DOMA), which defines marriage as between one man and one woman in the eyes of the federal government, none of the rights and benefits that LGBT couples have today in some states—whether legal marriages, civil unions, or domestic partnerships—are transferable to most other states. The so-called "mini-DOMAs" that have passed in more than forty states ensure that same-sex couples lose whatever rights they had previously when they enter mini-DOMA states.[74] In other words, legally married LGBT couples are legal strangers in almost every state of the union. DOMA allows states, as well as the federal government, to legally ignore the status of LGBT marriages, civil unions, and domestic partnerships.

In addition, even legal gay marriages inside Massachusetts, for example, only carry with them that state's rights and benefits—not Social Security, Medicare, family leave, health care, disability, military, or the other 1,049 federal rights and benefits belonging to married couples.[75] Gay married couples who go out of state on vacation lose their rights once they cross the state line. Thus, if a member of a married lesbian Massachusetts couple vacationing in Pennsylvania has a serious accident requiring hospitalization, her wife has no legal visitation rights or the right to make any decisions on her behalf in the event of incapacitation until the patient is moved back to a state that recognizes their marriage. In the event of death, no matter what state, she would receive no federal benefits that are due to spouses of heterosexual couples, she can be taxed the full 50 percent on all inheritance, and she would not be eligible for the federal exemption for spouses.[76] In addition, without federal same-sex marriage rights, LGBT immigrants who fall in love with American citizens have no right to move to the United States to be with their lover.

For a couple with domestic partnership or civil union rights, if the deceased spouse was the biological parent of any children the couple had, unless the surviving partner had the money to legally adopt the children, that partner could lose her kids.

Interestingly, the only time when the federal government acknowledged same-sex couple relationships was after September 11, 2001, when LGBT people who lost their partners in the Twin Towers and Pentagon fought successfully to win death benefits paid out to spouses. The government caved in the face of organized outrage—and as part of an attempt to win over gay and lesbian support for plans for imperial vengeance in the Middle East.[77]

The generation that participated in the Stonewall rebellion of 1969 that launched the modern gay liberation movement is becoming, or its members already are, senior citizens. If gay

San Francisco Board of Supervisors member Harvey Milk hadn't been assassinated thirty-one years ago, he would be seventy-nine today. Without same-sex marriage benefits, these gay seniors face a number of daunting financial realities, not the least of which is having no legal right to determine what happens to a partner they may have spent decades with at the time of their partner's death—not funeral arrangements, not burial or cremation or donations to science, or where and whether the body is buried.

In short, same-sex partners would be denied the same rights our government bestows on married heterosexual couples who tie the knot in a drunken night out in Vegas. The idea, common among some leftists, that right-wingers who poured tens of millions into getting Prop 8 passed are trying to force monogamy down gays' throats is wrong-headed as well. Consider what Republican troglodyte Newt Gingrich had to say about the anti–gay marriage victory in California:

> I think there is a gay and secular fascism in this country that wants to impose its will on the rest of us, is prepared to use violence, to use harassment. I think it is prepared to use the government if it can get control of it. I think that it is a very dangerous threat to anybody who believes in traditional religion.[78]

The right's opposition to gay marriage has to do with its desire to impose sexual and gender norms inside marriage as well outside. Socialists should neither advocate monogamy nor polyamory—that is, having more than one sexual relationship at a time. These are personal decisions for individuals and couples to decide for themselves. There is nothing implicitly radical about polyamory or reactionary about monogamy, but their forced imposition is reactionary and moralistic. Leftists ought to stand for the freedom to choose any consensual sexual arrangement, including marriage.

In 2007, on the fortieth anniversary of the court case *Loving v. Virginia*, which struck down anti-miscegenation laws in the United States and finally recognized marriages between Blacks and whites throughout the country, Mildred Loving, the Black female plaintiff in the case, came out in favor of gay marriage. "I believe all Americans, no matter their race, no matter their sex, no matter their sexual orientation, should have that same freedom to marry," she said. "Government has no business imposing some people's religious beliefs over others. Especially if it denies people civil rights."[79] Loving was right. The left should stand where it did when she and her white husband, Richard Loving, fought the system. Winning the right to biracial marriage did not divert the Black struggle for civil rights. It amplified and expanded it, just as the struggle for gay marriage today can and will.

The left shouldn't hand over the strategy and tactics for this fight to corporate-dominated gay organizations. It must stand with the thousands of angry and confident activists, and help shape the fight for a repeal of Prop 8—and demand that the Obama administration repeal DOMA as well.

Unite and fight

The enormous outpouring of tens of thousands of protesters in response to Prop 8's passage in cities across the United States begins to answer the crucial question: Where does change come from? From ending slavery and Jim Crow segregation to overturning sexist and anti-LGBT legislation, significant change often comes from organized struggle by ordinary peo-

ple catapulted into circumstances not of their choosing. Neo-
phyte activists Oskar and David Vidaurre, who initiated and organized a San Francisco protest of twenty thousand to thirty
thousand after Proposition 8 passed, banning gay marriage in
California, are among many examples of newly politicized gay
activists in what is shaping up to be a new political era under
President Obama. "Organizing this was mostly just out of
anger. I can't really call myself an activist," explained Oskar.[80]

We are encouraged to think of social transformation as inevitable, linear, and mostly the results of extraordinary leaders who swoop in to resolve problems as a result of their
wisdom or moral indignation in the face of economic or social
injustices. But the historical record proves otherwise. Even in
the circumstances where there have been leaders who played
important roles in shaping and advancing social justice, they
too have been transformed and elevated by a wider movement and political ferment. Harvey Milk, for example, was a
closeted political reactionary who morphed into an openly
gay progressive leader as a result of political debates and organizing in which he participated.

The trajectory of LGBT struggles has not been one of
even progress and advancement; rather, as the history in
these pages reveals, it has been filled with false starts, obstacles, setbacks, and lunges forward—often as a result of previously inactive or apolitical people coming into contact with
organized groups or politicized individuals who attempt to in-
volve broader layers of people to create a conscious force for
change. Just days following Thanksgiving 2008, nearly 250
workers in Chicago staged a factory occupation after being il-
legally dismissed from their jobs on three days' notice and
without severance pay. By deciding to occupy their factory—a

tactic used by labor in the 1930s but virtually unknown in this country since—the Republic Windows and Doors workers won nearly $2 million in compensation and sparked a solidarity movement that forced one of the biggest banks in the United States to pay two months of wages and health care benefits, even though the bank had no legal obligation to do so.[81] Hundreds of area LGBT activists, who had been marching for gay marriage rights, joined the workers' protests in solidarity. The night after Republic workers scored their historic victory, one of their members addressed a forum on LGBT liberation. Raúl Flores addressed the crowd, saying that our struggles are united and we must be too. "Our victory is yours," he said, "Now we must join with you in your battle for rights and return the solidarity you showed us."[82]

As 2009 began, more than fifty California labor unions representing more than two million workers signed on to an amicus brief urging that state's Supreme Court to overturn Proposition 8.[83] Their brief reads: "If a simple majority of voters can take away one fundamental right, it can take away another. If it can deprive one class of citizens of their rights, it can deprive another class too. Today it is gays and lesbians who are singled out. Tomorrow it could be trade unionists."[84] At the January 10, 2009, national day of action to repeal DOMA in Chicago, members of UNITE Here Local 2 joined with immigrant rights activists and two hundred others in a rally and march through a blizzard to stand with LGBT activists making demands on the new Obama administration.[85]

These are eloquent expressions of the old labor slogan, "An injury to one is an injury to all." They are also signs that LGBT people will not necessarily be isolated in making demands for rights and shifts in behavior and thinking in this era of economic uncertainty and expanding wars. Solidarity between working-class straight and LGBT people is no longer a distant dream, but can be forged and strengthened in a period that is throwing up all sorts of questions about the way our society is organized—from economic and racial inequality to the profit-driven exploits of industries that destroy the environment. The unquestioned transfer of wealth from workers to the rich on a colossal scale and the nasty culture wars that have dominated U.S. society for decades have ended. The right is ideologically in retreat. What ideas and organizing efforts will rise to take their place remains unclear.

New LGBT activists are shedding the hesitancy, defensiveness, and top-down strategies of recent years and have a sense of hope, as well as a healthy disdain for corporate-controlled tactics that have dominated in the recent past. If a new movement is to advance civil rights for all and raise larger questions about what sexual liberation would look like, it will need to engage with its own history and the political and theoretical limitations of the past.

CHAPTER NINE

Sexual Liberation for All!

What would sexual liberation mean? We can, perhaps, agree
on what must disappear—institutional and legal discrimination
against LGBT people, fixed gender roles and sexual identities,
legal constraints on consensual sex, and social repression of
sexual experimentation, etc. While many of us dream of a
world in which we are free to do as we choose with our bodies
and sex lives, living under capitalism, where sex is bought and
sold, bodies objectified, and relationships constrained by material forces out of our control, it seems that even our fantasies
must be limited somewhat by the world in which we live.

The ubiquitous use of sexual images to sell everything
from beer to toothpaste and shifts in popular culture that have
normalized skimpy clothing and near-nudity exist alongside a
culture of sexual repression and a formal educational policy of
denying crucial sexual knowledge to youth. Sex education in
the United States in the early twenty-first century has been reduced to puritanical "abstinence only" lectures—denying
young people knowledge about the most intimate functions of
their bodies, including how to use a condom in the age of
AIDS. According to the latest Centers for Disease Control and
Prevention survey, taken in 2007, nearly two-thirds of high

school seniors said they have had sexual intercourse, and 22 percent said they have been with at least four partners, yet they are provided little to no information about birth control or sexually transmitted diseases.[1] Under George W. Bush, $176 million was spent each year to promote abstinence-only "education," leading to an uptick in teen pregnancy and widespread ignorance among teens about their own bodies.[2] As one Joliet, Illinois, schoolteacher reported, many teens score a five out of twenty-five in quizzes on the reproductive system: "They don't even get the uterus right."[3]

The media and religious institutions, as well as schools, promote ideas that make many people feel too guilty or ashamed to explore their own bodies and sexuality. In one ABC News sex survey of a random sampling of adults, which recorded results typical of recent years, only 30 percent of women but 74 percent of men said they always have orgasms when they have sex. While 70 percent of those polled said they "enjoy sex a great deal," only 50 percent report that they are "very satisfied" with their sex lives. Though couples who openly discuss their sexual fantasies tend to have more fulfilling sex lives, only 51 percent of those polled report doing so.[4] In short, people's sex lives, regardless of sexual orientation, are not as enjoyable as many people would like. There is a wide range of explanations for this, from exhaustion to a lack of open communication between sex partners about desires and techniques. In a society in which television and movies are filled with youthful, skinny, white, straight bodies having Hollywood versions of sex, tens of millions remain too embarrassed to speak about their erotic desires with their sex partner/s. Millions of women go without attaining the joys of orgasm because they are either unaware that most women require clitoral stimulation or are too timid to ask their partners to pleasure them in that way.

LGBT people can rarely glimpse images of people like themselves on the screen—even lesbian porn is largely the domain of (some) straight men's fantasies, complete with spiked heels, cosmetically enlarged breasts, and women touching each other (with long, sharp nails) in ways very few women would ever find physically gratifying. Perhaps the virtual media blackout on LGBT sex has its upside since the images of straight sex on the screen are overwhelmingly dominated by conventionally good-looking and unimaginably toned young people who always appear to know exactly how to touch each other from the first moments and who invariably climax simultaneously, beating the statistical odds on such events. This constant bombardment of unreal sexual images and cosmetically altered or chiseled gym bodies not only promotes phony models of sex, but stokes feelings of sexual inadequacy and contributes to negative body images.

From the Kinsey Reports of the late 1940s and early 1950s on men's and women's sexual behavior to *The Hite Report* studies on men and women's sexuality in the 1970s, medical and social scientists have researched sexual practices and pleasures. The conclusion drawn by Shere Hite, who studies psychosexual behavior and has done extensive research on sex practices and attitudes, is "we haven't had a sexual revolution yet, but we need one."[5]

We are not the first to explore questions of sexual liberation. Every time society experiences profound upheaval, sexual relations too are called into question, as they were during the "sexual revolution" of the late 1960s and early 1970s in the United States, when racial, class, and international relations lay at the heart of the social explosions of that era. Similarly, after the First World War and the Russian Revolution of 1917, there was an explosion of debate and challenges to Victorian sexual mores in Europe and the United States.

Marxist psychoanalyst Wilhelm Reich founded the Socialist Society of Sexual Advice and Sexual Research in Vienna in 1929. There he set up clinics in working-class neighborhoods to aid people with their emotional problems and encouraged them to look for the roots of their maladies in the wider social organization of society.[6] He directed his attention to expanding Marx's understanding of alienation to the sexual realm. Ordinarily, we think of alienation as a feeling of isolation and separateness from others and the world around us. For Marxists, alienation doesn't describe an emotional condition, but an economic and social reality of class society. Marxist alienation refers to the way in which work and the products of our work are outside our control and dominate us. In his *Economic and Philosophical Manuscripts of 1844,* Marx wrote, "The object that labor produces, its product, stands opposed to it as something alien, as a power independent of the producer."[7]

As Paul D'Amato explains:

> Most of us own neither the tools and machinery we work with nor the products that we produce—they belong to the capitalist that hired us. But everything we work on and in at some point comes from human labor. The irony is that everywhere we turn, we are confronted with the work of our own hands and brains, and yet these products of our labor appear as things outside of us, and outside of our control.
>
> Work and the products of work dominate us, rather than the other way around. Rather than being a place to fulfill our potential, the workplace is merely a place we are compelled to go in order to obtain money to buy the things we need.[8]

Because of this, Marx argued, "the worker feels himself only when he is not working; when he is working, he does not feel himself.... His labor is, therefore, not voluntary but forced; it is forced labor. It is, therefore, not the satisfaction of a need but a mere means to satisfy needs outside itself. Its alien character is clearly demonstrated by the fact that as soon as no physical or other compulsion exists, it is shunned like the plague."[9]

By extrapolating from Marx's theory of alienation and his own studies of working-class people's neuroses in 1930s Berlin, Reich concluded that even our unconscious attitudes about such things as sex and intimacy are shaped by society. He doesn't argue that people simply needed to have more and varied sex, though he did challenge Victorian sexual temperance. Instead, Reich argued for overturning the social and economic order, which require sexual repression, in order for people to lead sexually liberated lives. He concluded that the nuclear family plays a central role in sexual repression and social conditioning:

> Its cardinal function, that for which it is mostly supported and defended by conservative science and law, is that of serving as a factory for authoritarian ideologies and conservative structures. It forms the educational apparatus through which practically every individual of our society, from the moment of drawing his first breath, has to pass...it is the conveyor belt between the economic structure of conservative society and its ideological superstructure.[10]

Reich continues,

> The sexual restraint which adults had to bear in order to tolerate marital and familial existence is perpetuated in their children. And since the latter, for economic reasons,

must eventually sink back into the family situation, sexual inhibition is perpetuated from one generation to the next.[11]

It is no wonder then that each generation's rebellion against the social status quo has involved some rebellion against the institution of the family. As explained earlier, however, the experience of the Russian Revolution showed that the process of replacing the family with something else is not merely a matter of laws or will, but requires a certain material level before such major cultural and social transformations can take place.

The Russian Revolution of 1917 pushed the contradictions of people's intimate lives to the fore in a society undertaking a monumental political and economic reordering. Alexandra Kollontai, a leading Bolshevik revolutionary, wrote and spoke widely on questions surrounding sexual relations, including the material link between loneliness and the drive people in class societies exhibit for totally possessing a partner. She wrote:

> We are people living in the world of property relationships, a world of sharp class contradictions and of an individualistic morality. We still live and think under the heavy hand of an unavoidable loneliness of spirit. Man experiences this "loneliness" even in towns full of shouting, noise and people, even in a crowd of close friends and work-mates. Because of their loneliness men are apt to cling in a predatory and unhealthy way to illusions about finding a "soul mate" from among the members of the opposite sex. They see sly Eros as the only means of charming away, if only for a time, the gloom of inescapable loneliness.[12]

Kollontai advocated "free love," meaning sexual relations free from the possessiveness born of private property relations and the alienation people experience in bourgeois society that often leaves them feeling trapped in loveless relationships. Her insights about the need to alter the material organization of society in order to open the way for a profound and lasting sexual reorganization remain useful to this day. Kollontai wrote that in order to resolve the "sexual crisis...a basic transformation of the socio-economic relationships along communist lines,"[13] was needed. That is, the socialization of child care, cooking, laundry, and other household services was necessary to enable new forms of intimate life to flourish.

Any attempt to try and live sexually liberated lives under the current material circumstances will always come up against the real limitations of people's daily existence. The economic constraints placed on all working-class people are not merely physically harsh but have a psychological impact as well. In our society it is hardly surprising that people harbor jealousies when a lover has sex with another person or that they desire a soul mate to ward off loneliness and insecurity. These emotions and desires cannot simply be willed out of existence, because they are human responses to real conditions in our society. A long day at work preceded and followed by a lengthy, often tension-filled commute to a household where the cooking, cleaning, child care, and other life needs must be attended to are not the ideal circumstances for sexually liberating experiences. At the same time, living in a society in which people are pitted against one another to find a job, housing, and education encourages people to seek out a person who can be their emotional life raft amid hostility and competition.

This does not mean that LGBT people and others are powerless today to challenge the repressive social and legal structures that confine our desires and oppress us all. Engaging in LGBT struggles in the here and now against the economic and social status quo, as well as sharing and debating ideas about sexual liberation, cannot wait for some future society. The inability to realize sexual liberation instantaneously need not be an excuse for inactivity in this realm any more so than in any other. The progress in social attitudes and the freedoms that activists have won in just the last forty years alone militates against passivity. However, individual lifestyle choices, from rejecting marriage to engaging in unconventional sexual practices, do not themselves pose a challenge to the dominant order. A thoroughgoing transformation of the system that keeps repressive structures and ideologies in place requires collective struggle.

Reich provides a glimpse of a genuine sexual revolution in a new society:

> In time of revolution, when the old order is shattered and everything outdated sinks into oblivion, when we are standing knee-deep in the debris of a corrupt, predatory, cruel, rotten social system, we must not moralize if the sexual contradictions among the youth are at first intensified. We must see the sexual revolution in the context of general historical change, we must place ourselves alongside youth, we must help youth so far as we are able, but more than anything else we must realize that we are living in a time of transition. To be put off by the confusions of such a transitional period, to take fright at the "crazy youngsters" and to fall back into bourgeois attitudes, such as asceticism and moralizing, attitudes which it is one of the tasks of the proletarian revolution to eradicate, means being left behind by historical events and standing in the way of progress.
>
> After the revolution, when the people liberated from their exploiters can at last begin to build socialism, to transform the economy into a socialist one and to destroy the rotten remains of capitalism in every sphere, the question

is once again entirely different. The workers' society is then faced with the important task of thinking about the future order of sexual life and preparing for it. This future order cannot and will not be other than, as Lenin put it, a full love-life yielding joy and strength. Little as we can say about the details of such a life, it is nevertheless certain that in the communist society the sexual needs of human beings will once more come into their own. To the degree that working hours and working pressures are reduced as a result of socialist rationalization of work and increased productivity of labor, sexual life, side by side with cultural and sports activities and no longer corrupted by money and brutality, will once again take its place on a higher level in human society. And human beings will once again become capable of enjoying their sexuality, because private economy, which is the basis of sexual oppression and which makes people incapable of enjoyment and therefore sick or crazy in the true sense of the word, will drop away.[14]

As this book has tried to flesh out, even the most intimate and seemingly individual aspects of our lives—the ways we express our gender and sexuality—are molded by the physical realities of our world. This central fact points to the need to revolutionize our material circumstances in order to truly liberate our sexual lives. The condition of the one is the precondition of the other. It is for this reason that sexual liberation appears impossible without the political, economic, and social liberation that lies at the heart of socialism.

Notes

INTRODUCTION

1. See "Anti-Lesbian, Gay, Bisexual and Transgender Violence in 2007," National Coalition of Anti-Violence Programs, 2008, http://www.ncavp.org/common/document_files/Reports/2007H vReportFINAL.pdf.

2. Poll results cited from Arian Campo-Flores, "A Gay Marriage Surge," *Newsweek*, December 5, 2008.

3. Quoted in W. E. B. DuBois, *Black Reconstruction in America 1860–1880* (New York: Simon and Schuster, 1999), 299.

4. Karl Marx and Frederick Engels, *Collected Works, 1845–1847*, (*MECW*) vol. 5 (New York: International Publishers, 1976), 54.

5. For more on the factory occupation, see Robert Mitchum, "What Does Deal for Chicago's Republic Windows & Doors Workers Mean?" *Chicago Tribune*, December 12, 2008.

6. The author was a speaker at this forum and recorded his words.

7. Ibid.

8. Cited in Lillian Faderman and Stuart Timmons, *Gay L.A.: A History of Sexual Outlaws, Power Politics, and Lipstick Lesbians* (New York: Basic Books, 2006), 224.

9. Gerald Hunt, ed., *Laboring for Rights: Unions and Sexual Diversity Across Nations* (Philadelphia: Temple University Press, 1999), 60.

10. Gary Kinsman, "Allan Bérubé, 1946–2007: A Queer Working-

Class Community-Based Historian," *Against the Current* 135 (July 3, 2008).

11. Cited in Susan Stryker, "Marine Cooks and Stewards Union," PlanetOut.com, http://www.planetout.com/news/history/archive/marine.html.

12. Campo-Flores, "Gay Marriage Surge."

CHAPTER ONE
The Roots of Gay Oppression

1. Matthew Shepard was a gay student at the University of Wyoming in October 1998 when he was tortured and killed by men who left him strung from a fence post in Laramie, Wyoming. Public outrage led to protests in many cities around the country and his name has become synonymous with fighting gay bashings. For a compilation of polls on public attitudes toward LGBT people, see "Same-Sex Marriage/Gay Rights" at PollingReport.com.

2. Martin Duberman, Martha Vicinus, and George Chauncey, eds., *Hidden from History: Reclaiming the Gay and Lesbian Past* (New York: Meridian, 1989), 20.

3. Karl Marx, *Grundrisse: Foundations of the Critique of Political Economy* (Harmondsworth: Penguin, 1973), 83.

4. Quoted in David F. Greenberg, *The Construction of Homosexuality* (Chicago: University of Chicago Press, 1988), 149.

5. Ibid., 44.

6. Quoted in Will Roscoe, *Changing Ones: Third and Fourth Genders in Native North America* (New York: Macmillan, 2000), 4.

7. Duberman, Vicinus, and Chauncey, *Hidden from History*, 5.

8. Michel Foucault, *The Use of Pleasure*, vol. 2, *The History of Sexuality* (New York: Pantheon, 1986), 187–88.

9. Greenberg, *Construction of Homosexuality*, 399.

10. Quoted in Jonathan Ned Katz, *The Invention of Heterosexuality* (Chicago: University of Chicago Press, 2007), 67.

11. Elizabeth Weil, "A Swimmer of a Certain Age," *New York Times*, June 29, 2008.

12. Sandra Steingraber, "The Falling Age of Puberty in U.S. Girls: What We Know, What We Need to Know," Breast Cancer Fund, August 2007, http://www.breastcancerfund.org/site/c.kwKXLd-PaE/6.3266509/k.27C1/Falling_Age_of_Puberty_Main_Page.htm.

13. "How Common Is Intersex?" Intersex Society of North America, http://www.isna.org/faq/frequency.

14. See, for example, Karen Sacks, "Engels Revisited: Women, the Organization of Production, and Private Property," in Rayna R. Reiter, ed., *Toward an Anthropology of Women* (New York: Monthly Review Press, 1976). See also Eleanor Burke Leacock, *Myths of Male Dominance: Collected Articles on Women Cross-Culturally* (Chicago: Haymarket Books, 2008).

15. For a fuller explanation of Engels's theory, see Sharon Smith, "Engels and the Origin of Women's Oppression," *International Socialist Review*, Fall 1997, 37–46.

16. Leacock, *Myths of Male Dominance*, 140.

17. Chris Harman, *A People's History of the World* (London: Bookmarks, 1999), 24–25.

18. Leacock, *Myths of Male Dominance*, 140.

19. Frederick Engels, *The Origin of the Family, Private Property and the State* (New York: International Publishers, 2001), 125.

20. Ibid., 129.

21. Jeffrey Weeks, *Sex, Politics and Society: The Regulation of Sexuality Since 1800*, 2nd ed. (London: Longman Limited, 1989), 99.

22. John D'Emilio and Estelle B. Freedman, eds., *Intimate Matters: A History of Sexuality in America* (New York: Harper and Row Publishers, 1988), 16.

23. Ibid., 30.

24. Katz, *Invention of Heterosexuality*, 38.
25. John D'Emilio, "Capitalism and Gay Identity," in *Making Trouble: Essays on Gay History, Politics, and the University* (New York: Routledge, 1992), 13.
26. Weeks, *Sex, Politics and Society*, 29.
27. Colin Wilson, *Socialists and Gay Liberation* (London: Socialist Workers Party, 1994), 11.
28. Quoted in Frederick Engels, *The Condition of the Working Class in England* (New York: Penguin Books, 2005), 81.
29. Greenberg, *Construction of Homosexuality*, 356–58.
30. Ibid., 388.
31. Sharon Lerner, "Bush's Marriage Proposal," *Village Voice*, May 1–7, 2002.
32. California's Supreme Court struck down the gay marriage ban, but on November 4, 2008, voters approved Proposition 8 reversing that right and setting off a new wave of activism for equal marriage rights across the United States. At the time of this writing, January 2009, it is unclear how this issue in California will be resolved.
33. D'Emilio, "Capitalism and Gay Identity," 7.
34. Ibid.
35. Noel Halifax, *Out Proud and Fighting: Gay Liberation and the Struggle for Socialism* (London: Socialist Workers Party, 1988), 11.
36. Rictor Norton, *The Myth of the Male Homosexual: Queer History and the Search for Cultural Unity* (London: Cassell, 1997), 14–15.
37. Here I emphasize that Marxists' constructionism is both materialist and dialectical because there are others, such as the queer theorists discussed in chapter 6 who are also constructionists and philosophical idealists, for whom there are no material determinates (biological or otherwise) for sexual or gender behavior.
38. Allan Bray, *Homosexuality in Renaissance England* (London: Gay Men's Press, 1982), 81–114.

39.   Gary Kinsman, *The Regulation of Desire: Homo and Hetero Sexualities* (New York: Black Rose Books, 1996), 49.

40.   John Lauritsen and David Thorstad, *The Early Homosexual Rights Movement (1864–1935)* (Ojai, CA: Times Change Press, 1995), 3.

41.   Ibid., 7.

42.   Ibid., 22.

43.   Katz, *Invention of Heterosexuality*, 67.

CHAPTER TWO

Repression, Resistance, and War: The Birth of Gay Identity

1.   Quoted in Joseph Pearce, *The Unmasking of Oscar Wilde* (San Francisco: Ignatius Press, 2004), 346.

2.   Lillian Faderman, *Odd Girls and Twilight Lovers: A History of Lesbian Life in Twentieth-Century America* (New York: Penguin Books, 1991), 9.

3.   Quoted in D'Emilio and Freedman, *Intimate Matters*, 125.

4.   Cited in Duberman, Vicinus, and Chauncey, *Hidden from History*, 184.

5.   Faderman, *Odd Girls and Twilight Lovers*, 43.

6.   Quoted in Weeks, *Sex, Politics and Society*, 105.

7.   Faderman, *Odd Girls and Twilight Lovers*, 14.

8.   Ibid., 32.

9.   Quoted in ibid., 34.

10.   Ibid., 38.

11.   Ibid,, 49.

12.   Ibid., 57.

13.   Quoted in Weeks, *Sex, Politics and Society*, 107.

14.   Quoted in D'Emilio and Freedman, *Intimate Matters*, 123.

15.   D'Emilio, "Capitalism and Gay Identity," 9.

16. Faderman, *Odd Girls and Twilight Lovers*, 73.
17. Quoted in George Chauncey, *Gay New York: Gender, Urban Culture, and the Making of the Gay Male World 1890–1940* (New York: HarperCollins, 1994), 261.
18. Chauncey, *Gay New York*, 261.
19. Ibid., 48.
20. John D'Emilio, *Sexual Politics, Sexual Communities: The Making of a Homosexual Minority in the U.S. 1940–1970* (Chicago: University of Chicago Press, 1983), 20.
21. Chauncey, *Gay New York*, 75.
22. Cited in ibid., 136.
23. Nan Alamilla Boyd, *Wide-Open Town: A History of Queer San Francisco to 1965* (Los Angeles and Berkeley: University of California Press, 2003), 26.
24. Quoted in Chauncey, *Gay New York*, 105–06.
25. Radclyffe Hall, *The Well of Loneliness* (New York: Covici Friede Publishers, 1932), 506.
26. Wilson, *Socialists and Gay Liberation*, 14.
27. Ibid., 15.
28. D'Emilio, *Sexual Politics, Sexual Communities*, 20.
29. Chauncey, *Gay New York*, 9.
30. Allan Bérubé, *Coming Out Under Fire: The History of Gay Men and Women in World War Two* (New York: Plume, 1991), 3.
31. D'Emilio, *Sexual Politics, Sexual Communities*, 24.
32. See "America at War," Something About Everything Military, http://www.jcs-group.com/military/war0000.html.
33. Martin Taylor, ed., *Lads: Love Poetry of the Trenches* (London: Duckbacks, 2002).
34. Quoted in Neil Miller, *Out of the Past: Gay and Lesbian History from 1869 to the Present* (New York: Alyson Books, 2006), 86.
35. Bérubé, *Coming Out Under Fire*, 10.
36. Ibid., 12.

37. Ibid., 19.

38. Ibid., 22.

39. D'Emilio, *Sexual Politics, Sexual Communities*, 25.

40. Ibid., 26.

41. Bérubé, *Coming Out Under Fire*, 30.

42. Ibid., photo inserts, 4.

43. Ibid., 33.

44. Quoted in Randy Shilts, *Conduct Unbecoming: Gays and Lesbians in the U.S. Military* (New York: St. Martin's Press, 1994), 107–08.

45. D'Emilio, *Sexual Politics, Sexual Communities*, 31.

46. Wilson, *Socialists and Gay Liberation*, 18.

47. Duberman, Vicinus, and Chauncey, *Hidden from History*, 4.

48. See Randy Dotinga and Gregg Drinkwater, "The U.S. Gives $500,000 to Nazis' Gay Victims," PlanetOut.com, June 1, 2001. See also "Pink Tringle Coalition—Restitution for gay survivors" at http://www.xs4all.nl/~kmlink/07gayhistory/03linkstogayresources/pinktrianglecoalition.htm.

49. Peter Tatchell, "Hidden from History—the Gay Holocaust," *Thud*, October 30, 1997.

50. Pierre Seel, *Liberation Was for Others: Memoirs of a Gay Survivor of the Nazi Holocaust* (New York: Da Capo Press, 1997), 43.

51. D'Emilio, *Sexual Politics, Sexual Communities*, 35.

52. Ibid., 36.

53. D'Emilio, "Capitalism and Gay Identity," 12.

54. Robert J. Corber, *Homosexuality in Cold War America* (Durham, NC: Duke University Press, 1997), 2.

55. Arthur M. Schlesinger, *The Vital Center: The Politics of Freedom* (New York: Westview Press, 1988), 127.

56. D'Emilio, *Sexual Politics, Sexual Communities*, 46.

57. Ibid.

58. Quoted in John D'Emilio, *Making Trouble: Essays on Gay History, Politics and the University* (New York: Routledge, 1992), 68.

59. Chapter 3 discusses the treatment of homosexuality before, during, and after the Russian Revolution in greater detail.

60. Quoted in Van Gosse, *The Movements of the New Left 1950–1975* (New York: St. Martin's Press, 2005), 40.

61. D'Emilio, *Making Trouble*, 37.

62. Ibid., 34.

63. C. Todd White, *Pre-Gay L.A.: A Social History of the Movement for Homosexual Rights* (Urbana and Chicago, IL: University of Illinois Press, 2009), 34, 237. Guy Rousseau was the pseudonym for Bailey Whitaker, ibid., 231.

64. D'Emilio, *Sexual Politics, Sexual Communities*, 108–10.

65. This author accompanied Harry Hay and his lover John Burnside to the Los Angeles protest in 1999, three years before Hay's death, and spent the afternoon discussing Mattachine's history and Hay's reflections on his past.

66. D'Emilio, *Sexual Politics, Sexual Communities*, 109.

67. Del Martin, "President's Message," October 1956, in Robert B. Ridinger, *Speaking for Our Lives: Historic Speeches and Rhetoric for Gay and Lesbian Rights (1892–2000)* (New York: Harrington Park Press, 2004), 52–53.

68. "The Homosexual in America," *Time*, January 21, 1966.

69. Kyle Dropp and Jon Cohen, "Acceptance of Gays in Military Grows Dramatically," *Washington Post*, July 19, 2008.

70. Ibid.

71. Studies, charts, and polls are available on the Servicemembers Legal Defense Network website, http://www.sldn.org/templates/index.html.

72. Karl Bryant, PhD and Kristen Schilt, PhD, "Transgender Veterans Survey," conducted December 13, 2007, to May 1, 2008, The Palm Center, http://www.tavausa.org/PressRelease/TAVASurveyPressRelease.html.

73. Ibid.

74. Eric Konigsberg, "Gays in Arms: Can Gays in the Military Work? In Countries Around the World, They Already Do," *Washington Monthly*, November 1992.

75. John D'Emilio, William B. Turner, and Urvashi Vaid, eds., *Creating Change: Sexuality, Public Policy, and Civil Rights* (New York: St. Martin's Press, 2000), 237.

76. Ibid.

77. Ibid., 242.

78. Quoted in ibid., 249.

79. Urvashi Vaid, *Virtual Equality: The Mainstreaming of Gay and Lesbian Liberation* (New York: Anchor Books, 1995), 127.

80. Ibid., 128.

81. "Colin Powell Reiterates Support for Review of 'Don't Ask, Don't Tell,'" *Advocate*, December 12, 2008.

82. The combined number of active-duty and reserve military personnel, en.wikipedia.org/wiki/Military_of_the_United_States, accessed September 2008.

CHAPTER THREE

The Myth of Marxist Homophobia

1. For the entry "Socialism and LGBT Rights," Wikipedia cites Saskia Poldervaart, "Theories about Sex and Sexuality in Utopian Socialism," *Journal of Homosexuality* 29 nos. 2/3 (September 30, 1995): 41, http://en.wikipedia.org/wiki/Socialism_and_LGBT_rights#_note-4.

2. Quoted in Terence Kissack, *Free Comrades: Anarchism and Homosexuality in the United States, 1895–1917* (Oakland, CA: AK Press, 2008), 168–69.

3. Ibid., 169.

4. Quoted in DuBois, *Black Reconstruction in America*, 299.

5. V. I. Lenin, *What Is to Be Done?* (New York: Progress Publish-

ers, 1992), 69.

6.   "Socialism and LGBT Rights," Wikipedia.com, http://en.wiki
      pedia.org/wiki/Socialism_and_LGBT_rights#_note-8.

7.   Engels to Marx, June 22, 1869, in *MECW*, vol. 43, 295.

8.   Marx to Engels, *MECW*, vol. 42, 120.

9.   Karl Marx, *Capital*, vol. 1 (New York: International Publishers,
      1967), 301.

10.   Marx, *Capital*, vol. I, 925–26.

11.   Dana Cloud, "Queer Theory and 'Family Values': Capitalism's
      Utopias of Self-Invention," in *Transformation 2: Marxist Bound-
      ary Work in Theory, Economics, Politics and Culture*, ed. Mas'ud
      Zavarzadeh, Teresa L. Ebert, and Donald Morton, (Syracuse,
      NY: The Red Factory, 2001) 78.

12.   This phrase is taken from the final line of a poem, "Two Loves,"
      written by Wilde's reputed young lover, Lord Alfred Douglas,
      which first appeared in the *Chameleon* in 1894; see
      http://www.law.umkc.edu/faculty/projects/ftrials/wilde/poem-
      sofdouglas.htm. "The love that dares not speak its name" has
      been a euphemism for homosexuality ever since Wilde's trial.

13.   Florence Tamagne, *A History of Homosexuality in Europe:
      Berlin, London, Paris 1919–1939*, vols. 1 and 2 (New York: Al-
      gora Publishing, 2006), 29.

14.   Hubert Kennedy, "Johann Baptiste von Schweitzer: The Queer
      Marx Loved to Hate," available in *Four in Gay History*, home.
      att.net/~clairnorman/Four.pdf. This is credited as the main source
      of proof of Marx's homophobia on Wikipedia.

15.   Ibid.

16.   Frederick Engels, *The Origin of the Family, Private Property and
      the State* (New York: International Publishers, 2001), 128.

17.   Jeffrey Weeks, "Where Engels Feared to Tread," *Gay Left: A So-
      cialist Journal Produced by Gay Men*, 1 (Autumn 1975): 3, Gay
      Left Collective.

18. Engels, *Origin of the Family*, 145.
19. John Lauritsen and David Thorstad, *The Early Homosexual Rights Movement (1864–1935)* (Ojai, CA: Times Change Press, 1995), 11.
20. Ibid.
21. Ibid., italics in original, 66.
22. Ibid., 63.
23. Ibid., 68.
24. Quoted in ibid., 70.
25. Sheila Rowbotham and Jeffrey Weeks, part I, "Edward Carpenter: Prophet of the New Life," in *Socialism and the New Life: The Personal and Sexual Politics of Edward Carpenter and Havelock Ellis* (London: Pluto Press, 1977), 25–138.
26. Ibid., 110.
27. Ibid., 151.
28. Ibid., 159.
29. Ibid., 181.
30. Quoted in Philip Foner, ed., *The Bolshevik Revolution: Its Impact on American Radicals, Liberals and Labor* (New York: International Publishers, 1967), 20.
31. See Igor S. Kon, *The Sexual Revolution in Russia* (New York: The Free Press, 1995) and Gregory Carleton, *Sexual Revolution in Bolshevik Russia* (Pittsburgh: University of Pittsburgh Press, 2005) for examples of a few of the more trenchant attacks on these gains.
32. Kon, *Sexual Revolution in Russia,* 59.
33. Women in the United States won the right to vote, codified in the Nineteenth Amendment to the U.S. Constitution in 1920, following decades of struggle. The U.S. Supreme Court struck down all sodomy laws in a 6–3 vote in Lawrence et al. v. Texas on June 26, 2003.
34. Leon Trotsky, *Stalin* (New York: Grosset and Dunlap, 1941), 422.

35. Dan Healey, *Homosexual Desire in Revolutionary Russia: The Regulation of Sexual and Gender Dissent* (Chicago: University of Chicago Press, 2001).

36. Quoted in Lauritsen and Thorstad, *Early Homosexual Rights Movement,* 71–73.

37. Healey, part I, "Same-Sex Eros in Modernizing Russia," in *Homosexual Desire in Revolutionary Russia*, 21–76.

38. Ibid., 29.

39. Ibid., 54.

40. "Capitalism and Homophobia: Marxism and the Struggle for Gay/Lesbian Rights," in Donald Morton, ed., *The Material Queer* (Boulder, CO: Westview Press, 1996), 369–79.

41. Cited in Healey, *Homosexual Desire in Revolutionary Russia*, 101.

42. Ibid., 112.

43. Ibid.

44. Duncan Hallas, "Toward a Revolutionary Socialist Party," *International Socialist Review* July–August 2002, 68–69.

45. Quoted in Wilhelm Reich, *The Sexual Revolution: Toward a Self-Regulating Character Struggle* (New York: Farrar, Straus & Giroux, 1974), 195.

46. Quoted in Ibid., 194.

47. Ibid., 179.

48. Healey, *Homosexual Desire in Revolutionary Russia*, 122.

49. Kissack, *Free Comrades,* 187.

50. Quoted in Duberman, Vicinus, and Chauncey, *Hidden from History*, 352–53.

51. Healey, *Homosexual Desire in Revolutionary Russia*, 132.

52. Ibid., 141.

53. Ibid., 168–69.

54. Ibid, 169.

55. Alexandra Kollontai, "Sexual Relations and the Class Struggle," http://www.marxists.org/archive/kollonta/1921/sex-class-

struggle.htm.

56. Reich, *Sexual Revolution*, 170.

57. Ibid., 161–67.

58. Ibid., 174.

59. Leon Trotsky, *Problems of Everyday Life* (New York: Pathfinder Press, 1994), 81.

60. Quoted in Healey, *Homosexual Desire in Revolutionary Russia*, 189.

61. Healey, *Homosexual Desire in Revolutionary Russia*, 196.

62. Ibid., 197–98.

63. Bettina Aptheker, "Keeping the Communist Party Straight, 1940s–1980s," *New Politics* 12, no. 1 (Summer 2008): 116.

64. Ibid., 120.

65. "China Decides Homosexuality No Longer Mental Disorder," Associated Press, *South China Morning Post*, March 8, 2001.

66. "The China Law Center Holds Conference on Homosexuality in China," January 26, 2006, Yale Law School, http://www.law.yale.edu/intellectuallife/1699.htm.

67. Ian Lumsden, *Machos, Maricones, and Gays: Cuba and Homosexuality* (Philadelphia: Temple University Press, 1996), Chapter 3.

68. Ibid., 70.

69. Quoted in Allen Young, *Gays Under the Cuban Revolution* (San Francisco: Grey Fox Press, 1981), 8.

70. Quoted in Ian Lekus, "Queer Harvests: Homosexuality, the U.S. New Left, and the Venceremos Brigades to Cuba," *Radical History Review* no. 89 (Spring 2004): 77, originally appeared in *Granma Weekly Review*, May 9, 1971.

71. Deirdre Griswold, "One-Fourth of Humanity Is Freed," *Workers World*, http://www.workers.org/ww/1999/china1014.php.

72. Quoted in Gert Hekma, James Steakley, and Harry Oosterhuis, eds., *Gay Men and the Sexual History of the Political Left* (Philadelphia, PA: Haworth Press, 1995), 330.

73. Kipp Dawson, *Gay Liberation: A Socialist Perspective* (New York:

Pathfinder Press, 1975), Deering Library Archives, Northwestern University.

74. Steve Forgione and Kurt T. Hill, eds., *Gay Liberation and Socialism: Documents from the Discussion on Gay Liberation Inside the Socialist Workers Party (1970–1973)*, 2nd ed., unauthorized informal publication of internal documents, 1. This copy (of a total twenty printed) was loaned to the author by David Whitehouse.

75. Jack Barnes, "Report of Membership Policy Given to the Political Committee of the SWP," November 13, 1970, 5–6 in ibid.

76. Barry Sheppard, "Concerning the Discussion," August 29, 1972, 67–71 in ibid.

77. Revolutionary Union, "Position Paper of the Revolutionary Union on Homosexuality and Gay Liberation," 1969, Tamiment Library, New York University.

78. Young, *Gays Under the Cuban Revolution*, 98–100.

79. Quoted in Lekus, "Queer Harvests," 83.

80. "Gay Rights in Cuba: How Much Has Changed?" Mariela Castro Espín interview by Eduardo Jiménez García, *Green Left Weekly*, February 29, 2004.

81. Quoted in Patricia Grogg, "Rights: Cuba Launches Anti-homophobia Campaign," Inter Press Service, March 30, 2009.

82. Paul D'Amato, "Race and Sex in Cuba," *International Socialist Review*, January–February 2007, 57.

83. Christopher Phelps, "A Neglected Document on Socialism and Sex," *New Politics* 12, no. 1 (Summer 2008): 12–21.

84. Quoted in ibid., 12.

85. Quoted in ibid., 13.

86. Quoted in ibid.

87. "The Nature of the Gay Struggle, Its Importance, and Its Place in Our Work," *IS Bulletin* no. 15, January 14, 1972, 3, mimeographed copy loaned to author by Bill Roberts.

88. Ibid.

89. Quoted in Bob Cant, "A Grim Tale: The IS Gay Group," *Gay Left* 3 (Autumn 1976).
90. Dennis Altman, "The State, Repression and Sexuality," *Gay Left* 6 (Autumn 1978).
91. Marx and Engels, *MECW*, vol. 5.

CHAPTER FOUR
The Birth of Gay Power

1. Sometimes the date Friday, June 27, 1969, is given, though the actual raid took place after midnight.
2. David Carter, *Stonewall: The Riots That Sparked the Gay Revolution* (New York: St. Martin's Press, 2004), 15.
3. D'Emilio, Turner, and Vaid, *Creating Change*, 11.
4. Carter, *Stonewall*, 14–15.
5. Del Martin and Phyllis Lyon, interview by Terry Gross, *Fresh Air*, NPR, December 29, 1992. Del Martin died on August 27, 2008, two months after she and Phyllis Lyon married in San Francisco after fifty-five years together as lovers.
6. Cited in D'Emilio, *Sexual Politics, Sexual Communities*, 138.
7. Ibid., 173.
8. Quoted in ibid., 186.
9. Quoted in ibid., 167.
10. Quoted in ibid., 164.
11. Donn Teal, *Gay Militants: How Gay Liberation Began in America, 1969–1971* (New York: St. Martin's Press, 1971), 37.
12. Carter, *Stonewall*, 109.
13. Susan Stryker, *Transgender History* (Berkeley, CA: Seal Press, 2008), 70.
14. Carter, *Stonewall*, 80.
15. Quoted in ibid., 74.
16. Ibid., 77, 79.

17. Jerry Lisker, "Homo Nest Raided, Queen Bees Are Stinging Mad," *Daily News*, July 6, 1969.

18. Quoted in Teal, *Gay Militants*, 2–3.

19. Quoted in Carter, *Stonewall*, 160.

20. Quoted in Teal, *Gay Militants*, 7.

21. Quoted in Carter, *Stonewall*, 196.

22. The Youth International Party (Yippies) was a hippie movement established in the late 1960s that adhered to anti-authoritarian methods and used guerrilla theater as a means of advancing its countercultural platform.

23. Quoted in Teal, *Gay Militants*, 19.

24. Quoted in Martin Duberman, *Stonewall* (New York: Plume, 1994), 229.

25. D'Emilio, *Sexual Politics, Sexual Communities*, 235.

26. Ibid., 236.

27. Lydia Saad, "Tolerance for Gay Rights at High-Water Mark," May 29, 2007, http://www.gallup.com/poll/27694/Tolerance-Gay-Rights-HighWater-Mark.aspx.

28. Quoted in Carter, *Stonewall*, 219.

29. Ibid., 220.

30. Ibid., 226.

31. Teal, *Gay Militants*, 57.

32. Quoted in ibid., 54.

33. Carter, *Stonewall*, 242.

34. Quoted in Teal, *Gay Militants*, 110.

35. Eric Marcus, *Making History: The Struggle for Gay and Lesbian Equal Rights, 1945–1990* (New York: HarperCollins, 1992), 253.

36. Quoted in Teal, *Gay Militants*, 151.

37. Chicago Gay Liberation, "Working Paper for the Revolutionary Peoples' Constitutional Convention," *Gay Flames,* pamphlet no. 13, September 1970, Deering Special Collections, Northwestern University Library.

38. Quoted in Teal, *Gay Militants*, 77.

39. Ibid., 80.

40. Forgione and Hill, *Gay Liberation and Socialism*.

41. Historian Simon Leys describes the Cultural Revolution this way: "The Cultural Revolution had nothing revolutionary about it except the name and nothing cultural about it except the initial tactical pretext. It was a power struggle waged at the top between a handful of men and behind the smokescreen of a fictitious mass movement. As things turned out, the disorder unleashed by this power struggle created a genuinely revolutionary mass current, which developed spontaneously at the grass roots in the form of army mutinies and workers' strikes on a vast scale. These had not been prescribed in the program, and they were crushed pitilessly." Simon Leys, *The Chairman's New Clothes: Mao and the Cultural Revolution* (New York: Palgrave Macmillan, 1977), 13.

42. Eldridge Cleaver, *Soul on Ice* (New York: Delta, 1968), 102.

43. Leroi Jones, "To Survive 'the Reign of the Beasts,'" *New York Times*, November 16, 1969.

44. Duberman, *Stonewall*, 258.

45. Carter, *Stonewall*, 231.

46. Ibid.

47. Jo Freeman, "The Tyranny of Structurelessness," JoFreeman.com, http://www.jofreeman.com/joreen/tyranny.htm.

48. Carter, *Stonewall*, 232.

49. Teal, *Gay Militants*, 155.

50. Quoted in ibid., 160.

51. Katha Pollitt, "Betty Friedan, 1921–2006," *Nation*, February 9, 2006.

52. Radicalesbians, "The Woman-Identified Woman," 1970, document from the Women's Liberation Movement, an online archival collection, Special Collections Library, Duke University, http://scriptorium.lib.duke.edu/wlm/womid/.

53. Ibid.
54. The Red Butterfly, "Gay Liberation," New York, 1970, Deering Special Collections, Northwestern University Library.

CHAPTER FIVE

Whatever Happened to Gay Liberation?

1. Sharon Smith, *Subterranean Fire: A History of Working Class Radicalism in the United States* (Chicago: Haymarket Books, 2006), 228–30.
2. Ibid., 232.
3. "Anita Bryant," Wikipedia, http://en.wikipedia.org/wiki/Anita_Bryant.
4. Smith, *Subterranean Fire,* 232.
5. A controversial and nonpolitical HRC-sponsored Millennium March on Washington for Equality took place on April 30, 2000. This music concert and marketing fair was boycotted by Pride at Work, National Gay and Lesbian Task Force, National Association of Black and White Men Together, as well as virtually every other progressive and left-wing gay organization and publication for being "a profit-making business enterprise masquerading as a lesbian/gay/bisexual/transgender civil rights rally." HRC executive director Elizabeth Birch said of the "march": "For a lot of people who dreamed of a different kind of world, the very notion that the Human Rights Campaign was involved in calling for this march was an anathema." Quoted in Joshua Gamson, "Whose Millennium March?" *Nation,* March 30, 2000.
6. For a detailed account of this process in the labor, Black, and women's liberation movements as well, see Lance Selfa, *The Democrats: A Critical History* (Chicago: Haymarket Books, 2008).
7. D'Emilio, Turner, Vaid, *Creating Change,* 152.

8.   Jean O'Leary, "From Agitator to Insider: Fighting for Inclusion in the Democratic Party," ch. 5 in ibid., 89.

9.   Quoted in Carter, *Stonewall*, 41.

10. See O'Leary, "From Agitator to Insider."

11. Ibid., 93.

12. Selfa, *The Democrats*, 116.

13. Quoted in D'Emilio, Turner, and Vaid, *Creating Change*, 87.

14. Ibid., 87.

15. David Mixner, *Stranger Among Friends* (New York: Bantam Books, 1996).

16. Quoted in Vaid, *Virtual Equality*, 111.

17. Ibid.

18. D'Emilio, Turner, Vaid, *Creating Change*, 60.

19. Ibid., 99.

20. Ibid., 100–01.

21. "About 'Don't Ask, Don't Tell,'" Servicemembers Legal Defense Network, http://www.sldn.org/pages/about-dadt.

22. "White House Apologizes for Rubber Gloves," *New York Times*, June 15, 1995.

23. Vaid, *Virtual Equality*, 185.

24. D'Emilio, Turner, and Vaid, *Creating Change*, 179.

25. David Herszenhorn, "House Approves Ban on Anti-Gay Discrimination," *New York Times*, November 7, 2007.

26. "Good Jobs Now!" Transgender Law Center and *San Francisco Bay Guardian*, 2006, http://www.transgenderlawcenter.org/pdf/Good%20Jobs%20NOW20%report.pdf.

27. Stryker, *Transgender History*, 151.

28. Valentina Simmons, "An Open Letter to Barney Frank About ENDA," Tina's Views blog, October 9, 2007, tinasviews.blogspot.com/2007/10/open-letter-to-barney-frank-about-enda.html. and see also Kevin M. Cathcart to Frank, LAMBDA Legal, http://data.lambdalegal.org/pdf/ltr_enda_frank.pdf.

29. "Statement of Barney Frank on ENDA, the Employment Non-Discrimination Act," accessed September 28, 2007, http://www.house.gov/frank/ENDASeptember2007.html. See also Kevin M. Cathcart to Frank, LAMBDA Legal, http://data.lambdalegal.org/pdf/ltr_enda_frank.pdf.

30. Robert E. Goss and Amy Adams Squire Strongheart, eds., *Our Families, Our Values: Snapshots of Queer Kinship* (New York: Routledge, 1997), xviii.

31. D'Emilio, Turner, and Vaid, *Creating Change*, 108–09.

32. J. Jennings Moss, "Bill Clinton," *Advocate*, June 25, 1996.

33. Vaid, *Virtual Equality*, 112.

34. Quoted in Dean E. Murphy, "Some Democrats Blame One of Their Own," *New York Times*, November 5, 2004.

35. Ibid.

36. "Do You Approve or Disapprove of Marriage Between Whites and Non-whites?" Gallup poll, June 26–July 1, 1968, pollingreport.com/race.htm.

37. "Same-Sex Marriage, Gay Rights," Time magazine poll, July 31–August 4, 2008, pollingreport.com/civil.htm.

38. Carter, *Stonewall*, 252.

39. Amy Gluckman and Betsy Reed, eds., *Homo Economics: Capitalism, Community, and Lesbian and Gay Life* (New York: Routledge, 1997), xvii.

40. Leslie Bennetts, "k. d. lang's Edge," *Vanity Fair*, August 1993 and Esther Rothblum, "Lesbians Coming Out Strong: What Are the Limits of Tolerance?" *Newsweek*, June 21, 1993.

41. Ibid., 4.

42. Quoted in Riccardo A. Davis, "Marketers Game for Gay Events," *Advertising Age*, May 30, 1994.

43. Amy Gluckman and Betsy Reed, "The Gay Marketing Moment: Leaving Diversity in the Dust," *Dollars and Sense*, November–December 1993.

44. Gluckman and Reed, *Homo Economics*, 4.
45. "A Dream Market," *Wall Street Journal*, July 18, 1991.
46. Gluckman and Reed, *Homo Economics*, 12.
47. Ibid., 67.
48. Katherine Sender, *Business, Not Politics: The Making of the Gay Market* (New York: Columbia University Press, 2005), 151.
49. Ibid., 151–52.
50. Gay and Lesbian Consumer Index, Community Marketing, Inc., http://gayconsumerindex.com/.
51. Gary Gates, "Income of Gay Men Lags Behind that of Men Partnered with Women," The Urban Institute, http://www.urban.org/url.cfm?ID=900631.
52. David Zurawik, "Final Ratings Report on HBO's 'The Wire,'" *Baltimore Sun*, March 11, 2008.
53. Gluckman and Reed, *Homo Economics*, 19.
54. Quoted in Vaid, *Virtual Equality*, 251–52.
55. Ibid., 252.
56. Ibid., 252–53.
57. Quoted in Alexandra Chasin, *Selling Out: The Gay and Lesbian Movement Goes to Market* (New York: Macmillan, 2001), 38.
58. Ibid., 39.
59. Quoted in ibid., 30.
60. Log Cabin Republicans, "About Log Cabin," http://online.log-cabin.org/about/.
61. "Bush Wins Same Portion of Gay Vote as '00," *Washington Blade*, November 3, 2004.
62. Maddow is quoted in Sarah Warn, "Rachel Maddow to Host MSNBC News Show," AfterEllen.com, April 20, 2008, http://www.afterellen.comV/2008/8/rachelmaddow.
63. Former vice president Dick Cheney's daughter Mary and Congressman Newt Gingrich's half-sister Candace are both open lesbians.

64. Quoted in Paul Robinson, *Queer Wars: the New Gay Right and Its Critics* (Chicago: University of Chicago Press, 2005), 94.

65. Richard Goldstein, "The Real Andrew Sullivan Scandal," *Village Voice*, June 19, 2001.

66. Quoted in ibid.

67. Quoted in Robinson, *Queer Wars*, 97.

68. Richard Goldstein, *Homocons: The Rise of the Gay Right* (New York: Verso, 2002), 6.

69. Gabriel Rotello, *Sexual Ecology: AIDS and the Destiny of Gay Men* (New York: Dutton, 1997), 3.

70. Ibid., 36.

71. Ibid., 10.

72. AVERT, "Worldwide HIV & AIDS Statistics Commentary," http://www.avert.org/worlstatinfo.htm.

73. Ibid, "United States Statistics Summary," http://www.avert.org/usa-statistics.htm.

74. Ibid.

75. Gardiner Harris, "Price of AIDS Drug Intensifies Debate on Legal Imports," *New York Times*, April 14, 2004.

76. See chapter 6, "In Defense of Materialism: Postmodernism, ID Politics, and Queer Theory in Perspective."

CHAPTER SIX

In Defense of Materialism: Postmodernism, ID Politics, and Queer Theory in Perspective

1. Marx and Engels, *MECW*, vol. 5, 5.

2. Lenin, *What Is to Be Done?*, 25.

3. Terry Eagleton, *After Theory* (New York, Penguin Books, 2003), 13.

4. Structuralism is a theory of language, associated with linguists

such as Ferdinand de Saussure, and culture, associated with anthropologist Claude Levi-Strauss, which examines these phenomena as parts of complex systems that have a structural
relationship to each other. *Post*structuralism seeks to destabilize,
"decenter," and subvert foundational assumptions, calling into
question traditional views of individuals in society, and rejecting
or "deconstructing" determinate meanings of texts. As with postmodernism, poststructuralism challenges the notion of universality and objective truths in the realm of literary and cultural theory.

5.   See Daniel Singer, *Prelude to Revolution: France in May 1968*
     (Cambridge, MA: South End Press, 2002), xvi–xxvi.

6.   Ibid., xv.

7.   Ibid., 69.

8.   Ibid., 205.

9.   William B. Turner, *A Genealogy of Queer Theory* (Philadelphia:
     Temple University Press, 2000), 18.

10. David M. Halperin, *Saint Foucault: Towards a Gay Hagiography*
     (New York: Oxford University Press, 1995), 31.

11. "New Times," *Marxism Today*, October 1988.

12. C. H. Feinstein, "Structural Change in the Developed Countries
     in the 20th Century," *Oxford Review of Economic Policy* 15, no. 4
     (Winter 1999): table A1.

13. Sharon Smith, "Mistaken Identity—or Can Identity Politics Liber-
     ate the Oppressed?" *International Socialism* 62, (Spring 1994): 7.

14. Herbert Marcuse, "Socialism in the Developed Countries," *In-
     ternational Socialist Journal*, no. 8 (April 1965): 150–51.

15. Ernesto Laclau and Chantal Mouffe, *Hegemony and Socialist Strat-
     egy: Towards a Radical Democratic Politics* (London: Verso, 1985).

16. Quoted in Smith, "Mistaken Identity," 16.

17. Cloud, "Queer Theory and 'Family Values,'" 90.

18. Cindy Patton, *Inventing AIDS* (New York: Routledge, 1990), 124.

19. Ibid.

20. Quoted in Smith, "Mistaken Identity," 16.

21. Cindy Patton, *Sex and Germs: the Politics of AIDS* (Cambridge, MA: South End Press, 1985), 153.

22. Heidi Hartmann, "The Unhappy Marriage of Marxism and Feminism," *Capital and Class,* no. 8 (Summer 1979): 14.

23. See chapter 1.

24. Text from the original flyer is posted at http://www.qrd.org/qrd/misc/text/queers.read.this.

25. Quoted in Smith, "Mistaken Identity," 19.

26. See polls cited in chapter 1.

27. John D'Emilio, *The World Turned: Essays on Gay History, Politics and Culture* (Durham, NC: Duke University Press, 2002), 143.

28. Ibid.

29. Quoted in Alex Callinicos, *Against Postmodernism: A Marxist Critique* (Cambridge, MA: Polity Press, 1989), 3.

30. Ibid.

31. Ellen Meiksins Wood, *The Retreat from Class: A New "True" Socialism* (New York: Verso, 1986), 54.

32. Stuart Hall, "The West and the Rest: Discourse and Power," in Stuart Hall and Bram Gieben, eds., *Formations of Modernity* (Open University/Polity Press, 1992), 275–330.

33. Michel Foucault, *History of Sexuality*, vol. I (New York: Pantheon Books, 1976), 36.

34. Marnie Holborow, "Putting the Social Back into Language: Marx, Volosinov and Vygotsky Reexamined," *Studies in Language and Capitalism* 1 (2006): 2.

35. Quoted in Callinicos, *Against Postmodernism*, 76.

36. Marx and Engels, *MECW*, vol. 5, 36–37.

37. Callinicos, *Against Postmodernism,* 145.

38. Terry Eagleton, *The Illusions of Postmodernism* (Malden, MA: Blackwell Publishers, 1996), 5.

39. Marx and Engels, *MECW*, vol. 5, 59.

40. Foucault, *History of Sexuality*, 93.
41. Ibid.
42. Quoted in Colin Gordon, ed., *Power/Knowledge: Selected Interviews and Other Writings* (New York: Pantheon Press, 1980), 98.
43. Halperin, *Saint Foucault*, 16–17.
44. Ibid., 18.
45. Quoted in Smith, "Mistaken Identity," 18.
46. Ibid.
47. The author attended Queer Nation's early meetings in New York City in the spring and summer of 1990.
48. Eve Kosofsky Sedgwick, *Tendencies* (Durham NC: Duke University Press, 1993), 4.
49. Quoted in Cloud, "Queer Theory and 'Family Values,'" 90.
50. Phil Gasper, "The German Ideology," *International Socialist Review*, January–February 2004, 84.
51. Marx and Engels, *MECW*, vol. 5, 30.
52. Riki Wilchins, *Queer Theory, Gender Theory: An Instant Primer* (Los Angeles: Alyson Publications, 2004), 103.
53. Patton, *Inventing AIDS*, 161.
54. Allen White, "Reagan's AIDS Legacy: Silence Equals Death," *San Francisco Chronicle*, June 8, 2004.
55. Larry Kramer, "The Beginning of ACTing Up," (1987) in *We Are Everywhere: A Historical Sourcebook of Gay and Lesbian Politics*, ed., Mark Blasius and Shane Phelan, (New York: Routledge, 1997), 609.
56. Kramer, "1,112 and Counting," in ibid., 578.
57. Quoted in White, "Reagan's AIDS Legacy."
58. Quoted in John-Manuel Andriote, *Victory Deferred: How AIDS Changed Gay Life in America* (Chicago: University of Chicago Press, 1999), 67–68.
59. Ibid., 69.
60. Quoted in ibid.

61. Andriote, *Victory Deferred*, 161.
62. Quoted in Jason Deparle, "Rude, Rash, Effective, Act Up Shifts AIDS Policy," *New York Times*, January 3, 1990.
63. Jeffrey Schmalz, "Whatever Happened to AIDS?" in Blasius and Phelan, *We Are Everywhere*, 694.
64. Mark Harrington, "From Therapeutic Utopianism to Pragmatic Praxis: Some Transitions in the History of AIDS Treatment Activism," May 1996, excerpts from this speech given at the "Acting on AIDS" conference, Institute for Contemporary Art in London, TheBody.com, http://thebody.com/content/art1461.html.
65. Quoted in Andriote, *Victory Deferred*, 252.
66. Ibid.
67. The author was an active participant in ACT UP's New York City chapter from 1988 through the early 1990s. For documentation on the composition, some debates, and the character of ACT UP meetings and actions, see Deparle, "Rude, Rash, Effective," and "ACT UP Capsule History," http://www.actupny.org/documents/capsule-home.html.
68. Emily Douglas, "ACT UP's New Urgency," *Nation*, April 3, 2007.
69. Bob Nowlan, "Post-Marxist Queer Theory and the 'Politics of AIDS,'" in Zavarzadeh, Ebert, and Morton, *Marxism, Queer Theory, and Gender*, 115–54.
70. Ibid., 130–32.
71. See Zoe Leonard, "Lesbians in the AIDS Crisis," in *The ACT UP New York Women and AIDS Book Group, Women, AIDS and Activism* (Boston: South End Press, 1990).
72. Centers for Disease Control and Prevention, "HIV/AIDS among Women Who Have Sex with Women," June 2006, http://www.cdc.gov/hiv/topics/women/resources/factsheets/wsw.htm.
73. Andriote, *Victory Deferred*, 250.
74. Christopher Heredia, "S.F.'s ACT UP Ordered to Back Off," *San Francisco Chronicle*, November 11, 2000.

75. Tara Shioya, "Men Behaving Viciously," *San Francisco Weekly*, March 19, 1997.
76. Craig A. Rimmerman, "ACT UP," TheBody.com, 1998, http://www.thebody.com/content/art14001.html.
77. Contents of the Women's Action Coalition records from 1992–1997 can be found at the New York Public Library, http://www.nypl.org/research/chss/spe/rbk/faids/wac.html. The author attended New York WAC's weekly organizing meetings.
78. "Historical Presidential Zap," ACT UP New York, http://www.actupny.org/campaign96/rafsky-clinton.html.
79. "ACT UP Capsule History for 1992," http://www.actupny.org/documents/cron-92.html.
80. See "ACT UP Capsule History" for timeline of all actions.
81. Church Ladies for Choice, MySpace page, profile.myspace.com/index.cfm?fuseaction=user.viewprofile&friendID=110549818.
82. Centers for Disease Control and Prevention, "HIV/AIDS and African Americans," 2005, http://www.cdc.gov/hiv/topics/aa/.
83. Halperin, *Saint Foucault*, 67.
84. Lisa Duggan, "Queering the State," *Social Text* 39 (Summer 1994): 11.
85. "Judith Butler," interview by Jill Stauffer, *Believer*, May 2003.
86. Max H. Kirsch, *Queer Theory and Social Change* (New York: Routledge, 2000), 8.
87. Turner, *Genealogy of Queer Theory*, 16.
88. Halperin, *Saint Foucault*, 61–62.
89. Turner, *Genealogy of Queer Theory*, 10.
90. Quoted in Annamarie Jagose, *Queer Theory, An Introduction* (New York: NYU Press, 1996), 1.
91. Sarah Salih and Judith Butler, eds., *The Judith Butler Reader* (Hoboken, NJ: Wiley-Blackwell, 2004), 120–21.
92. Marx and Engels, *MECW,* vol. 5, 467.
93. Wilchins, *Queer Theory, Gender Theory,* 100.

94. "There Is a Person Here: Interview with Judith Butler," *International Journal of Sexuality and Gender Studies* 6, nos. 1/2, 2001.

95. Quoted in Martin Manalansan IV, "Queer Love in the Time of War and Shopping," in *A Companion to Lesbian, Gay, Bisexual, Transgender, and Queer Studies*, Blackwell Companions in Cultural Studies, ed. George E. Haggerty and Molly McGarry, (Malden, MA: Blackwell, 2007) 82.

96. Thomas Piontek, *Queering Gay and Lesbian Studies* (Chicago: University of Illinois Press, 2006), 23.

97. Michael Warner, *The Trouble with Normal: Sex, Politics and the Ethics of Queer Life* (Cambridge, MA: Harvard University Press, 2000), 59.

98. Quoted in Piontek, *Queering Gay and Lesbian Studies*, 90.

99. Rona Marech, "Radical Transformation: Writer Patrick Califia-Rice Has Long Explored the Fringes. Now the Former Lesbian S/M Activist Is Exploring Life as a Man," *San Francisco Chronicle*, October 27, 2005, http://www.sfgate.com/cgi-bin/article.cgi?file=/chronicle/archive/2000/10/27/WB78665.DTL.

100. Quoted in Piontek, *Queering Gay and Lesbian Studies*, 84.

101. Pat Califia, *Public Sex: The Culture of Radical Sex* (San Francisco, CA: Cleiss Press, 2000), 158.

102. Cloud, "Queer Theory and 'Family Values,'" 87.

103. Quoted in Nowlan, "Post-Marxist Queer Theory,'" 136.

104. "Sexual Relations and the Class Struggle," *Selected Writings of Alexandra Kollontai* (Westport, CT: Lawrence Hill, 1977), 237.

105. Judith Butler, *Gender Trouble: Feminism and the Subversion of Identity* (New York: Routledge, 1990), 33.

106. Ibid.

107. Ibid., 200.

108. Cloud, "Queer Theory and 'Family Values,'" 92.

109. Judith Butler, "Doing Justice to Someone" in *The Transgender Studies Reader*, ed. Susan Stryker and Stephen Whittle (New

York: Routledge, 2006), 183.

110. Butler, *Gender Trouble*, 6.

111. Ibid.

112. Harriet Malinowitz, *Textual Orientations: Lesbian and Gay Students and the Making of Discourse Communities* (Portsmouth, NH: Boynton/Cook Publishers, 1995), 12.

113. Butler, *Gender Trouble*, 50.

114. April Herndon, "Why Doesn't ISNA Want to Eradicate Gender?" ISNA, February 17, 2006, http://www.isna.org/faq/not_eradicating_gender.

115. Kirsch, *Queer Theory and Social Change*, 17–18.

116. Ibid., 4.

CHAPTER SEVEN

Biology, Environment, Gender, and Sexual Orientation

1.   David Gelman, "Is This Child Gay? Born or Bred: The Origins of Homosexuality," *Newsweek*, February 24, 1992.

2.   "Are You Born Gay?" ABC News 20/20 Reports, March 28, 2008.

3.   John D'Emilio, interview by Sherry Wolf, *International Socialist Review*, May–June 2009, 21–22.

4.   Edward Stein, *The Mismeasure of Desire: The Science, Theory, and Ethics of Sexual Orientation* (New York: Oxford University Press, 1999), 120.

5.   Simon LeVay, "A Difference in Hypothalamic Structure in Heterosexual and Homosexual Men," *Science* 253 (August 30, 1991): 1034–37.

6.   Robert Alan Brookey, *Reinventing the Male Homosexual: The Rhetoric and Power of the Gay Gene* (Bloomington, Indiana: Indiana University Press, 2002), 17.

7.   Quoted in David France, "The Science of Gaydar," *New York*,

308 SEXUALITY AND SOCIALISM

June 18, 2007.

8. Ruth Hubbard and Elijah Wald, *Exploding the Gene Myth* (Boston: Beacon Press, 1993), 97.

9. Cited in Stein, *Mismeasure of Desire*, 148–53.

10. Ibid., 149.

11. Quoted in Tim Taylor, "Twin Studies of Homosexuality," Tim-Taylor.com, December 17, 1997, http://www.tim-taylor.com/papers/ twin_studies/stud.

12. Brookey, *Reinventing the Male Homosexual*, 65. Also cited in Stein, *Mismeasure of Desire*, 196.

13. Stein, *Mismeasure of Desire*, 221.

14. Phil Gasper, e-mail correspondence with the author, October 23, 2008.

15. Anne Fausto-Sterling, *Myths of Gender: Biological Theories About Women and Men* (New York: Basic Books, 1992), 75.

16. Ibid., 76.

17. Ibid., 74–76.

18. Cited in Brookey, *Reinventing the Male Homosexual*, 5.

19. Gelman, "Born or Bred?"

20. Dr. Albert Mohler, Jr., "Is Your Baby Gay? What If You Could Know? What If You Could Do Something About It?" Albert-Mohler.com, http://almohler.com/blog_read.php?id=891.

21. Fausto-Sterling, *Myths of Gender*, footnote: "A staggering amount of information goes into the development of a human being. We all have twenty-three pairs of chromosomes (one set contributed from each parent) and each chromosome contains one enormously long DNA molecule. Estimates suggest that there is enough DNA in each of our cells to contain information for from ten thousand to fifty thousand different proteins," 71.

22. Quoted in Stein, *Mismeasure of Desire*, 210.

23. Ibid.

24. Alfred C. Kinsey, Wardell R. Pomeroy, and Clyde E. Martin, *Sex-*

ual Behavior in the Human Male (Bloomington, IN: University of Indiana Press, 1998), 638–39.

25. Brookey, *Reinventing the Male Homosexual*, 45.
26. See Richard Green, *The "Sissy Boy Syndrome" and the Development of Homosexuality* (New Haven, CO: Yale University Press, 1995). Green's book title has come into frequent use in gender theory literature to refer to gender-atypical young men.
27. Quoted in Jeffrey Weeks, *Sexuality* (New York: Routledge, 2003), 43.
28. Quoted in Ibid., 53.
29. Margaret Mead, *Sex and Temperament in Three Primitive Societies* (New York: Routledge, 1948).
30. Stein, *Mismeasure of Desire*, 32.
31. Anne Fausto-Sterling, *Sexing the Body: Gender Politics and the Construction of Sexuality* (New York: Perseus Books, 2000), 109.
32. Weeks, *Sexuality*, 55.
33. Fausto-Sterling, *Sexing the Body*, 243–55.
34. Quoted in ibid., 247.
35. Janet Shibley Hyde, "The Gender Similarities Hypothesis," *American Psychologist* 60 (September 2005): 581.
36. "Anti-Lesbian, Gay, Bisexual, and Transgender Violence in 2007," National Coalition of Anti-Violence Programs, New York, 2008.
37. "The 2007 National School Climate Survey: The Experiences of Lesbian, Gay, Bisexual, and Transgender Youth in Our Nation's Schools," Gay, Lesbian, and Straight Education Network, 2008, 30, http://www.issuelab.org/research/2007_national_school_climate_survey_the_experiences_of_lesbian_gay_bisexual_and_transgender_youth_in_our_nations_schools.
38. Green, *"Sissy Boy Syndrome,"* 6.
39. Cited in Stryker, *Transgender History*, 111.
40. Ibid., 112.
41. Stein, *Mismeasure of Desire*, 237.

42. D'Emilio, *International Socialist Review*, 21.

43. Amanda Schaffer, "The Sex Difference Evangelists, Meet the Believers," Slate.com, July 1, 2008, http://www.slate.com/id/2194486/entry/2194487.

44. Quoted in ibid.

45. "Mars vs. Venus," video interview between Amanda Schaffer and Emily Bazelon, Slate.com, July 1, 2008.

46. Ibid.

47. Janice L. Ristock, *No More Secrets: Violence in Lesbian Relationships* (New York: Routledge, 2002), x–xi.

48. Ibid., 10.

49. Cited in Wilchins, *Queer Theory, Gender Theory*, 74.

50. Cited in Fausto-Sterling, *Sexing the Body*, 45–46.

51. Ibid., 51.

52. Ibid., 1. The idea that "masculine" women must prove their gender at the Olympic Games so that no male can pose as female giving a team an unfair advantage is fraught with problems. Aside from the obvious sexism—there is no proving manliness at the games—it also presumes that gender is a more significant advantage than, say, how much a country is capable of spending on training, outfitting, and paying an athlete, which would clearly confer tremendous advantages that every wealthy country takes for granted.

53. *Herculine Barbin*, introduction by Michael Foucault, trans. by Richard McDougall (New York: Pantheon, 1980).

54. Ibid., 45–54.

55. Cited in Wilchins, *Queer Theory, Gender Theory*, 73.

56. Herndon, "Why Doesn't ISNA."

57. Leacock, *Myths of Male Dominance*, 190.

58. Fausto-Sterling, *Sexing the Body*, 239.

59. Ibid., 162.

60. Ibid., 188–89.

61. Ibid., 111.
62. Stephen Jay Gould, *Ever Since Darwin: Reflections in Natural History* (New York: Norton, 1977), 257.
63. Fausto-Sterling, *Sexing the Body*, 255.
64. Phil Gasper, "Is Biology Destiny?" part one of a two-part series, *International Socialist Review*, November–December 2004, 64.

CHAPTER EIGHT
An Injury to One Is an Injury to All

1. Harris Interactive, "Pulse of Equality: A Snapshot of U.S. Perspectives on Gay and Transgender People and Policies," December 2, 2008, 8, http://www.sun-sentinel.com/media/acrobat/2008-12/43696052.pdf.
2. Ibid., 31.
3. Gary Gates, "In Cities, Suburbs, and the Sticks," Urban Institute, September 4, 2004, http://www.urban.org/publications/9007 34.html.
4. Ibid.
5. Adam P. Romero, Amanda K. Baumle, M. V. Lee Badgett, and Gary J. Gates, "U.S. Census Snapshot," Williams Institute, December 2007, http://www.law.edu/williamsinstitute/publications/USCensusSnapshot.pdf.
6. Smith, "Mistaken Identity," 39.
7. Antonio Gramsci, *Excerpts from the Prison Notebooks*, trans. and ed. Quintin Hoare and Geoffrey Nowell Smith (New York: International Publishers, 1971), 333.
8. Romero, et al., "U.S. Census Snapshot."
9. Ibid.
10. Ibid.
11. George A. Appleby, *Working-Class Gay and Bisexual Men* (Binghamton, NY: Haworth Press, 2001), 51–62.

12. Quoted in ibid., 60.
13. Susan Raffo, *Queerly Classed: Gay Men and Lesbians Write About Class* (Cambridge, MA: South End Press, 1997).
14. Quoted in Carol Anne Douglas, "Queerly Classed: Gay Men and Lesbians Write About Class," *off our backs*, July 1997.
15. Gary Kinsman, "Allan Bérubé, 1946–2007: A Queer Working-Class Community-Based Historian," *Against the Current*, July 3, 2008.
16. Stryker, "Marine Cooks and Stewards Union."
17. Quoted in Hunt, *Laboring for Rights*, 59.
18. Cited in Stryker, "Marine Cooks and Stewards Union."
19. Hunt, *Laboring for Rights*, 60.
20. Quoted in ibid.
21. The Human Rights Campaign Web site has a state-by-state listing of legal codes regarding sexual and gender identity, http://www.hrc.org.
22. Quoted in Dudley Clendinen, "Anita Bryant, b. 1940, Singer and Crusader," *St. Petersburg Times*, November 28, 1999.
23. Marcus, *Making History*, 258.
24. Randy Shilts, *The Mayor of Castro Street: The Life and Times of Harvey Milk* (New York: Macmillan, 1988), 171.
25. Ibid., 173.
26. Ibid., 83.
27. "On the Front Lines with Howard Wallace," *Political Affairs*, April 2004, http://www.political affairs.net/article/artview/113/.
28. Quoted in ibid.
29. Shilts, *Mayor of Castro Street*, 98.
30. Fred Fejes, "The Briggs Initiative Goes National," *Gay and Lesbian Review Worldwide*, July–August 2008, http://findarticles.com/p/articles/mi_hb3491/is_4_15/ai_n29452455/.
31. Ibid.
32. Gluckman and Reed, *Homo Economics*, 223.
33. Fejes, "Briggs Initiative Goes National."
34. Quoted in "On the Front Lines with Howard Wallace."

35. Hunt, *Laboring for Rights*, 64.

36. Ibid., 66.

37. Gluckman and Reed, *Homo Economics*, 231–32.

38. Quoted in Margaret Cruikshank, *The Gay and Lesbian Liberation Movement* (New York: Routledge, 1992), 73.

39. Shilts, *Mayor of Castro Street*, 281.

40. Rob Epstein, *The Times of Harvey Milk*, documentary film (San Francisco, CA: New Yorker Studios, 1984).

41. Cruikshank, *Gay and Lesbian Liberation Movement*, 74.

42. This excerpt from Nina D'Amato's letter is published here for the first time, with permission from her brother, Paul D'Amato. Tragically, fifteen years after this riot, Nina D'Amato died of complications from AIDS as a result of a blood transfusion. This young woman, who acted in solidarity with gays and lesbians in her youth, died of a disease whose global spread was enabled by government indifference and homophobia.

43. Quoted in Hunt, *Laboring for Rights*, 90.

44. Ibid.

45. Gluckman and Reed, *Homo Economics*, 224.

46. Hunt, *Laboring for Rights*, 72.

47. Ibid., 71–72.

48. Ibid., 77–80.

49. Meg Sullivan, "UCLA: U.S. Union Rates Up Substantially in 2008 for First Time Since 1970s, Study Shows," UCLA news, August 31, 2008, http://newsroom.ucla.edu/portal/ucla/PRN-u-s-union-memberships-up-substantially-56265.aspx.

50. Selfa, *The Democrats*, 88.

51. Hunt, *Laboring for Rights*, 109.

52. Ibid.

53. Ibid., 110.

54. See Human Rights Campaign, "GLBT Equality at the Fortune 500," http://www.hrc.org/issues/6989.htm.

55. Human Rights Campaign, "The State of the Workplace for Gay,

Lesbian, Bisexual and Transgender Americans 2006–2007," 4, http://www.hrc.org/documents/State_of_the_Workplace.pdf.

56. Nicole Raeburn, *Changing Corporate America from Inside Out: Lesbian and Gay Workplace Rights* (Minneapolis, MN: University of Minnesota Press, 2004), 24.

57. Ibid., 38.

58. Ibid., 61.

59. Harris Interactive, "Pulse of Equality."

60. Ibid., 22.

61. Ibid.

62. Patrick Egan and Kenneth Sherrill, "California's Prop 8: What Happened and What Does the Future Hold?" NGLTF, January 2009, http://haasjr.org/design/plain/downloads/Proposition8Study.pdf.

63. Marcus Wohlsen, "Exit Poll: Black Voters Back Calif. Marriage Ban," Associated Press, November 5, 2008.

64. Timothy Stewart-Winter, "Gay Marriage and the Black Vote," *Los Angeles Times*, August 14, 2008.

65. Ibid.

66. Newsweek Poll, December 3–4, 2008, PollingReport.com.

67. Christopher Curtis, "Jesse Jackson: Gay Marriage Rights Are Not Civil Rights," Gay.com, February 17, 2004, http://planetout.com/news/article/html?date=2004/02/17/6.

68. "HIV/AIDS and African Americans," Centers for Disease Control and Prevention, http://www.cdc.gov/hiv/topics/aa/index.htm.

69. Julian Bond, "Black America Must Confront AIDS," *Washington Post*, August 14, 2006.

70. Quoted in Gluckman and Reed, *Homo Economics*, 200.

71. Ibid.

72. Harris Interactive, "Pulse of Equality."

73. Alexander Cockburn, "Gay Marriage: Sidestep on Freedom's Path," CounterPunch, March 20–21, 2004, http://www.couterpunch.org/cockburn.03202004.html.

74. The Human Rights Campaign website has a state-by-state listing of each state's marriage laws and restrictions, www.hrc.org.

75. Davina Kotulski, PhD, *Why You Should Give a Damn About Gay Marriage* (Los Angeles: Alyson Publications, 2004). See ch. 5, "Why Marriage Lite Doesn't Work."

76. Ibid., 39.

77. Ibid., 47–48.

78. Quoted in Patricia Nell Warren, "Newt Gingrich and Gay Fascists," HuffingtonPost.com, November 25, 2008, http://www.huffingtonpost.com/patricia-nell-warren/newt-gingrich-and-gay-fas_b_146498.html.

79. Quoted in Lisa Keen, "Same-Sex Marriage Supporter Loving Dies," *Washington Blade*, May 9, 2008.

80. "Giving a Voice to the Anger Over Prop 8," interview by Amanda Maystead, *Socialist Worker*, November 12, 2008.

81. Mitchum, "What Does Deal."

82. Quoted in Sherry Wolf, "Teamsters and Trannies, Unite!" *International Socialist Review,* January–February 2009. The author was a speaker at this forum and recorded Flores's words.

83. "Big Labor Backs Overturn of Proposition 8," *Sacramento Bee*, January 13, 2009.

84. Ibid.

85. Video coverage of the rally and march can be found at http://www.outworld.tv/media/136/The-march-against-DOMA-begins/.

CHAPTER NINE

Sexual Liberation for All!

1. Tara Malone, "Sex Ed: Abstinence-Only Programs under Review," *Chicago Tribune*, April 22, 2009.

2. Ibid.

3. Ibid.

4. "Poll: American Sex Survey: A Peek Beneath the Sheets," *ABC News*, October 21, 2004, http://a.abcnews.com/Primetime/Poll-Vault/Story?id=156921&page=2.

5. Shere Hite, *The Hite Report: A Nationwide Study of Female Sexuality* (New York: Seven Stories Press, 2004), 397.

6. Bertell Ollman, "Social and Sexual Revolution: From Marx to Reich and Back," Dialectical Marxism: the Writings of Bertell Ollman, http://www.nyu.edu/projects/ollman/docs/ssr_ch06.php.

7. Karl Marx, *Economic and Philosophic Manuscripts of 1844*, trans. Martin Milligan (Moscow: Foreign Languages Publishing House, 1959), 324.

8. Paul D'Amato, "Alienation in Capitalist Society," *Socialist Worker*, September 12, 2003.

9. Marx, *Economic and Philosophic Manuscripts,* 73.

10. Reich, *The Sexual Revolution*, 75.

11. Ibid., 80. One problem with Reich's theories of sexual repression, though, is that he offered no outlet by which this repressive structure could be challenged. He tended toward a very pessimistic idea of how trapped people are because of sexual repression, and, as a result, placed too much emphasis on it. This is partly what led him away from Marxism in later years, and toward the idea that our psychic structure, anchored by sexual repression, was the most important determinant of the social structure of society, rather than economic forces.

12. Kollontai, "Sexual Relations and the Class Struggle," http://www.marxists.org/archive/kollonta/1921/sex-class-struggle.htm.

13. Ibid.

14. Wilhelm Reich, "Politicizing the Sexual Problem of Youth," *Sex-Pol Essays 1929–1934,* ed. Lee Bandaxall (New York: Vintage Books, 1972), 272–73. Reich eventually abandoned Marxism and emigrated to the United States where he was hounded by authorities for his sexual theories and died in an American prison in 1957. See Ollman, "Social and Sexual Revolution," for details.

Selected Readings

David F. Greenberg, *The Construction of Homosexuality* (Chicago: University of Chicago Press, 1988).

This is a fascinating and detailed account of the social construction of homosexuality. Greenberg's work covers everything from homosexual relations in kinship societies to the rise of market economics and provides some extremely insightful analysis.

Eleanor Burke Leacock, *Myths of Male Dominance: Collected Articles on Women Cross-Culturally* (Chicago: Haymarket Books, 2008).

This is a classic anthropological work that draws on extensive cross-cultural research to challenge the conception that women's oppression is inherent in human nature.

Frederick Engels, *The Origin of the Family, Private Property and the State* (New York: International Publishers, 2001).

This book, originally published in 1884, lays out a historical materialist understanding of the rise of class society and its role in shaping the modern nuclear family and women's oppression, which are so crucial to the understanding of the oppression of LGBT people.

John D'Emilio, "Capitalism and Gay Identity," in *Making Trouble: Essays on Gay History, Politics, and the University* (New York: Routledge, 1992).

This groundbreaking essay by one of the foremost American LGBT historians, originally published in 1983, provides a short and accessible materialist history of how modern capitalism shaped the formation of gay and lesbian identities.

John Lauritsen and David Thorstad, *The Early Homosexual Rights Movement (1864–1935)* (Ojai, CA: Times Change Press, 1995).

Lauritsen and Thorstad's short book remains the most authoritative and widely cited introduction to the earliest efforts at gaining social acceptance and civil rights for gays and lesbians. Evidence of the role of organized socialists in these struggles is highlighted.

Lillian Faderman, *Odd Girls and Twilight Lovers: A History of Lesbian Life in Twentieth Century America* (New York: Penguin Books, 1991).

Faderman's many works on lesbian history, especially this one, are a joy to read and provide much needed documentation and analysis of how women with erotic desires for other women came to discover their sexuality, find one another, and organize.

George Chauncey, *Gay New York: Gender, Urban Culture, and the Making of the Gay Male World 1890–1940* (New York: HarperCollins, 1994).

Chauncey's history of gay and lesbian pioneers in New York City uses newspapers, interviews, and other documents from the late nineteenth and early twentieth centuries to explode some myths about one of the largest and earliest homosexual subcultures in the United States.

John D'Emilio, *Sexual Politics, Sexual Communities: The Making of a Homosexual Minority in the U.S. 1940–1970* (Chicago: University of Chicago Press, 1983).

D'Emilio's essays on the early U.S. gay and lesbian movements don't simply provide facts but offer important insights about why gays and lesbians thought and organized as they did from the early twentieth century through the turbulent 1970s.

Nan Alamilla Boyd, *Wide-Open Town: A History of Queer San Francisco to 1965* (Berkeley and Los Angeles: University of California Press, 2003).

This historical narrative of one of the biggest LGBT meccas in the world explains how and why San Francisco came to be one of, if not *the*, premiere global cities for sexual minorities.

Allan Bérubé, *Coming Out Under Fire: The History of Gay Men and Women in World War Two* (New York: Plume, 1991).

Bérubé's scintillating history of gays and lesbians during the Second World War is one of the best historical examples of the law of unintended consequences.

Randy Shilts, *Conduct Unbecoming: Gays and Lesbians in the U.S. Military* (New York: St. Martin's Press, 1994).

Any hesitancy anyone might have about lifting the ban on gays and lesbians in the military is put to rest in this work. In addition, Shilts's research describes in detail the lives and relationships of LGBT and straight members of the armed forces.

Dan Healey, *Homosexual Desire in Revolutionary Russia: The Regulation of Sexual and Gender Dissent* (Chicago: University of Chicago Press, 2001).

So far, this book provides the best source of English-language material regarding the history of LGBT people before, during, and after the Russian Revolution—much needed given the misinformation that dominates most histories of this period.

David Carter, *Stonewall: The Riots That Sparked the Gay Revolution* (New York: St. Martin's Press, 2004).

This is the definitive blow-by-blow description of the event that more than any other shaped the modern LGBT movement. The inclusion of conversations with the riot's participants and documents from 1969 and 1970 help any scholar and activist to grasp the era through the eyes of the people who lived it.

Susan Stryker, *Transgender History* (Berkeley, CA: Seal Press, 2008).

Stryker provides a clear and accessible history of the rise of a transgender identity in the late twentieth century and is a must-read for modern-day LGBT activists.

Sharon Smith, *Women and Socialism: Essays on Women's Liberation* (Chicago: Haymarket Books, 2005).

In a sharp departure from most current writings on women and sexism, Smith refuses to shy away from political theorizing and takes on debates in anthropology and foreign affairs with a journalistic style that is engaging, fact-filled, and often witty.

Amy Gluckman and Betsy Reed, eds., *Homo Economics: Capitalism, Community, and Lesbian and Gay Life* (New York: Routledge, 1997).

This varied collection of essays answers the question about how a once reviled group of outcasts became a sought-after market niche.

Terry Eagleton, *After Theory* (New York, Penguin Books, 2003).

Eagleton uses sarcasm and class politics in equal measure to explain the depoliticized preoccupation with sex and pop culture that has come to dominate some LGBT studies departments in the current period.

Terry Eagleton, *The Illusions of Postmodernism* (Malden, MA: Blackwell Publishers, 1996).

In addition to his trenchant critique of postmodernism, Eagleton, in his usual witty manner, explains how and why these ideas are so dominant inside the U.S. academy.

Ellen Meiksins Wood, *The Retreat from Class: A New "True" Socialism* (New York: Verso, 1986).

Though a bit dated, Wood's Marxist analysis of postmodernism's anti-working-class outlook remains a classic.

Anne Fausto-Sterling, *Myths of Gender: Biological Theories About Women and Men* (New York: Basic Books, 1992).

Beyond tearing apart the myths of gender, Fausto-Sterling exposes the faux science behind premenstrual syndrome and menopause.

Anne Fausto-Sterling, *Sexing the Body: Gender Politics and the Construction of Sexuality* (New York: Perseus Books, 2000).

If every scientist wrote like Fausto-Sterling, millions more of us would actually understand what the often impenetrable world of biological science is about. *Sexing the Body* is simply fascinating in scientifically taking on the false male-female binary and demystifying intersex people and, in doing so, all of our bodies.

Index

326	SEXUALITY AND SOCIALISM

Also from Haymarket Books

Black Liberation and Socialism • Ahmed Shawki

A sharp and insightful analysis of historic movements against racism in the United States—from the separatism of Marcus Garvey, to the militancy of Malcolm X and the Black Panther Party, to the eloquence of Martin Luther King Jr., and much more—with essential lessons for today's struggles. ISBN 9781931859264

Annotated Communist Manifesto: A Road Map to History's Most Important Political Document • Edited by Phil Gasper

An authoritative, accessible introduction to *The Communist Manifesto*. This beautifully organized, fully annotated edition of *The Communist Manifesto* is complete with historical references and explication, additional related texts and a thorough glossary, bringing the Manifesto to life for today's readers. ISBN 9781931859257

No One Is Illegal: Fighting Racism and State Violence on the U.S.-Mexico Border • Mike Davis and Justin Akers-Chacón

No One Is Illegal debunks the leading ideas behind the often violent right-wing backlash against immigrants, revealing deep roots in U.S. history. The authors also remember the long tradition of resistance among immigrants organizing in the factories and the fields, and chart a course toward justice and equality for immigrants in the U.S. ISBN 9781931859356

Women and Socialism:
Essays on Women's Liberation • Sharon Smith

Thirty years have passed since the heyday of the women's liberation struggle, yet women remain second-class citizens. Feminism has shifted steadily rightward since the 1960s. This collection of essays examines these issues from a Marxist perspective, badly needed today. ISBN 9781931859110

About Haymarket Books

Haymarket Books is a nonprofit, progressive book distributor and publisher, a project of the Center for Economic Research and Social Change. We believe that activists need to take ideas, history, and politics into the many struggles for social justice today. Learning the lessons of past victories, as well as defeats, can arm a new generation of fighters for a better world. As Karl Marx said, "The philosophers have merely interpreted the world; the point, however, is to change it."

We take inspiration and courage from our namesakes, the Haymarket Martyrs, who gave their lives fighting for a better world. Their 1886 struggle for the eight-hour day, which gave us May Day, the international workers' holiday, reminds workers around the world that ordinary people can organize and struggle for their own liberation. These struggles continue today across the globe—struggles against oppression, exploitation, hunger, and poverty.

It was August Spies, one of the Martyrs targeted for being an immigrant and an anarchist, who predicted the battles being fought to this day. "If you think that by hanging us you can stamp out the labor movement," Spies told the judge, "then hang us. Here you will tread upon a spark, but here, and there, and behind you, and in front of you, and everywhere, the flames will blaze up. It is a subterranean fire. You cannot put it out. The ground is on fire upon which you stand."

We could not succeed in our publishing efforts without the generous financial support of our readers. Many people contribute to our project through the Haymarket Sustainers program, through which donors receive free books in return for their monetary support. If you would like to be a part of this program, please contact us at info@haymarketbooks.org.

Order these titles and more online at www.haymarketbooks.org or call 773-583-7884.

ABOUT THE AUTHOR

Sherry Wolf is a leading socialist activist, writer, and public speaker, and is an associate editor of the *International Socialist Review*. She is a popular public speaker on campuses and at community centers and has spoken widely on topics including the war in Iraq and the occupation of Palestine, as well as about the fight for lesbian, gay, bisexual, and transgender liberation. She has written for publications and websites such as CounterPunch, Alternet, Znet, DissidentVoice, *New Politics*, *Socialist Worker*, MRZine, and others as well as done interviews with Amy Goodman on *Democracy Now!*, on Pacifica Radio, and in *BusinessWeek*.